H.L. MENCKEN

Portrait by Nikol Schattenstein, 1927

H. L. Mencken in his heyday

H.L. MENCKEN

ICONOCLAST
FROM
BALTIMORE

Douglas C. Stenerson

The University of Chicago Press
Chicago and London

International Standard Book Number: 0-226-77249-7
Library of Congress Catalog Card Number: 78-158683

The University of Chicago Press, Chicago 60637
The University of Chicago Press, Ltd., London

To the memory of my parents

CHRISTOPHER P. STENERSON (1886–1960)

MAXINE DALTON STENERSON (1888–1963)

Contents

Illustrations

Preface

H.L. Mencken believed that—at least this side of unrestrained violence and anarchy—free discussion, dissent, and controversy are signs of cultural health. "Literature," he asserted, "always thrives best . . . in an atmosphere of hearty strife." From "God's controversy with New England" in colonial times to the Transcendentalist revolt, and from the antislavery crusade to the civil-rights movement of the 1960s, the leaven of unrest has continually enriched and reshaped the American experience. Whether the questioners and repudiators of the status quo have been poets, novelists, dramatists, literary critics, historians, social and political pundits, or professional reformers, they have been disturbed and sometimes shocked by the discrepancy between the ideal and the real, between their vision of what America should be and their perception of what it is. Often the values sustaining their efforts have, as in Mencken's case, clustered about nostalgic images of certain cherished portions of the American past.

This book examines and evaluates Mencken's part in precipitating and perpetuating the great quarrel within American culture which developed between his boyhood in the 1880s and 90s and his heyday in the 1920s. It is not a conventional biography, but an intensive study of his temperament, his famed "prejudices," and his career in journalism as they were affected by his interactions with and reactions against various aspects of the American tradition. It interprets that tradition much as he did—not as monolithic and static, but as pluralistic and dynamic.

My main purposes are, first, to trace the genesis and development
of his typical ideas and attitudes and of the coruscating and
forceful style which became his trademark, and, second, to estimate the significance that his views and his manner of dramatizing them had for him and for American culture generally.
As a means of posing the problems to be dealt with, chapter
1 concentrates on Mencken's editorial personality and interests
as revealed in *The American Mercury* from 1924 through 1926
when his reputation was reaching its height and the magazine
was approaching its peak circulation. This introductory chapter
also discusses the tensions implicit in his views which, by both
attracting him to and repellng him from the American scene,
help account for the remarkable extent to which his thought
and writing focused primarily within and upon America. Finally, in addition to showing tentatively how his standards are
related to certain trends in American thought and feeling, a topic
explored more fully in later sections, the opening pages consider
the characteristics of his mature style.

This background gives perspective to the issues faced in chapters 2 through 7. Beginning with a study of Mencken's interactions with his boyhood world, these chapters proceed chronologically. They are concerned with five main lines of investigation:
first, to trace the origins of his "prejudices" and style as these
are embodied in the *Mercury;* second, to determine under what
main influences and through what channels they developed;
third, to analyze the tensions in his thought which made his
attitude toward American life basically ambivalent; fourth, to
indicate how these tensions provide much of the motive power
behind his peculiar blend of artistry and iconoclasm; and, fifth,
to explain how and why his opinions and the delight in combat
expressed in his style fitted many of the needs and moods of
the twenties. Chapter 8 sums up the main conclusions and makes
a final estimate of Mencken's significance.

H.L. Mencken was always friendly and helpful to anyone
who wished to write about him. He continued to be so even
after the massive cerebral thrombosis which, in 1948, not only
impaired his memory and speech, but also made it impossible
for him to read or put words on paper, the two activities which

had been the most vital in his past life and career. When I was in the early stages of my research, August Mencken acted on behalf of his brother and arranged for me to consult the unpublished materials in the Enoch Pratt Free Library in Baltimore and in the libraries of Princeton University and the University of Pennsylvania. On one memorable summer evening in 1952, and on another in 1953, the Menckens entertained me in the little garden back of their home in Baltimore. Between sips of ice-cold gin and ginger beer, I had the chance to ask all the questions I pleased. With some help from his brother, H.L. Mencken was able to answer, or at least comment on, most of my queries. His cordial manner and his eagerness to aid an inquisitive stranger were much the same as they would undoubtedly have been before his illness. After H.L. Mencken's death in 1956, I remained in touch with August Mencken for several years and incurred further obligations to him. His death in 1967 deprived serious students of his brother's work of one of their staunchest friends and supporters. Both he and his brother were glad to correct errors of fact, but neither of them wanted in any way to influence or direct how the facts should be interpreted.

In 1957, while teaching at the University of Miami, Coral Gables, Florida, I received a grant from the Southern Fellowships Fund which relieved me of teaching duties for a year and enabled me to make substantial progress in writing the earliest version of this study. I am also pleased to acknowledge that chapter 4 in its original form, presented as an essay entitled "The Literary Apprenticeship of H.L. Mencken," was the winner of a McKnight Foundation Humanities Award for 1960. Neither the Southern Fellowships Fund nor the McKnight Foundation is at all responsible for any of the statements and judgments made herein.

Since joining the Department of English at Roosevelt University in 1967, I have benefited from several reductions in teaching load which enabled me to make more rapid progress in putting this book into publishable form.

For much assistance through correspondence and in person, I am grateful to Mr. Richard Hart, head of the humanities division at the Enoch Pratt Free Library; Miss Betty Adler, the same library's Mencken specialist; and Mrs. Neda Westlake, secretary to the Theodore Dreiser Committee and curator of the Rare Book Collection, University of Pennsylvania Library. Officials of the Princeton University Library saved me a great deal of time and expense by arranging an interlibrary loan of the microfilmed Mencken letters collected by Julian P. Boyd. I also owe a debt of thanks to staff members in the American Literature Collection, Yale University Library, and in the manuscripts divisions of the Library of Congress, the New York Public Library, and the Houghton Library, Harvard University.

I am indebted to the executor of the Henry L. Mencken estate, the Mercantile–Safe Deposit and Trust Company of Baltimore, represented by Mr. William G. Frederick, for authorization to quote from letters and other unpublished writings by Mencken; to the University of Pennsylvania Library for the use of an unpublished letter of Theodore Dreiser to H.L. Mencken, August 23, 1907; to the University of Pennsylvania Press for the right to cite extracts from Robert H. Elias, ed., *Letters of Theodore Dreiser*, 3 vols., 1959; and to Alfred A. Knopf, Inc., for permission to quote from *The American Mercury* and from copyrighted works by Mencken published by that firm. The latter, listed in order of publication, include *A Book of Prefaces; In Defense of Women; The American Language; A Book of Burlesques; Prejudices*, first through sixth series; *Notes on Democracy; The Days of H.L. Mencken; A Mencken Chrestomathy; Minority Report;* and *Letters of H.L. Mencken*, ed. Guy J. Forgue.

I appreciate being granted permission by the editors of the journals listed below to incorporate into chapters 1 and 4, in somewhat altered form, my own articles. "The 'Forgotten Man' of H.L. Mencken" appeared in *American Quarterly*, XVIII (Winter 1966) ; "Mencken's Early Newspaper Experience: The Genesis of a Style" in *American Literature*, XXXVII (May 1965) ; and "Short-story Writing: A Neglected Phase of Mencken's Literary Apprenticeship" in *Menckeniana*, no. 30 (Summer 1969) . I am under similar obligations to the Johnson Reprint Corporation for allowing me to reproduce in chapter 5 a few passages from my introduction to its reprinting of Percival Pollard, *Their Day in Court*, 1969.

To many of my coworkers in modern American thought and letters, I have expressed my acknowledgments in the Notes at the end of this volume. For valuable criticisms when this work was in its initial phase, I wish to voice my appreciation to Professors Bernard Bowron, Mulford Q. Sibley, Clarke A. Chambers, David Cooperman, and David W. Noble, all of whom participate in the American Studies program at the University of Minnesota. In 1965–66, while serving as a Fulbright lecturer at the University of Helsinki, Finland, I had some stimulating discussions of Mencken and the twenties with Professor Napier Wilt of the University of Chicago. I am especially grateful to him for his kindness in looking through a large portion of my typescript. I am similarly obliged to my friends and former colleagues, Roger Blakely and John H. Randall III, for many perceptive remarks and suggestions based on their reading of the entire revision.

My final word of thanks goes to my wife Marjorie for her constant encouragement and discriminating advice.

H.L. MENCKEN

1

MENCKEN AND *THE AMERICAN MERCURY*, 1924–1926

From *The Smart Set* to the *Mercury*

The founding of *The American Mercury*[1] gave H.L. Mencken precisely the opportunity he wanted to defend those aspects of the American tradition he cherished and to denounce or satirize those he disliked. The new magazine reflected his fascination with the American people—their culture, language, literature, institutions, and politics. In his first editorial, he commented on the extent to which many American magazines concentrated on publicizing ideas originating on the Continent or in Great Britain. The *Mercury* in contrast, would "lay chief stress at all times upon American ideas, American problems and personalities because it assumes that nine-tenths of its readers will be Americans and that they will be more interested in their own country than in any other." In a skeptical and urbane manner, untinged by any moral purpose or reformist impulse, it would examine critically the features of American life and thought most magazines neglected.[2]

Just after Christmas, 1923, the first number of the *Mercury* appeared on the newsstands. Browsers attracted by the Paris-green cover noted that it was dated January 1924, the editors were Mencken and George Jean Nathan, the publisher was Alfred A. Knopf, and the price was fifty cents per copy or five dollars per year. The attractive and dignified format, fine quality paper, and tastefully chosen type suggested that the newcomer was not intended to compete with "slick" magazines aimed at a mass audience. In literary merit it rivaled *Harper's* and *The Atlantic,* and as a commentator on current affairs it competed with *The Nation* and *The New Republic.*

Mencken and Nathan had long been associated as friends and coworkers. They first met in May 1909,[3] when Nathan started as drama critic of *The Smart Set,* on which Mencken had already served a few months as book reviewer. Late in 1914, Nathan, on being invited to take over the editorship, accepted only on condition that Mencken should be coeditor. Mencken and the publisher's representative agreed to this arrangement. Nathan took charge of the New York office, and Mencken came up from Baltimore once or twice a month to consult with him.

Superficially, the most striking characteristics of the new editors of *The Smart Set* were a boisterous egoism and a bohemian disregard for the accepted formalities of the publishing business. Their office featured colored portraits of Follies girls and a marble slab spread with refreshments and labeled "Poet's Free Lunch." When Mencken visited New York, they were likely to decide on the tone and pattern of the next issue over drinks at the Beaux Arts or during dinner at Lüchow's.

But beneath this frivolous exterior lay their serious determination to print what best satisfied their own tastes. In 1921 Mencken summed up their view by declaring, "Magazine editing is simply a tournament in autobiography. The more an editor tries deliberately to please the public, the quicker he comes a cropper."[4] In accord with this philosophy, the image they projected in *The Smart Set* was a composite of their personalities and interests. As they had done in their critical departments prior to 1914, they now, as editors, opposed the shoddy, the pretentious, and the merely genteel, and championed writing which either transcended the old formulas or filled them with new life. They searched diligently for genuine literary talent—especially new talent. Although they could not compete in the open market for work by recognized authors, they took advantage of the fact that much of the material which appealed to them could find no outlet in conventional magazines. Many writers were grateful to get published even though the pay was small.

The editorial procedures Mencken and Nathan followed also helped to offset the difficulty caused by their limited funds.

They alerted every friend or acquaintance who had any chance of either contributing, or persuading someone else to contribute, something worthwhile. They acted quickly in considering manuscripts, and paid promptly for those accepted. Mencken won the support of many contributors by speaking to them not as editor to author, but as one writer to another. Instead of the usual businesslike notes or printed rejection slips, he wrote friendly and amusing letters varied to fit the author and the situation. He and Nathan were able to attract such authors of growing reputation as Joyce, Lord Dunsany, Cabell, Dreiser, Willa Cather, and Sherwood Anderson, and to bring out early work by Ben Hecht, Thomas Beer, Ruth Suckow, O'Neill, and Fitzgerald.

Although the editors shared many opinions, social habits, and literary enthusiasms, Mencken's interests were much more broadly social and political than Nathan's. In listing "certain fundamentals" on which he and Nathan agreed, Mencken included a number of economic, social, and political views:

Both of us are opposed to all such ideas as come from the mob, and are polluted by its stupidity: Puritanism, Prohibition, Comstockery, evangelical Christianity, tin-pot patriotism, the whole sham of democracy. Both of us, though against socialism and in favor of capitalism, believe that capitalism in the United States is ignorant, disreputable, and degraded, and that its heroes are bounders.[5]

But such issues were not of primary importance to Nathan. "What interests me in life," he wrote, ". . . is the surface of life: life's music and color, its charm and ease, its humor and loveliness. The great problems of the world—social, political, economic and theological—do not concern me in the slightest. . . . What concerns me alone is myself, and the interests of a few close friends."[6] To Nathan, the confirmed aesthete, "the great problems of the world" were worth only occasional amused and satirical comment. To Mencken, they were central issues.

The Smart Set maintained a kind of compromise between the editors' partially conflicting interests, but by 1922 Mencken was eager to scrap it and start a new review. Back in 1911, he and

Nathan, stimulated by H.G. Wells's description in *The New Machiavelli* of a "Blue Weekly" intended for enlightened Tories, had dreamed of originating a quarterly with an American motif and titled *The Blue Review*. From time to time, Mencken had revived this hope. He disliked the title of *The Smart Set,* with its misleading implication that the magazine specialized in society and fashion news. He was sensitive about the unsavory reputation for society scandal and risqué fiction it had acquired under some of its earlier editors. He balked at the restricted budget which made it impossible to pay the prices demanded by certain writers—Joseph Conrad, for example—whom he and Nathan would have liked to publish. He felt that the magazine's literary orientation did not offer enough leeway for social and political commentary. Finally, he was worried about its drop in circulation and the consequent decline in revenue from advertising, as a result of which it was no longer able to hold its own against such competitors as *Judge, Life,* and *Vanity Fair.*

Early in March 1923, Mencken and Nathan talked with Eltinge Warner, publisher of *The Smart Set,* about how to improve and revitalize it. Mencken favored starting a nonfiction sister publication, while Nathan preferred experimenting with the journal as it was. When Warner rejected both of these alternatives, they discussed the problem with Alfred A. Knopf, who had been publishing Mencken's books since 1917. Knopf responded sympathetically. Either he or his father, Samuel Knopf, negotiated through a friend to buy *The Smart Set,* but Warner refused to sell. When Mencken and Knopf waxed enthusiastic about founding an entirely new review, Nathan consented, but stipulated that he and Mencken should continue to operate *The Smart Set.* This compromise soon proved impracticable. In August, Warner demanded the removal from the September issue of a satirical piece about President Harding's funeral train. This violation of his long-standing agreement not to interfere with the magazine's contents led to a quarrel which convinced Nathan, as well as Mencken, that they must abandon *The Smart Set* and establish a new journal.[7]

The *Mercury* as Mencken's Self-portrait

In contrast to the composite personality embodied in *The Smart Set*, the *Mercury* projected chiefly the editorial personality of Mencken. This was true in spite of the fact that, in part, the pattern and tone as well as the editorial practices of the *Mercury* continued those established by Nathan and Mencken jointly in *The Smart Set.* Nathan's drama criticism and Mencken's book reviews were to be retained. The satirical "Americana" department, compiled by the editors and published under the pseudonym Major Owen Hatteras, was carried over to the *Mercury* without any credit line. "Répétition Générale," written jointly by Nathan and Mencken, was transferred to the *Mercury* under the heading "Clinical Notes."[8] But, unless Nathan's "The Theatre" is excepted, none of these departments clashed with Mencken's determination "to shake up the animals, in politics, economics, the sciences, etc., as well as in the fine arts."[9]

The opening editorial announced that in the fine arts the editors "will not deviate from their old program—to welcome sound and honest work, whatever its form or lack of form, and to carry on steady artillery practice against every variety of artistic pedant and mountebank." Since "they belong to no coterie and have no aesthetic theory to propagate," the editors dissociated themselves from both the Greenwich Village avant garde, with its "transcendental, gibberishy theory," and the academic critics, with their "harsh, moral, patriotic theory." In addition to the drama and book reviews, the *Mercury* would print one or two short stories each month and, occasionally, a short play or a small amount of verse. In artistic matters the *Mercury* had the same general aim as *The Smart Set*, but it would subordinate what had been the primary concern of the latter to the broader purpose of portraying "the whole field of American life."

The first editorial presented Mencken's conception of the approach and standards appropriate for that purpose. Because the editors were "entirely devoid of messianic passion," they hoped to introduce some novelty in achieving their major aim: "to ascertain and tell the truth." They had no "sovereign balm," economic, political, or aesthetic, to offer; for "the world, as they see it, is down with at least a score of painful diseases, all of them chronic and incurable." They were convinced that "many of the great problems of man . . . are intrinsically insoluble," but nevertheless, they cling to the notion that human existence remains predominantly charming. Especially is it charming in this unparalleled Republic of the West, where men are earnest and women are intelligent, and all the historic virtues of Christendom are now concentrated. The Editors propose, before jurisprudence develops to the point of prohibiting skepticism altogether, to give a realistic consideration to certain of these virtues, and to try to save what is exhilarating in them, even when all that is divine must be abandoned.

This passage implies that the editors spoke for an elite class which found human existence charming because it was conscious of its own superiority, was capable of social and political realism, and derived an ironic enjoyment from the discrepancies between human pretensions and human performance. The beliefs and actions of the mass of Americans and their leaders and heroes provided the best opportunity for the contemplation of such discrepancies. What Mencken intended by his ironic reference to "the historic virtues of Christendom" can be indicated by quoting once more the list of notions that "come from the mob, and are polluted by its stupidity: Puritanism, Prohibition, Comstockery, evangelical Christianity, tin-pot patriotism, the whole sham of democracy." It was these and similar "virtues," produced by "the ponderous revolutions of the mass mind," which the *Mercury* would dissect.

The editorial also made it clear that the elite, as represented by the editors, would enjoy the literary methods the *Mercury* planned to use. Mencken proposed "to undertake the business in a polished and aseptic manner, without indignation on the one hand and without too much regard for tender feelings on the other."

A statement announcing the withdrawal of Mencken and Nathan from *The Smart Set* accurately expressed Mencken's view, but not Nathan's, in saying that the editors' "desire and interests now lead them beyond belles lettres."[10] Nathan, it turned out, would not compromise his aesthetic principles, an attitude which made him disagree frequently with Mencken's recommendations. By the fall of 1924, Mencken was convinced that he and Nathan could no longer work effectively as a team and that Knopf must make his choice between them. Knopf sided with Mencken and entrusted him with the dissolution of the partnership. As a result, in February 1925, Nathan retired as coeditor to become contributing editor, but his name was linked with Mencken's on the front cover until July, after which Mencken's name alone was featured.[11]

Through the "tournament in autobiography" represented by the *Mercury*, Mencken became a truly national figure. *The Smart Set* had given him the chance to marshal his prejudices, perfect his style, and learn the art of editing, but it was not fully satisfactory as a vehicle for his mature work as a social and political commentator. He knew that *The Smart Set* reached many intelligent readers, such as the "young intellectuals" and some college students, but at times he envisioned its audience as "fat women trying to keep awake in Pullman cars after heavy greasy meals."[12] Its circulation, dependent chiefly on newsstand sales, had ranged as high as 50,000 between 1914 and 1920, but by 1923 it had declined to only 22,000.[13] In the *Mercury*, by contrast, Mencken had a review whose policies he could shape and whose budget was adequate to attract the authors he needed. He expected to appeal to an audience which was skeptical of the "infallible elixirs" of the liberals but at the same time scorned the "Tories" to whom any kind of discontent looked like subversion. This middle group of readers, the first editorial asserted, included "the leading men of science and learning, the best artists, in all the arts," and "such men of business as have got any imagination."

Even so, the editors considerably underestimated the number of Americans aspiring to belong to the "civilized minority." They had anticipated that the *Mercury* would reach a circulation of twenty or twenty-five thousand, about the same as that of *The Smart Set*. But, after a sale of 14,000 for the initial issue, the net paid circulation climbed to nearly 43,000 for the December 1924 number. In round figures, the circulation reached 69,000 in 1926 and 77,000 in 1927, after which it gradually declined, but it did not drop below 68,000 until the 1929 crash.[14]

Two-thirds of the *Mercury* readers were concentrated in the eleven largest American cities. Although *The Smart Set*, too, had appealed primarily to an urban audience, *Mercury* readers were not only more numerous but also represented a greater variety of occupations and classes. "The subscription list," Mencken remarked, "makes very instructive and exhilarating reading. It includes all the most lively and enlightened of Americans—from the wetter university presidents to the editorial writers of the better newspapers, from business men to orchestral conductors, and from theologians to cheer leaders."[15] The popularity of the *Mercury* among college students received much notice both locally and nationally. Those who attacked as well as those who praised added to the publicity which made Mencken and his magazine nationally important. The vogue of the *Mercury* became one of the major journalistic and literary phenomena of the twenties.

Loving and Loathing American Life

When the *Mercury* was in the planning stage, Nathan objected to what he called its "messianic" aspects, but Mencken disavowed any such impulse and liked to pose as a sardonic spectator of the American circus, amused but not rendered indignant by the gaudy show of bigotry, conceit, fraud, and sham. In a quip titled "Catechism," he asked and countered the inevitable question:

Q. If you find so much that is unworthy of reverence in the United States, then why do you live here?
A. Why do men go to zoos?

Was Mencken, as this pose suggests, merely a debunker laughing cynically at the faults of his society but refusing to assume any responsibility for them? Hostile critics could easily answer yes to this question and cite passages from the *Mercury* to support their contention. In a piece called "Nostalgia," for example, Mencken's ironic vein implies personal detachment from the problems of World War I. Mencken listed such "entertaining" features of the war as "the daily bulls and ukases of the eloquent Woodrow," "the enchanting dawn of the Ku Klux Klan, 100% Americanism and the American Legion," "the first alarms about

Debs, the I.W.W. and the Bolsheviki," and "the tall talk about self-determination, saving the world for democracy, breaking the heart of humanity." Or, with similar apparent detachment, he could say of the presidential campaign of 1924, with Coolidge and Davis as the candidates, "It is, at bottom, wholly senseless— a furious but meaningless joust of stuffed shirts, actors, quacks, shadows. Its result is worth no man's concern. But while it lasts it is at least genuinely diverting."[16]

But no sooner does the reader catch this glimpse of Mencken chortling from the sidelines of American life than a seemingly contradictory phase of his editorial personality emerges. He was, in his own way, much more fully committed to the American enterprise than his pose as a cynical spectator indicates. In "On Being an American" (1922), he had announced his reasons for staying in America rather than joining the disillusioned young intellectuals on the next boat to Europe. After presenting his bill of indictment against the federal government, the administration of justice in America, United States foreign policy, and the American people, he concluded that nevertheless his happiness was best served by staying put:

To be happy (reducing the thing to its elements) I must be:
  a. Well-fed, unhounded by sordid cares, at ease in Zion.
  b. Full of a comfortable feeling of superiority to the masses of my fellow-men.
  c. Delicately and unceasingly amused according to my taste.

The first objective was more readily attained in America than in any other country because of the ease with which "an educated and forehanded man" could make a living. The second required little effort because "any man who knows his trade, does not fear ghosts, has read fifty good books, and practices the common decencies . . . is thrown willy-nilly into a meager and exclusive aristocracy." The third was easily within reach because "the daily panorama . . . of private and communal folly . . . is so inordinately grotesque and preposterous . . . that only the man who was born with a petrified diaphragm can fail to laugh himself to sleep every night."[17] These reasons, as Mencken phrased them, were cynically selfish, but concealed in them is the truth that he needed America at least as much as America needed him.

"On Being an American," however, presents only part of the truth about his concern for America and her fate. He was incapable of maintaining consistently the ironic detachment he sometimes professed. When he commented on American life, he did so as one who saw it from within and had strong feelings about it. He often used language showing that it really offended him that such phenomena as Prohibition and infringement of civil rights not only existed but even had widespread support in the United States. At such times he was likely to oversimplify complex problems and portray a stereotype as typical of a whole group.

An editorial later revised and reprinted as "The Husbandman" illustrates these tendencies. Mencken sometimes admitted that other groups besides farmers had brought about the national ban on liquor, as when he declared, "It was not primarily the Christian faithful of the backwoods who fastened Prohibition upon us; it was the rustic *curés* working upon the Christian faithful, whose heat, in turn, ran the State legislators amok."[18] But in "The Husbandman" editorial, he held that the farmers alone are responsible for "Prohibition, Sunday Blue Laws, Comstockery, the whole insane complex of statutes against free speech and free thought." Setting up the harassed city man as his hero, he proceeded to explode the ancient stereotype of "the virtuous husbandman":

There, where the cows low through the still night, and the jug of Peruna stands behind the stove, and bathing begins, as at Biarritz, with the vernal equinox—there is the reservoir of all the nonsensical legislation which now makes the United States a buffoon among the great nations. It was among country Methodists, practitioners of a theology degraded almost to the level of voodooism, that Prohibition was invented, and it was by country Methodists . . . that it was fastened upon the rest of us, to the damage of our bank accounts, our dignity and our ease. What lies under it, and under all the other crazy enactments of its category, is . . . the yokel's congenital and incurable hatred of the city man—his simian rage against everyone who, as he sees is, is having a better time than he is.[19]

The humor evident in the description of the farmer's habits and immediate environment heightens, by contrast, the invective dominant in the rest of the passage. The underlying tone is at least partly one of vexation, not of detached superiority.

When Mencken concealed his indignation by guffawing from the sidelines, or revealed it by damning whole groups of the population, he seemed to express chiefly a negative response to American life. But his negative reactions, important though they were, were not in themselves enough to account either for his deep absorption in things American or for the special quality of his iconoclasm. To notice only that he rejected certain popular beliefs and trends is to leave out of account the gusto which gave his negative attitudes an infectiously vital quality. As Walter Lippmann put it, "this holy terror from Baltimore is splendidly and contagiously alive. He calls you a swine and an imbecile, and he increases your will to live."[20]

Mencken's negative prejudices, moreover, implied a whole set of positive preferences which strongly attracted him to some features of the American scene. His vitality spilled over into an admiration for anything that had life and vigor in it, and he found many evidences of those qualities in America and Americans, both past and present. Although convinced that "the normal, average Americano is not an outlaw, but a goose-stepper," he noted at the same time "a maverick and outlaw strain" in his countrymen which makes "certain men find the restraints of what is called Christian civilization unbearable, and break into insurrection against it."[21] Many of the writers he admired were Americans who, like Poe, Mark Twain, Bierce, Huneker, Sinclair Lewis, and Ring Lardner, had a capacity for irreverent wit and humor and the strength to resist, at least much of the time, the pressures making for conformity. The lives and works of such writers formed part of a native tradition of dissent with which he could ally himself. The "maverick and outlaw strain" presumably survived also in the "civilized minority" the *Mercury* sought to entertain and console. This superior group, it should be remembered, was as thoroughly American as the tyrannous majority and dominant minorities, and Mencken was quite aware of this fact.

Another illustration of his absorption in the American scene, with all its rawness and color, was his eagerness to have both artists and scholars portray it realistically. He could look back with satisfaction on his efforts in *The Smart Set* to defy the genteel tradition, oppose literary commercialism, and encourage talented authors to make honest use of American materials. By 1923 he felt that the critical movement he had helped forward had achieved its main objectives, and his social and political concerns overshadowed his more purely literary interests. Yet in the *Mercury* he did not lose sight of his earlier aims. In his first editorial he maintained that "the young American artist is quite as free as he needs to be," but he also promised him "aid against the obscurantists who occasionally beset him." In his reviews, he often crowded together scanty and rather perfunctory comments on several volumes of fiction, but he continued to hail novelists who resembled Dreiser in their "courageous destruction of . . . old taboos" and their "sense of the tragedy that may play itself out among the lowly."[22] He also drew attention to American types and locales he believed had been slighted by serious novelists.

His reviews of nonfiction show his delight in portrayals of prominent Americans, particularly the vigorous and colorful ones. Brigham Young, for instance, struck him as "an organizer of high skill, a serpentine politician, a shrewd trader, a mobmaster of the first order." John L. Sullivan was "a salient and joyous figure in the incomparable comedy of life in America." Mencken also welcomed studies dealing cogently with "the history of ideas in the Republic." In his "Editorial Notes," he often suggested topics for articles, as when he asked young journalists to comment on the current state of journalism, or urged Indian writers to discuss Indian problems.[23]

Mencken tirelessly championed the language of his compatriots, including the "boobs" and the "yokels." In *The American Language* (1919) and its three later editions and two supplements, he demonstrated that American usage had a versatility and vigor making it distinct from British usage. He opened up the pages of the *Mercury* to such distinguished linguists as Edward Sapir ("The Grammarian and His Language," February 1924), George Philip Krapp ("The English of the Negro," June 1924), and Louise Pound ("Notes on the Vernacular," October 1924). Mencken himself made skillful use of American idiom, to which he contributed such coinages as *bootician* (bootlegger), *homo boobiens,* and *booboisie.* Mark Twain's command of the vernacular was one reason for Mencken's judgment that *Huckleberry Finn* is "the greatest work of the imagination that These States have yet seen."[24] Other writers Mencken praised for their effective use of colloquial speech included George Ade, Sherwood Anderson, and Ring Lardner.

This brief survey is enough to illustrate the tensions implicit in Mencken's attitudes—tensions that both repelled him from and attracted him to the American scene. He expressed his views in forms that ranged from outright affection and good-humored banter to invective sustained by indignation and even to the apparently cynical amusement of his pose as a spectator viewing a magnificently banal farce. The tensions between simultaneous loving and loathing in his work resemble those he detected in Thackeray's portrayal of the picaresque Irish rogue, Barry Lyndon. "The true humorist," Mencken observed, "loves as he snickers. . . . Even Thackeray, convinced that he was a cynic and trying hard to be bitter, couldn't smother his tolerant affection for Barry Lyndon." Similarly, Mencken, even when seeming most incensed or claiming to by cynically detached, could not consistently suppress his real affection for the United States. It was only natural that his "insatiable interest in ideas . . . and more than the average facility for putting them into words"[25] came to focus primarily within and upon America.

The Faith of an Agnostic

Impressed by his aggressive manner, some critics have considered Mencken an almost entirely destructive force. Elmer Davis, for example, asserted in 1927 that "the only positive doctrine which emerges from the sacred writings of Mr. Mencken himself is that Germany was right in the late war."[26] Such an opinion overlooks the marked preferences and positive standards which formed the obverse side of Mencken's negative prejudices. These standards embraced a militant agnosticism, an ideal of truth-seeking, and a staunch libertarianism.

Mencken's agnosticism and scientism embodied assumptions which came into prominence during what he himself called "an era of rising doubt, with the name of Darwin on every Christian's lips and Huxley in full eruption." Throughout his lifetime Mencken maintained with relative fixity beliefs resting on the postulates of the mechanistic scientific naturalism and the social Darwinism of the late nineteenth century. By the 1920s many of these postulates, which did not go unchallenged even at the turn of the century, were intellectually outmoded, but for Mencken and many of his contemporaries they were the basis of a world view that had burst upon them with the force of revelation. The ideas and attitudes which could be interpreted as following from the postulates were so comprehensive and diverse that each individual could select from them those most congenial to his own tastes and temperament. Accepting the assumption of scientific naturalism that the universe is a vast mechanism operating inexorably under immutable laws, Mencken held to a philosophy of materialism and determinism which, at least in theory, admitted no duality between man and nature. "I believe," he declared, "that the phenomena of life are wholly chemical and mechanical. . . . I am a strict determinist and do not believe in free will, though I admit in ordinary thinking free will must be assumed."[27]

He also accepted as gospel some of the conclusions popularly drawn from the analogy the social Darwinists made between the natural laws governing the biologic evolutionary process and the economic "laws" operating in human society under capitalism. For those whose views, like Mencken's, were at least partially conservative, that analogy could be used to justify as the inevitable result of the laws of social evolution the economic and social inequalities and competitiveness existing under capitalism. For those who, again like Mencken, had a temperamental distaste for conventional religion, the new world view offered a plausible alternative to that of Christianity. Mencken commented in the *Mercury* that it was with "the general rise of skepticism" in the eighteenth century "that Christianity first took to its bed, and as its strength slowly oozed out men had to look elsewhere for light and leading. Having tried philosophy and found it lacking, they turned to science—and science had a curious way of exalting what was natural, of making it seem inevitable."[28] In Thomas Huxley, in particular, Mencken had discovered a rationale for his home-bred agnosticism, and also the example of a style fully equal to its task of waging a vigorous campaign, in the name of science, against the entrenched positions of conventional religion.

Mencken's scientism is properly called that because, although it purported to have scientific validity, it was actually grounded in faith in certain dogmas of the Darwinian dispensation. Henry Adams, shortly after 1900, had sensed the religious quality of the era's confidence in science when he wrote, "The atomic theory; the correlation and conservation of energy; the mechanical theory of the universe; the kinetic theory of gases, and Darwin's Law of Natural Selection, were examples of what a young man had to take on trust." To Adams, "Natural Selection seemed a dogma to be put in place of the Athanasian creed; it was a form of religious hope." Mencken was too convinced of the validity of his commitments and clung to them too tenaciously to be capable of that kind of insight. Despite his claim that a superior man "is full of a skepticism which plays like a spray of acid upon all the ideas that come within his purview, including especially his own," his writings show no sign that any such process made him alter substantially his own beliefs. Fortunately, he was too much the humorist to take himself with deadly seriousness, and the play of humor over his own ideas as well as those of others usually saved him from adopting a strident or pontifical tone. He also admitted, on occasion, that he might be mistaken, or even that on certain points he had been mistaken, but he never lost confidence sufficiently to make him feel a need to overhaul his whole critical system. His skepticism was mainly directed outward at the opinions of others and was sustained by his sense of the rightness of his own views. Had he been more fully skeptical about his own beliefs, he would almost certainly have been less vigorous in asserting them. In speaking of "the doctrine of a new religion which . . . may as well be called Mercurianity,"[29] Elmer Davis suggested with considerable shrewdness the element of dogmatism in Mencken's opinions and the self-assurance with which he presented them.

Agnosticism, for both Thomas Huxley and Mencken, was much more militant than "a state of not professing to know," the literal meaning of the term, implies. In its aggressive faith in the methods of science, its animus against religious orthodoxy, and the scope it gave for his delight in controversy, Mencken's agnosticism closely paralleled Huxley's. While invoking the name of science, Mencken, perhaps more often than Huxley, indulged in language more emotional in its appeal than strict adherence to a logical method would permit.

The Scopes trial and the issues it raised explain why Mencken, writing in the *Mercury* in 1925 and 1926, commented at length upon the revival of "the old conflict between science and religion."[30] Although not present at the close of the trial, he was on hand for most of it as a correspondent for the *Baltimore Sun*.[31] He enjoyed the show as sheer spectacle, but he also felt that no one with any pretensions to intellect could consent even tacitly to the antievolution laws without being either mentally flabby or hypocritical and cowardly. Appropriately enough, he found in Huxley the example of leadership he recommended to scientists (and, by implication, to all *Mercury* readers). Under the "Millikins and other such amiable bunglers" who try to reconcile science with conventional religion, "science exposes itself to be shot at, but agrees not to shoot back." Huxley's strategy was much wiser. When the Gladstones and Bishop Wilberforces denounced the new biology, Huxley "made a bold and headlong attack upon Christian theology—an attack so vigorous and so skillful that the enemy was soon in ignominious flight."[32]

Although Mencken had real sympathy for rationalist critiques of theology and scripture in the Huxley manner, he did not undertake in his own right to restate in any detail the arguments against specific theological positions. He seemed to assume that a preference for agnosticism or modernism as against Fundamentalism, and a knowledge of the chief arguments in their favor, were part of the common heritage of the enlightened minority. In regard to the issues raised by the Scopes trial, for instance, he directed his attack not on Fundamentalist theology as such, but on its adherents and on those southern intellectuals who did not openly oppose it. He wanted not primarily to champion science against orthodoxy, but to oppose the efforts of religious groups to force their conception of life upon Americans generally. The state antievolution laws were only one example of the influence wielded by the evangelical sects: Prohibition imposed through an amendment to the federal Constitution was an even more ominous one. Mencken asserted that, because of Prohibition, "at least two-thirds" of America's adult citizens, "not to mention millions of its younger ones, have been inoculated with the notion that breaking the law, and even violating the Constitution, is, after all, no serious thing, but simply a necessary incident of a civilized social life."[33] Thus, for Mencken, what Huxley called the "ecclesiastical spirit" is not only the enemy of science, but also the enemy of civilized living. It violates all reasonable standards of what is honorable and decent. In his indictments of such groups as the evangelical clergy, the Ku Klux Klan, and the supporters of Prohibition, he mixed stereotyping and invective with shrewd judgments and vividly humorous portrayals of types and situations.

As editor of the *Mercury*, Mencken showed that he had a genuine interest in both the natural and the social sciences and a considerable knowledge of the literature in each of those broad areas. In "The Arts and Sciences" department, he printed short essays on topics in both fields, and he welcomed longer articles on similar themes. He was particularly well informed about biology and medicine. In reviewing books with such titles as *Malignancy and Evolution: A Biological Inquiry Into the Nature and Causes of Cancer,* he could handle competently "questions of embryology, physiology and paleontology quite as much as questions of pathology."[34]

Since he was not, however, conscious of the religious quality of his faith in a rather narrowly conceived empirical method, his agnosticism imposed certain limits upon the range of his vision. A naive rationalism colored his conceptions of science and religion. In defending the facts and truths of science as opposed to religious faith, he specifically denied "that science itself is based upon faith, and that it cannot explain that faith." The scientist "gives no credit to anything he cannot see—if not with his physical eyes, then at least with machines that compensate for their infirmities." Mencken could say of a work like William Osler's *Principles and Practice* that the author poured into it not only his vast knowledge but also "all his fascination as a man,"[35] but the statements he makes about science as such do

not leave much room for the personal equation. His assumption
that science is simply a process of collecting and verifying data
and generalizing from them gave the scientific method a certain
aura of infallibility, but it overlooked the part that the scientific
imagination and intuitive hunches play both in directing research and in analyzing its results. It also revealed little awareness that the whole rationale of science rests ultimately on what
Santayana called "animal faith"—faith, for example, in the existence of an external world, the efficacy of human reasoning,
and the possibility of controlling natural forces.

The agnostic faith in an empirical method is a satisfying one
for those who, like Mencken, are, in the conventional sense,
nonreligious. "I am," he wrote,

incapable of religious experience, in any true sense. Religious
ceremonials often interest me aesthetically, and not infrequently
they amuse me otherwise, but I get absolutely no stimulation
out of them, no sense of exaltation, no mystical *katharsis*. . . .
When I am low in spirits and full of misery I never feel any
impulse to seek help, or even mere consolation, from supernatural powers. Thus the generality of religious persons remain
mysterious to me, and vaguely offensive, as I am unquestionably
offensive to them. I can no more understand a man praying than
I can understand him carrying a rabbit's foot to bring him luck.

The restrictions the agnostic vision imposed upon Mencken become apparent in his review of Howard A. Kelly's *A Scientific
Man and the Bible*. How could his friend and fellow Baltimorean be at one and the same time an eminent surgeon and
man of science and "a Fundamentalist of the most extreme
wing"? As a young man, Kelly, while recuperating from snow
blindness, suddenly felt "an overwhelming sense of a great light
in the room." To Kelly this was the central event of his life and
signified the presence of God. Mencken could only refer Kelly's
experience "to the violent conjunctivitis from which he was suffering—in other words to a purely physical cause." Perhaps
Mencken was right about the physical cause, but no matter what
he might say, the sense of God's presence remained a reality
to Kelly. As William James pointed out, "mystical states of a
well-pronounced and emphatic sort *are* usually authoritative
over those who have them. They have been 'there,' and know.

It is vain for rationalism to grumble about this."[36] However skeptical Mencken might be about the possibility of a non-empirical order of truth, mystic communion with the divine exists as a reality in the lives of those who, like Kelly, experience it. Mencken was not equipped to understand that reality and the power it exerts. Instead of realizing he was pitting his own faith and dogmas against those of orthodox religion, he conceived of science as the citadel of truth and of orthodox religion as the citadel of superstition and error. These limitations help explain his tendency to stereotype Fundamentalists unfavorably and denounce them unceremoniously.

The "Forgotten Man"

Critics who have hailed Mencken as a libertarian or damned him as a reactionary have not seen the whole man. The truth is that he was both. His social and political thought is particularly fascinating because it embodied so many conflicting elements in the American heritage. He remained faithful throughout his lifetime not only to Huxley's agnostic ideal of iconoclasm and truth-seeking, but also to many of the more conservative aspects of the Darwinian revelation as interpreted by such thinkers as Herbert Spencer and William Graham Sumner.[37] He was equally indebted, as we shall see later, to an idealized conception of the plantation society of the Old South and to the German-American way of life as he had known it in Baltimore, but the ideas and values that contrasted most strikingly with his conservative views were those stemming from the tradition of the Enlightenment. Since he took over concepts from these different sources without attempting to reconcile the assumptions on which they were based, the opinions he expressed in his social criticism are often inconsistent. Through an analysis of his interpretation of the "Forgotten Man," an image · he borrowed from Sumner and adapted to his own purposes, it is possible to identify and examine some of the major contradictions in his attitudes.

In the first issue of *The American Mercury*, Mencken declared that the reader to whom he and George Jean Nathan wished to appeal was "what . . . Sumner called the Forgotten Man— . . . the normal, educated, well-disposed, unfrenzied, enlightened

citizen of the middle minority." Sumner had portrayed the Forgotten Man as "the clean, quiet, virtuous, domestic citizen" who
"is independent, self-supporting, and asks no favors."[38] Like this
definitely middle-class figure, Mencken cultivated the virtues
associated with the Protestant ethic, and for him, as frequently
for the Forgotten Man, these virtues had lost all trace of religious
feeling. He exhibited, and admired in others, individual initiative, hard work, punctuality, thrift, and prompt payment of
debts.

His approval of these qualities is implied in his description
of himself as "a larva of the comfortable and complacent
bourgeoisie."[39] In his writings, he scourged not the bourgeoisie,
as such, but the booboisie. That is, he resisted and ridiculed
only those members of the middle class who were lodge-joiners,
back-thumpers, do-gooders, and goose-steppers and thus, in his
lexicon, qualified as boobs.

Like Sumner and many other social Darwinists, Mencken
assumed that the law of natural selection operates in human
society much as it does, according to Darwin, among the lower
animals. In 1883, Sumner had protested that the Forgotten Man
had to bear the expense of laws and agencies designed "to
protect people . . . against the results of their own folly, vice,
and recklessness." We should not, he argued, spend money for
measures that do not really prevent vice, but merely ward off
Nature's penalty for it. For "a drunkard in the gutter is just
where he ought to be. Nature is working away at him to get him
out of the way, just as she sets up her processes of dissolution to
remove whatever is a failure in its line." Similarly, when Mencken
opposed laws to control "fortune-tellers, layers on of hands,
communists, Ku Kluxers, Holy Rollers, . . . heroin addicts,
cancer quacks, and a hundred and one other varieties of fanatics
and mountebanks," it was partly on the ground that "There
is evil, indeed, in every effort to relieve the stupid of the biological consequences of their stupidity."[40]

Both Sumner and Mencken personified Nature as a kind of
nemesis for those who fail in the struggle for survival. For
Mencken, heredity and natural selection, rather than the cultural milieu and cultural opportunities, were the main deter-
minants of social divisions. Society consisted basically of an elite

versus the mob. Apropos of birth control, he argued that we should "promote and not hinder the multiplication of the lower orders, for if they do not multiply then there will be insufficient coal miners, ashmen and curve-greasers in the next generation." Sometimes he went so far as to maintain that a whole race was far behind in its evolutionary development. After praising a volume of essays by a group of Negro intellectuals, he asserted that one of the chief problems confronting them was that "the vast majority of the people of their race are but two or three inches removed from gorillas."[41]

For Sumner, the elite—those who presumably proved themselves most fit in the struggle for survival—were the economically secure captains of industry and the relatively secure Forgotten Men. Mencken's beliefs carried a kind of tacit approval of these agents of the free-enterprise gospel. On its conservative side, his opposition to big government manifested the sort of economic individualism Sumner advocated when he wrote, "All experience is against state regulation and in favor of liberty." Mencken's admiration for the economic virtues made him recognize similar traits in successful capitalists and industrialists, even though in some respects he might subject them to severe criticism. Henry Ford, for instance, was "the most adept and ingenious manufacturer ever heard of," despite the fact that when "lured into discussing all sorts of public questions, most of them quite beyond his comprehension, . . . he made a fool of himself almost daily."[42]

But Mencken, unlike Sumner, did not define his elite almost exclusively in economic and material terms. For Mencken, the group who paralleled Sumner's captains of industry were the "Tories" who, in the twenties, dominated business and politics and controlled the press. In his opinion, these Tories were an uncivilized plutocracy, not part of a true elite. Even the Forgotten Man, as Mencken described him, was "enlightened" and represented scholars, scientists, and artists as well as businessmen. For Mencken, indeed, intellectual and artistic superiority was the prime requisite, with economic security also a desideratum, but in second place.

The social and political realism stressed in the first *Mercury* editorial had a forerunner in Sumner's observation "that cupidity, selfishness, envy, malice, lust, vindictiveness, are constant vices of human nature." Much as Sumner counseled "that if you learn to look for the Forgotten Man and to care for him, you will be very skeptical toward all philanthropic and humanitarian schemes," Mencken editorialized that in politics

utopianism is not only useless; it is also dangerous, for it centers attention upon what ought to be at the expense of what might be. Yet in the United States politics remains mainly utopian—an inheritance, no doubt, from the gabby, gaudy days of the Revolution. The ideal realm imagined by an A. Mitchell Palmer, a King Kleagle of the Ku Klux Klan or a Grand Inquisitor of the Anti-Saloon League, with all human curiosity and enterprise brought down to a simple passion for the goose-step, is as idiotically utopian as the ideal of an Alcott, a Marx or a Bryan.[43]

Although Mencken was as fervent as Sumner in opposing liberal or radical reformism, he differed from Sumner in being as skeptical of "utopianism" on the right as of "utopianism" on the left. He saw no reason why Americans should fear radical doctrines and persecute their advocates. He ridiculed the widely held assumption that leftist agitators seriously threatened American capitalism. Americans, he held, were full of delusions running directly counter to those of the radicals. Because Americans refused to admit they might be "doomed to life imprisonment in the proletariat," they always hoped to move upward economically and socially. As a result, they suffered from "the delusion that class barriers are not real." They were even likely to believe "that the interests of capital and labor are identical—which is to say, that the interests of landlord and tenant, hangman and condemned, . . . are identical." Capitalism would endure in the United States as long as the notion that any bright boy can rise to the top remained part of the national religion.

It seemed to Mencken that the Forgotten Man, representing "the middle minority," was always in danger of being victimized by the dominant social and political groups. If the Forgotten Man indulged in a harmless bottle of wine, he ran the risk of trial and imprisonment. If he spoke up vigorously on behalf of the Bill of Rights, he might be denounced as an agent of the Bolsheviks. Neither the liberals nor the tories could offer him any real help. "There is no middle ground of consolation,"

Mencken claimed, "for men who believe neither in the Socialist fol-de-rol nor in the principal enemies of the Socialist fol-de-rol —and yet it must be obvious that such men constitute the most intelligent and valuable body of citizens that the nation can boast."[44]

When his individualism operated in the context of the harsh competitive world envisaged by Sumner, with Nature siding with a self-styled elite and inexorably stalking the allegedly unfit, Mencken often gave the impression that only he and the enlightened minority could lay claim to true individuality. At such times he tended to stereotype a whole group unfavorably as "the nether rabble of cowherds, lodge-joiners and Methodists," or the like. If Swamp Root hastened the death of the yokels who drank it, so much the better; they were merely reaping "the biological consequences of their stupidity." The elite, meanwhile, could preen themselves on the superior intelligence which prompted them to take their medical problems to a doctor. The logical outcome of this attitude is an atomistic and inhumane individualism, with its pitting of the rights of the privileged few against efforts to help what Sumner called "the nasty, shiftless, criminal, whining, crawling, and good-for-nothing people." To the extent that Mencken carried the outmoded assumptions of social Darwinism into his analyses of socioeconomic problems, he overlooked the possibility "that the life of man in society, while it is incidentally a biological fact, has characteristics which are not reducible to biology and must be explained in the distinctive terms of cultural analysis."[45]

Mencken's seeming callousness reflected the harshness of the dogmas of social Darwinism, but it was also in part an impression created by his literary technique. Stereotyping is a form of exaggeration with considerable value for writers who, like Mencken, specialize in invective and ridicule. Such an author wants his readers to share his animus against a particular group or a type representative of the group. Stereotyping enables him to ignore all the differences among the members of the group which make them unique personalities and which might enlist his readers' sympathies with his victims. If he has the stylistic resourcefulness, he can portray the evil traits he attributes to the group so vividly that he succeeds in making many readers accept his judgments. The danger is that stereotyping may become not a conscious technique but a habitual manner of thought.

Although Mencken sometimes seemed to assume that his stereotypes summed up the whole truth, his quick response to anything vital and colorful in individuals saved him from consistently taking his own sweeping generalizations at their face value. Whenever he looked upon the yokels or the boobs as individuals, not mere ciphers, the more humane aspects of his social and political thought began to emerge. He then realized that even "the Rotarian and his humble brother, the Kiwanian," "the Americanizers, the Law Enforcers, the boosters and boomers" have aspirations distinctly and appealingly human. They glimpse "a dim and disturbing mirage of a world more lovely and serene than the one the Lord God has doomed them to live in." What they lack is "the vision of Liberty" which would give them "a rational conception" of what this lovelier world "ought to be, and might be."

Liberty, as Mencken defined it here, featured not economic individualism and free enterprise, but the right to moral and spiritual self-determination:

I preach reaction. Back to Bach! . . . The Fathers, too, had a Vision. . . . What they dreamed of and fought for was a civilization based upon a body of simple, equitable and reasonable laws. . . . The thing they imagined was a commonwealth of free men, all equal before the law.

Although convinced that "some of their primary assumptions were false," Mencken accepted their "premiss that the first aim of civilized government is to augment and safeguard the dignity of man."[46]

Responding sympathetically to Hamilton's aristocratic bias and distrust of the mob, Mencken did not accept all the implications of this liberal faith in human dignity. He rejected Jefferson's belief in the wisdom of the common people as having "a sweep and scope that took it far beyond the solid facts." To explain this point of view, he made a distinction between two kinds of political liberty:

There was, first, the liberty of the people as a whole to determine the forms of their own government, to levy their own taxes, and to make their own laws—freedom from the despotism of the King. There was, second, the liberty of the individual man to live his own life, within the limits of decency and decorum, as he pleased—freedom from the despotism of the majority.

"We have got the [first] half of liberty," he commented,

but the other half is yet to be wrested from the implacable fates. . . . Minorities among us have no rights that the majority is bound to respect; they are dragooned and oppressed in a way that would make an oriental despot blush. Yet behind the majority . . . there is always a sinister minority, eager only for its own advantage and willing to adopt any device, however outrageous, to get what it wants.[47]

In several respects, however, Mencken's concept of liberty was closer to Jefferson's than it was to Hamilton's. His elite resembled Hamilton's only superficially. Hamilton sought to preserve the powers and prerogatives of an economically privileged group, but Mencken wanted a guarantee of the moral and spiritual liberties which make it possible for the civilized minority to be civilized. Despite his preference for an aesthetic and intellectual elite and his distrust of "the lower orders," he acknowledged "that it is worth nothing to be a citizen of a state which holds the humblest citizen cheaply, and uses him ill." He praised Jefferson's "complete integrity," "immense intellectual curiosity, profound originality, and great daring."[48] Mencken's libertarianism was strongly Jeffersonian in tone because it insisted that *all* persons, not only members of the elite, have inalienable rights, and that any interference with these rights by either an agency of government or community mores is intrinsically evil.

Closely linked with the liberal aspect of Mencken's individualism were his concepts of honor and "common decency." Like his libertarianism, these values had an absolute validity for him. They transcended the materialism and dog-eat-dog ethic so resolutely expounded by Sumner. The Forgotten Man emerged, at this juncture, as a gentleman of humane sensibilities—a role which further transformed Sumner's image of him. In addition to intelligence, a concern for the arts, and courage, the gentleman upheld decency and honor. He knew that he must not violate privately commitments that he had made publicly. For example, he would not advocate Prohibition, thus encouraging invasions of the rights of his wet friends, and then accept hospitality from those friends.

The ideals of honor and decency also suggested the pattern Mencken would have liked society to take. To the "good American," who felt that "the notions of propriety . . . held by the mob are good enough for the state, and ought, in fact, to have the force of law," he opposed the citizen

who views the acts and ideas of his fellows with a tolerant and charitable eye, and wishes them to be free and happy. For the thing that makes us enjoy the society of our fellows is not admiration of their inner virtues but delight in their outward manners. It is not enough that they are headed for heaven, and will sit upon the right hand of God through all eternity; it is also necessary that they be polite, generous, and, above all, reliable. We must have confidence in them in order to get any pleasure out of associating with them. . . . It is the tragedy of the Puritan that he can never inspire this confidence in his fellowmen.

Mencken and his Forgotten Man wanted a stable, orderly society dominated by an elite to which they would belong, but they wanted everyone to have the right to self-determination. They wanted all members of the society to have the opportunity to act as men of honor, maintain the social amenities, and take an innocent enjoyment in the pleasures of the senses—"the nonpuritanical acts and whimsies that make life charming."[49]

Mencken would not ally himself with any of the existing political parties, but he identified himself imaginatively with such statesmen as Washington, Hamilton, and Jefferson. His nostalgia for the past and his distaste for many of the social and political trends of the twenties reinforced each other. During the Revolution and the early national period, gentlemen could enter politics and not be forced to compromise their honor. The dilemma of modern American politics was that, with few exceptions, gentlemen would not assume political duties, and even when they did, they could not long remain gentlemen. The "worst curse of democracy . . . is that it makes public office a monopoly of a palpably inferior and ignoble group of men. They have to abase themselves in order to get it, and they have to keep on abasing themselves in order to hold it."[50]

As for government generally, Jefferson was right in seeing "that it tended inevitably to become corrupt—that it was the common enemy of all well-disposed, industrious and decent men." Since 1914, in particular, Jefferson's worst fears had been realized. Although Mencken sometimes treated the events of World War I in a tone of ironic detachment, his real feelings came out in an editorial note in which he spoke of the war as causing "the appearance of organized and malignant Babbittry, and the complete destruction of all the old American ideas of freedom. Down to 1914, the United States was a refuge for the oppressed of all lands; now they are barred out, and the government is engaged gloriously in the oppression of its own citizens." At times, Mencken's opposition to government verged on anarchism. In the widespread evasion of the efforts to enforce Prohibition, he saw "the first glimmers of a revolt that must one day shake the world—a revolt, not against this or that form of government, but against the tyranny at the bottom of *all* government."[51]

Mencken's negative prejudices, as the preceding analysis has shown, implied a considerable number of positive, though contradictory, standards. He accepted, for example, much of the conservative creed of the American middle class, with its confidence in capitalism, its equation of natural and economic laws, its stress on the utility of the Protestant virtues, its skepticism about liberals and radicals. In part, like Sumner, looking down scornfully upon those who failed in the economic struggle, he called on the middle class to live up more fully to its ideal of self-reliance. In part, since he identified the Forgotten Man with an intellectual and artistic elite, he condemned the middle class for its philistinism and anti-intellectualism. In other instances, he measured American life by norms he believed had formerly prevailed but were now neglected, as when he contrasted the integrity and courage of Washington and Jefferson with the venality of politicians in the twenties. As a staunch libertarian, he opposed any interference with individual rights.

In its mixture of conservatism and liberalism, orthodoxy and iconoclasm, his social commentary showed the shrewdness of his judgments about the interests and needs of the middle-class

Americans who formed the bulk of his audience. It also embodied his two logically incompatible sets of standards. As a partisan of Sumner's Forgotten Man, he complacently ignored or accepted as inevitable some types of economic and social inequalities and injustices. He distrusted sudden innovations and proposals for transforming society and the existing political system. At the same time, as the champion of his more humane version of the Forgotten Man, he asserted his libertarianism. On behalf of "common decency," he attacked real evils: gentility, ignorance, philistinism, bigotry, intolerance, suppression of individual rights. What united his conflicting attitudes was the mood generated by his insistence that the individual counts more than the group. With all the strength of a powerful ego, he resisted the forces, both cultural and legal, which tended to impose conformity on him and his contemporaries.

A Fusion of Artistry and Iconoclasm

As an examination of his positive standards indicates, Mencken had the sensibility and talents of an artist-journalist, not those of a philosopher. He was not, and did not claim to be, either an original or a systematic thinker. He was interested in religion, philosophy, and politics, but he was not an adequate theologian, philosopher, or political theorist. He was a critic of the arts, but he had no consistent aesthetic. For the most part, he took for granted the generalizations and value judgments contained in his views. At his average, he was a superlative journalist, writing in moods that ranged from broad humor to savage satire on topics of current and sometimes ephemeral interest. At his best, he was an artist whose prejudices were the themes of his art.

He was so consistently an individualist that he wanted others to be individualists too. Even though he deplored the ideas of such an opponent as Paul Elmer More, one of the New Humanists, he admired More's unshakable fidelity to those ideas.[52] He did, of course, want an audience, but he did not want to organize members of that audience into a coterie, a school, or a movement. The intent of the *Mercury* was "to console and entertain" the civilized minority, not to organize it and urge it to adopt a particular program of social and political action.

Even if Mencken had wished to present a plan that would attract followers and start a movement, he was incapable of the kind of disciplined introspection he would have needed to develop a consistent philosophy. The inadequacy of his ideas as the stuff of social or political theory, or of a reform program, is at once apparent. In contemporary America, he could find no basis for a stable, orderly society dominated by an aristocracy. This social ideal is agrarian and at least partly anti-industrial in tone, but his explicit economic philosophy, if pressed to its logical conclusion, justified and even glorified big, corporate industry. He rejected the going equivalent of Sumner's captains of industry as a plutocracy, but the logic of his economic views was to elevate this same group to an elite status.

He observed that the chief defect in American culture was "the lack of a civilized aristocracy," which, along with its other qualifications, would be "secure in its position" and "superior to the sentimentality of the mob." But how can such an aristocracy be established or rendered secure if, as he demanded, the members of the "mob" are left free to air their opinions, and, by implication, exercise the tyranny of the majority? In *Notes on Democracy* (1926), he stated that "the practical choice is between the plutocracy on the one side and a rabble of preposterous impossibilitists on the other. One must either follow the New York *Times* or one must be prepared to swallow Bryan and the Bolsheviki." What democracy needs, he concluded, is "a party of liberty . . . that will separate the good that is in it theoretically from the evils that beset it practically, and then try to erect that good into a workable system," but it will never have a party of libertarians "until it invents and installs a genuine aristocracy, to breed and secure them."[53] The use of "invents" in that last statement suggests that Mencken, as a political theorist, was as much an "impossibilitist" as any of those he denounced. How does a society go about "inventing" an aristocracy?

In Mencken's writings in the *Mercury*, the iconoclastic and artistic impulses are almost indistinguishable. The tensions which generated his ambivalent attitude—the tensions between simultaneous loving and loathing—made all aspects of American life fascinating to him. His positive standards involved an acceptance of many typically American assumptions, but they also made him oppose much that was widely accepted in religion, morals, manners, and politics. The religious quality of his commitment to the ideals of agnosticism and libertarianism, honor and decency, and their violation by much that was happening in the United States, account for the intensity of feeling behind his protests. Because his dissent was not only extensive in range but deeply felt, he tended to cast his running commentary on American affairs in forms adopted to an iconoclastic purpose. Ideologically, the tasks of iconoclasm, in his view, were to expose error and sham, and, if possible, to discover and publicize the truth. Artistically, his iconoclasm was the vehicle for his strong urge to self-expression and his concern with the "clang-tints" of words.

At first glance, the conception of criticism as a kind of error-blasting and truth-seeking operation seems to conflict with the conception of it as an art. Despite Mencken's real interest in literature and the other arts, he sometimes declared that only the objective, verifiable data of science are really "true," and overlooked or put in second place the imaginative truth embodied in art. He was fully capable of painstakingly accumulating a body of data and putting them in logical and persuasive form, as he did in *The American Language*. But he was skeptical about the possibility of either finding hard-and-fast truths in social and political matters or of establishing in the public mind such truths as do emerge. Truth-seeking in the *Mercury* took the highly qualified form of demonstrating that man's problems are often insoluble and emphasizing that knowledge is less a matter of accumulating facts than a matter of destroying illusions assumed to be facts.[54] Mencken's iconoclasm, it is true, implied the hope that his bludgeoning of what he considered false or fraudulent would help create conditions in which something approximating the truthful and genuine could flourish. With vigor and consistency, Mencken opposed restrictions on individual rights and strove to improve the atmosphere in which American artists worked. The crucial question is whether in these efforts he was being loyal chiefly to an empirical method and the accumulation of facts, or to the truth of his prejudices—his reactions and insights as an artist-journalist.

The close identification of the iconoclastic and artistic impulses in his work suggests the answer. In the *Mercury* he did not usually carefully document the case for his own point of view. When he did make sustained use of logical form, it was usually with satiric purpose. In one editorial, for example, he linked argument after argument together in an ostensibly grave manner to justify a new way of dealing with corrupt officials, the gist of the proposal being that "it shall be no longer *malum in se* to pummel, cowhide, kick, gouge, cut, wound, bruise, burn, club, bastinado, flay or even lynch a job-holder, and that it shall be *malum prohibitum* only to the extent that the punishment exceeds the job-holder's deserts." More typically, in his onslaught against what he conceived to be error and fraud, he used some facts, but featured mainly a wide variety of nonlogical appeals, ranging from simile and metaphor to vivid caricature, from a feigned ironic detachment to stereotyping and invective, from controlled ridicule to unrestrained vituperation. In other words, he brought all his accumulated literary skill to his self-appointed task of functioning joyfully as an iconoclast. As he said of the iconoclast he depicted as a type in the first number of the *Mercury,* he was not so much concerned with giving a logical proof of his case as he was with proving "by his blasphemy that this or that idol is defectively convincing—that at least *one* visitor to the shrine is left full of doubts." "One horse-laugh," he added, "is worth ten thousand syllogisms."[55]

The iconoclastic and artistic impulses merged in Mencken's conception of the artist as one who can express with skill and power his dissent from whatever is crass and repressive in his culture. The same impulses also merged in the editorial interests and personality Mencken projected in the *Mercury.* Blasting the contentment of the "Tory" plutocracy on one hand, and of the rabble and the booboisie on the other, was his means of dramatizing his own dissent. Bringing all his gusto and literary skill to the blasting process was his means of fulfilling his strong urge to express his individuality. The blasting process consoled the civilized minority. The literary showmanship Mencken brought to the process entertained it.

2

CHILD OF
BALTIMORE

Looking to the Past

However zestfully Mencken, as editor of the *Mercury,* consoled
and entertained the civilized minority, he could not assure them
that their lot would be measurably more bearable in the future.
His version of social Darwinism did not imply that evolution
as it works out in human society makes progress necessary and
inevitable. In the arts, especially in literature, he believed that
America since the years just before the war of 1914 to 1918
had improved remarkably. In economic, social, and political
matters, on the other hand, he noticed some signs of potential
progress, but not many signs of progress achieved.

In his view, social and political progress occurs when "by
some occult process, half rational and half instinctive, the truth
gets itself found out and an ancient false assumption goes over-
board." The largely urban audience of the *Mercury* could take
comfort in his observation that they were far ahead of farmers
and villagers in getting rid of the notions crediting "the rev.
clergy with a mysterious wisdom and awful powers" and con-
ceiving of the police as "altruistic agents of a benevolent state."
"Delivered from the extortions of country politicians, and from
the oppression of country-made laws," American cities could
become "independent of the States, and mistresses in their own
houses." Once this happens, "civilization in the United States
will have a chance to spread its wings."[1]

The quality distinguishing such expressions of hope is what Mencken once called "a certain sough of rhetoric."[2] The wording suggests that the conditions required for progress will materialize rather quickly, but this optimistic tone, sometimes generated by his eloquence, is not typical of his thought. Ordinarily, his social and political commentary created the impression that the United States of the 1920s, including even his beloved Baltimore and Maryland, were on the decline from heights reached in the past.

As late as 1942, a local historian declared that Baltimore was reluctant to yield to the standardizing processes of the modern world, but in the early twenties Mencken was already noting how big industrialism, organized Babbittry, and mass entertainment were dissipating the graces of life in his native city and state. In "Maryland, Apex of Normalcy" (1922), he exposed the ambiguity of the concept that Gamaliel Harding and the Republican managers had proposed as an ideal for the postwar era. In a campaign speech in May 1920, Harding, inadvertently coining the word "normalcy," had proclaimed: "America's present need is not heroics, but healing; not nostrums but normalcy; not revolution, but restoration; . . . not experiment, but equipoise; not submergence in internationality, but sustainment in triumphant nationality." Alert Republicans quickly devised the imperative "Back to Normalcy!," a slogan with a strong appeal for millions of Americans weary of war and alarmed by the international responsibilities the country faced in its new role as a great world power. Harding, in effect, invited them to shove to one side the complexities of the present and to associate with "normalcy" the political ideal of the high-tariff Republicanism of the Hayes to McKinley era and the social ideal contained in a nostalgic image of small-town life. In one speech, after describing sentimentally the little town in which he had grown up in the seventies and eighties, he concluded, "What is the greatest thing in life, my countrymen? Happiness. And there is more happiness in the American village than in any other place on the face of the earth."[3]

After comparing Harding with the other presidential nominees in 1920—James Cox the Democrat, Debs the Socialist, and Parley Christenson the Farmer-Laborite—Mencken voted for

Harding as the least of the four evils, but he had no respect
for either Harding or his rhetoric. He regretted having to cast
his ballot for "an almost perfect specimen of a 100% American
right-thinker," the operations of whose brain resembled "the
rattlings of a colossal linotype charged with rubber stamps."
"The Gamalian style . . . ," said Mencken,

came to birth on the rustic stump, it developed to full growth
among the chautauquas, and it got its final polishing in a small-
town newspaper office. In brief, it reflects admirably the tastes
and traditions of the sort of audience at which it was first aimed,
to wit, the yokelry of the hinterland, naive, agape, thirsty for
the prodigious, and eager to yell.[4]

In "Maryland, Apex of Normalcy," Mencken catalogs the
realities of American life which had been glossed over or ignored
in the campaign oratory. "In brief," he summarized,

Maryland . . . represents . . . the ideal toward which the rest of
the Republic is striving. . . . It has all the great boons and usufructs of current American civilization: steel-works along the
bay, movies in every town, schools to teach the young how to
read and write, high-schools to ground them in a safe and sane
Americanism, colleges for their final training, jails to keep them
in order, a State police, a judiciary not wholly imbecile, great
newspapers, good roads. It has vice crusaders, charity operators,
drive managers, chambers of commerce, policewomen, Y.M.C.A.'s,
women's clubs, Chautauquas, Carnegie libraries, laws against
barking dogs, the budget system, an active clergy, uplifters of
all models and gauges. It is orderly, industrious, virtuous, normal, free from Bolshevism and atheism.

Despite these "great boons and usufructs," "life in arcadian
Maryland" is "depressing" and "steadily grows worse."

Everywhere in the United States, indeed, there is that encroach-
ing shadow of gloom. Regimentation in morals, in political
theory, in every department of thought has brought with it a
stiffening, almost a deadening in manners, so that the old goat-
ishness of the free democrat . . . has got itself exchanged for a
timorous reserve, a curious psychical flabbiness, an almost complete incapacity for innocent joy. To be happy takes on the
character of the illicit: it is jazz, spooning on the back seat, the

Follies, dancing without corsets, wood alcohol. . . . On all ordinary days, for all ordinary Americans, the standard carnality has come to be going into a silent and stuffy hall, and there, in the dark, gaping stupidly at idiotic pictures in monochrome. No light, no color, no sound![5]

Mencken's commentary in the *Mercury,* with its stress on urban and "civilized" as contrasted with rural and small-town standards, is a kind of counterimage to Harding's evocation of village life. Mencken's emphasis on a free and assertive individualism, decency and honor, and joy in life also presents a counterimage to the mechanizing and standardizing forces that were shaping "normalcy" as he saw it developing. His backward glances revealed more evidences of civilized living than he could detect in the present or imagine in any near future. America, he believed, formerly produced many men who were forcefully themselves if not always men of integrity, but in the twenties most men fitted a pattern. Americans once loved liberty, but now only scattered voices spoke up in its behalf. Americans could once openly enjoy such pleasures as moderate drinking, but now puritanical mores and oppressive laws gave an illicit and furtive quality to many phases of social life.

Mencken sometimes looked back beyond the range of his own memories to his idealized conceptions of antebellum colonial plantation life and of the early national period. He sometimes saw the decline of American culture as starting with Jacksonian democracy. But he had a special partiality for the eighties and nineties. Although he rejected Harding's assumption that the American village circa 1880 was an apt symbol of the happy life, he resembled Harding in cherishing a nostalgic image of his own boyhood and youth. Agreeing with Thomas Beer's contention in *The Mauve Decade* that near the turn of the century "the gaudy spectacle of American life reached its high point and the beginnings of its decline," he commented:

The American people, it seems to me, have never been genuinely happy since. Today they are rich, and if the laws are to be believed they are virtuous, but all the old goatish joy has gone out of their lives. Compare Coal Oil Johnny to young John D. Rockefeller. Compare Jim Fiske to the current J. Pierpont Morgan. . . .

Something is surely missing. . . . The Americano no longer dances gorgeously with arms and legs.[6]

This conception of the eighties and nineties is obviously highly selective. Alternative associations, stark in outline and grim in mood, quickly come to mind, such as those that would be remembered by families which suffered severely in the depression of 1893 to 1897, or were tragically affected by the militant action taken against union members in the Haymarket riot of 1886 or the Pullman strike of 1894.

As the focus of Mencken's nostalgic moods suggests, the standards against which he and the *Mercury* measured America in the twenties were the product of his formative years. "I can't recall ever changing my mind about any capital matter," he remarked in his posthumously published *Minority Report*. "My general body of fundamental ideas is the same today as it was in the days when I first began to ponder."[7] His prejudices, with the tensions implicit in them, originated within the context of thought and feeling available to him as he grew to maturity in Baltimore and the border state of Maryland. As he interacted with or reacted against the diverse traditions which clashed and intermingled in that setting, he formed the strong preferences and aversions, the definite preconceptions and norms, congenial to his temperament and emergent personality. His heritage may be summed up briefly as that of a bourgeois German-American who developed cosmopolitan interests but retained intense local attachments to a relatively provincial Tidewater city. By the time he started on the *Baltimore Herald* in 1899, his basic views were well established. His later experiences and his responses to such trends as social Darwinism and literary bohemianism considerably broadened the range of his interests and activities, but their chief effect was to confirm and strengthen the attitudes and ideas he had already formed.

Boyhood World

Between 1880 and 1900, when Mencken was growing up, Baltimore was notably different from most other American cities. After the Civil War, the city's commercial tradition, dating back to the days when it was a port for Tidewater planters, still remained strong. In fact, Baltimore became industrialized more slowly than any other leading American city.[8] As late as 1900 it was still in the intermediate stage of the shift from primarily commercial activities to big, corporate industrial development. As a result, such concomitants of industrial expansion as overproduction and economic insecurity for many workers took a much less acute form in Baltimore than in New York, Chicago, Philadelphia, Boston, and Pittsburgh. Mencken learned to take pride in Baltimore's resistance to sudden change, its tenacious hold on some of the amenities surviving from the antebellum era. As a boy growing up in this big seaport, he also glimpsed vistas stretching eastward to Europe as well as to north and south, the directions taken by the coastal trade.

Another characteristic of Baltimore which helped shape Mencken's attitudes was its firmly established German-American community. Since the members of this community constituted nearly one-fourth of the total population of 425,000, they could cope fairly well with the danger of having their way of life swallowed up by the dominant American culture. Mencken was particularly conscious of the German-American tradition because as the *Stammhalter,* the oldest son of the oldest son, he was potentially the next head of all the American branches of his family.

At least partly as the result of being brought up in Baltimore, Mencken was neither fully northern nor fully southern in his allegiance and thought. His city and state had close cultural and commercial ties with both North and South. Writing in 1922, he analyzed the enduring effects of this division of sympathies and interests:

A Marylander from St. Mary's County or from the lower reaches of the Eastern Shore is as much a stranger to a Marylander from along the Pennsylvania boundary, or even from Baltimore, as he would be to a man from Maine or Wisconsin. He thinks differently; he has different prejudices, superstitions, and enthusiasms. . . . During the Civil War the State was even more sharply divided than Kentucky or Missouri, and that division still persists. It results in constant compromises—an almost Swiss need to reconcile divergent traditions and instincts.

After the Civil War, Baltimore, though bound to the South by kinship and sentiment, was not prostrated by its defeat. The city had both the economic and cultural resources to make it of strategic importance as the South confronted the tasks of Reconstruction. In the words of C. Vann Woodward, "Baltimore was at one and the same time the last refuge of the Confederate spirit in exile and a lying-in hospital for the birth of the New Order."[9] Consequently, Mencken responded to two traditions relating to the South. One tradition, marked by nostalgia for a mighty past, upheld an idealized conception of the plantation society of the Old South. The other, much swayed by northern example, looked forward to a New South built on industrialism and a *laissez-faire* business philosophy. In Mencken's mind, elements from his German-American heritage intermingled in complex ways with elements from the venerable tradition of the Old South and the brashly adolescent one of the New.

Like many men of the middle class, H.L. Mencken's father, August, and his uncle Henry took advantage of the opportunities provided by the economic expansion of Baltimore after the Civil War. The city's easy access to transportation and its financial resources enabled it to meet much of the southern demand for capital and for manufactured goods. In 1895, when its total trade by ship and rail amounted to more than $350,000,000, three-fourths of it was with the southern states. At the same time, Baltimore became a financial center equipped to handle the millions of dollars its capitalists invested in southern railroads, streetcar lines, cotton mills, lumber tracts, and coal, iron, and phosphate mines.

These conditions favored those who, like the Mencken brothers, had the acuteness to detect economic opportunity and the drive to found small industrial firms. The markets, railroads, and ship lines that served the Baltimore merchants could serve its industrialists equally well. Between 1870 and 1900, the number of factories in Baltimore and the average number of workers employed in them almost trebled, and the amount of capital invested in industry increased nearly sixfold. By 1890, these companies employed an average of fifteen persons and had an average capital of $18,000.[10]

One of these firms was the cigar factory owned and managed by the Menckens. They took naturally to the tobacco trade because their father, Burkhardt Ludwig Mencken, had been trained in it before emigrating from Germany and had become a successful tobacco wholesaler. In 1875, when August was twenty-one and Henry was eighteen, they risked a total cash capital of $35.00 and boldly set themselves up as August Mencken & Bro. Because of their thorough knowledge of the trade and their initiative in claiming a share of the southern market, they were soon able to build a factory. With August as production and office manager, and Henry as sales manager, the firm continued to prosper. By the mid-eighties, the brothers had acquired several warehouses in tobacco-growing areas and had opened a branch office in Washington, D.C.

Although the younger generation of Menckens was not exclusively of German descent, the German-American influence was dominant in the family. Three years after emigrating from Saxony in 1848, when he was twenty, Burkhardt Ludwig had married Harriet McClellan, then sixteen. Her family was Scotch and English and had come to Baltimore from Kingston, Jamaica. After bearing five children, she died of tuberculosis in 1862, when August was eight and Henry was five. Since she knew no German, English was the language of the household, and this continued to be true even after Burkhardt remarried. Under these circumstances, August picked up only a smattering of German, but, because of his mother's early death, his strongly Germanic father was the central figure in his boyhood world. For his own wife, August chose Anna Margaret Abhau, a girl of thoroughly German background. They were married in November 1879. Henry Louis was born September 12, 1880, followed by Charles Edward in 1882, Anna Gertrude in 1886, and August in 1889. Within the family, Henry Louis was known as Harry, and Charles as Charlie.

A few weeks after his third birthday, Harry moved with his family to a new three-story brick house at 1524 Hollins Street, opposite the little park at Union Square in West Baltimore. His uncle Henry lived next-door in a house which, together with August's, formed part of a row of the kind typical of Baltimore.

1524 Hollins Street was the center of the stable, normal, happy world of H.L. Mencken's boyhood. The reminiscences and personal folklore he presented in the first volume of his autobiography, devoted to his life to age twelve, cluster around that home and its immediate environs.[11]

The dominant male personalities in Harry's childhood were his father and, somewhat more remotely, his grandfather Burkhardt. Both were staunch individualists and strongly inner-directed men, with a real love of family life and a keen sense of their responsibilities as heads of their families.

H.L. Mencken remembered Burkhardt as a bewhiskered patriarch who limped along with the aid of a tremendous cane. When grandfather "heaved into sight in his long-tailed black coat, his Gladstonian collar and his old-fashioned black cravat," the whole family was on its mettle and the children were warned to behave themselves. Burkhardt would announce his readiness to discuss and settle any matter of family importance. In August's family, it was he who chose the children's names and gave advice on topics ranging from infant feeding to interior decoration.

To young Harry, his father was "a man of illimitable puissance and resourcefulness." Mr. Mencken usually dispatched most of his business at the factory in the morning, and then returned home for a hearty lunch followed by a nap. After going back to his office, he spent the rest of the day in leisurely fashion, sometimes adjourning to the saloon next door to entertain a customer or leaving to attend a baseball game. This schedule was broken by a weekly business trip to Washington and by occasional trips to out-of-town tobacco markets or to Masonic conventions, but it gave him ample time in which to look after his family.

Although Mrs. Mencken usually had a Negro maid to help her, she was a resourceful and energetic cook and housewife in her own right. She was also a sympathetic and understanding mother. Speaking of himself, his brothers, and his sister, Mencken declared, "We were encapsulated in affection, and kept fat, saucy and contented."[12]

When Harry and Charlie were old enough to go to school, their parents saw to it that many of the children's activities continued to be planned and directed from within the family. Harry was only five or six when his father began to take him along occasionally on business trips. In Washington, while his father made the rounds of restaurants and saloons owned by customers, Harry sat on one brass rail after another, munched pretzels, and drank sarsaparilla. Sometimes they visited such landmarks as the Capitol, the Washington Monument, and the Smithsonian Institution.

Other activities which resulted from family planning were Harry's playing at being a printer and newspaperman and his study of music. At Christmas 1888 the chief gift for him was a small self-inker printing press. Soon he was turning out calling cards for his father and a four-page "newspaper" printed on scraps of wrapping paper. His piano lessons, starting the same year, formed the basis for his lifelong devotion to music as an amateur performer as well as a listener.

Even though the urban environment decisively shaped his attitudes, Harry learned to enjoy some aspects of rural life. He and Charlie had their first chance to roam the open countryside in the summers of 1889 and 1890, when their father and their uncle Henry rented a large double house near the village of Ellicott City, about ten miles northwest of Baltimore. Exploring Sucker Branch, a heavily wooded stream that flows into the nearby Patapsco, was an especially thrilling experience. Harry was also excited to discover the office of a real newspaper, the *Ellicott City Times,* and he went nearly every Thursday to watch it being printed on an old-fashioned handpress.[13] In 1892 the August Menckens bought a country home on a hill above the Jones Fall valley near Mount Washington, five miles from the city. From that time on, the family moved to the country in early May, returning to Hollins Street in September.

August Mencken and his brother Henry shared traits and opinions which foreshadowed certain of those typical of H.L. Mencken. Their concocting of elaborate hoaxes and practical jokes, for example, anticipated the younger Mencken's similar ingenuity as well, perhaps, as his broader talents as a humorist. One instance of the kind of humor H.L. Mencken appreciated was their invention of a mythical brother named Fred, who, they claimed, had become a clergyman in defiance of the wishes of their father, Burkhardt. Since the latter's reputation as an infidel was well known, they warned their hearers not to mention the clergy in his presence, lest grief over his renegade son should overwhelm him. Over a period of years, they added details so convincing that at least some Baltimoreans actually believed in Fred's existence.[14]

H.L. Mencken also derived from his father and uncle the rudiments of the conservative economic views for which he later found a fuller rationale in social Darwinism. He grew up believing that the capitalist-manager, as illustrated by their example and precept, was an admirable type. After describing his father as "a competent manager of men" who personally inspected the cigars in his factory and insisted on high standards of workmanship, Mencken called him "the archetype of the assiduous business man." H.L. Mencken's personal financial practices were like those he ascribed to August and Henry: "They paid spot cash for everything, and never borrowed money. They liked to live well, but were never extravagant." Since August expected Harry to succeed him at the factory, he often lectured him "on the mysteries of tobacco and credit, the accursed nature of workingmen, the laziness of drummers, questions of freight," and kindred topics.[15] His son quickly became aware of the distinctions between their own class and those classes which were inferior economically and also inferior, by implication, in the qualities making for competence and success. Although August and Henry had little labor trouble, they refused to negotiate with labor representatives or to employ union help.

August Mencken's political philosophy, though never very fully articulated, involved strong views, some of which were taken over by H.L. Mencken and survive in his mature writings. These views bear traces of his grandfather Burkhardt's social and political conservatism. Burkhardt emigrated in 1848, but had little in common with the true Forty-eighters, the small group of politically liberal idealists who found refuge in America after participating in the abortive revolution of that year. In his primary aim of seeking improved economic opportunities, he resembled the majority of German immigrants, but he differed from many of them in his consciousness of a proud family heritage, his possession of enough money to meet his immediate expenses, and the ease with which he obtained work after his arrival. "In world affairs," according to his grandson, "he was a faithful customer of Bismarck." Since Bismarck's mother was a Mencken, this loyalty may have been strengthened by family pride. In 1852 Burkhardt was naturalized as an American citizen. During the Civil War, he sympathized with the South, and after the war he generally favored the Democratic party. But he was not greatly concerned about politics and was rather contemptuous of the political process in a democratic system.[16] His sons were high-tariff Republicans, but they shared his distrust of politics and his disdain for most politicians.

Despite this heritage from Burkhardt, August Mencken's political views, like his economic views, can be traced most directly to the class interests of the bourgeoisie of his time and place. "He believed," wrote H.L. Mencken, "that free trade would ruin the cigar business; beyond that his political imagination did not go." August's experiences with local government convinced him that most politicians are rogues and that any change in the political status quo is likely to be a change for the worse. When August Mencken & Bro. put up a new factory building in 1885, $20.00 paid privately to the councilman for the district warded off for ten years all the taxes that might have been levied on the huge swinging sign outside. When a reform group came into power in 1895, and the councilman was voted out of office, the new administration horrified August by notifying him that a license to maintain the sign would cost $62.75 per year. "This," his son explained in *Happy Days*, "was proof to my father that reform was mainly only a conspiracy of prehensile charlatans to mulct taxpayers. I picked up this idea from him and entertain it to the present day."[17]

August Mencken also had a violent dislike for liberal and radical reformers who loomed up on the national scene: "Debs, Altgeld, Bryan—all these were devils in his eyes."[18] The panic of 1893 intensified the conflicts between management and labor and between eastern financial and industrial interests and the agrarian interests of the West and the South. As unemployment and economic unrest increased, as the number of strikes mounted, as many business firms and banks collapsed, and as one railroad after another went into the hands of receivers, many conservatives viewed all efforts to reform government and curb privilege as attempts to undermine the established order. In the early nineties, Eugene Debs was not yet converted to Socialism, but capitalists regarded him as an archfiend because of his career as a labor organizer and his leadership of the strike of the American Railway Union against the Pullman Palace Car Company in 1894. John Peter Altgeld earned the hatred of many conservatives by his defiant liberalism as governor of Illinois from 1892 to 1896. William Jennings Bryan, elected to Congress in 1890 as a spokesman for Nebraska farmers, became the target for the jibes of Republicans and some eastern Democrats because of his championship of free silver and his vigorous campaign as the Democratic-Populist presidential nominee in 1896.

In reviewing Waldo R. Browne's *Altgeld of Illinois* in the *Mercury*, Mencken indicated that it took him many years to modify his jaundiced view of the staunchly liberal governor. He probably had his father in mind as the chief among his "elders" when he wrote:

What I gathered from my elders, in the awful years of adolescence . . . was that Altgeld was a shameless advocate of rapine and assassination, an enemy alike to the Constitution and the Ten Commandments—in short, a bloody and insatiable anarchist.

Altgeld's popular reputation as an anarchist was part of the aftermath of the Haymarket bomb explosion in Chicago in 1886, as a result of which seven people were killed and over sixty injured. Although the persons directly responsible for the throwing of the bomb were never discovered, a jury found eight anarchists guilty of murder, and seven were sentenced to death and one to life imprisonment. Of the seven, two had their sentences commuted to life imprisonment. One of Altgeld's first acts as governor was to pardon the three anarchists still serving prison terms for a crime of which they were undoubtedly innocent. To dominant business groups and to the conservative press, this decision branded the governor as a subverter of public order and decency. In 1894 his notoriety among conservatives increased when he vigorously protested President Cleveland's authorizing a federal injunction and federal troops to be used in Illinois to put down the Pullman strike.

Mencken was surprised to find in later life that men who knew the governor personally—Theodore Dreiser, for example—had a high regard for him. From this he concluded "that Altgeld, though perhaps not an anarchist . . . was at least a blathering Socialist." Only after reading Browne's biography did he overcome his old prejudice sufficiently to say that "Altgeld was one of the first public men in America to protest by word and act against government by usurers and their bullies." In other words, Altgeld was a man of honor and integrity, the kind of gentleman that Mencken believed survived in American politics only as an anomaly.

Characteristically, however, Mencken, instead of seeing in Altgeld's election as governor a sign of hope for American democracy, concentrated on his defeat in his campaign for re-election. From this defeat, he derived the moral that the governor was excessively romantic in his faith that the common people would follow him. Thus even Mencken's modified opinion of Altgeld revealed the disdain for politics and politicians and the skepticism about the possibility of political reform which were part of his heritage. Mencken believed that, in recent times, nearly all American politicians had been out primarily for their own gain. Even if they started out as gentlemen, it was almost impossible for them to resist the forces tending to corrupt them. The rare exceptions who, like Altgeld, maintained their integrity, usually turned out to be idealists who took the democratic dogma too seriously. "Altgeld battled for the under dog all his life—and the under dog bit him in the end."[19]

The German-American Heritage

Since the middle-class German-Americans of Baltimore had the same economic base as the "native" middle class, both groups tended to develop similar economic views and, to some extent, similar political views. The German-American religious and moral outlook and patterns of social life did, however, differ significantly from those of their neighbors. In their consciousness of having a culture distinct from, and in their opinion superior to, the dominant native culture, the Menckens resembled millions of other German immigrants and their descendants. The nearly five million Germans who emigrated to the United States between 1830 and 1900 came from different religious groups, different economic and social classes, and different educational and occupational backgrounds, but they shared a common language and a common culture. Although some became almost completely Americanized within a generation and retained few distinctively German traits, the majority, and many of their descendants in the first and second American-born generations, became German-Americans. German-Americanism, as a complex of moral and social attitudes and a way of life, originated in their responses to American conditions. It arose in the 1850s, reached its peak near the end of the century, declined as the number of immigrants lessened, and suffered an almost fatal crisis when the United States declared war against Germany in 1917.[20]

Even if Mencken had been brought up a conventionally religious German Lutheran or Roman Catholic, he would almost certainly have opposed the puritanical attitude toward drinking, dancing, and other worldly pleasures which was officially common among American Protestants. Particularly offensive to the sociable, beer-drinking, music-loving German-Americans were such threatened curbs to their freedom as Sabbatarianism and temperance movements. Their dislike of righteous reformism was accompanied by a corresponding emphasis on social enjoyments and on a tolerant attitude toward the frailties and peccadilloes of others.[21]

More intensely antipuritanical than the common run of German-Americans was a small minority of free-thinkers who either tacitly or openly revolted against supernaturalism, clericalism, and conventional theology. Through Burkhardt and August, this free-thinking tradition came down to Harry Mencken. His mother sometimes attended an English Lutheran church, but both his grandfather and his father were outright skeptics. Burkhardt, though antireligious, was also an amateur theologian of sorts, and was on friendly terms with the Xaverian Brothers of St. Mary's Industrial School, where delinquent boys studied various trades, including cigar-making. Sometimes he took young Harry along when he called to sell the Brothers some leaf tobacco, and then settled down to drink beer and debate points of theology.[22] August, whose influence on Harry was more direct and more prolonged, was not only antireligious but also had an active dislike of the clergy.

The Menckens, nevertheless, had all of their children baptized. Beginning in 1886, they sent Harry and Charlie to Sunday school at a small Methodist chapel. Harry reveled in joining the other children in singing such lively hymns as "Are You Ready for the Judgment Day?," "Throw Out the Lifeline," and "Stand Up, Stand Up for Jesus." Two years later, the boys were transferred to a larger Sunday school at the English Lutheran church their mother attended. In this church Harry was confirmed on Palm Sunday, 1895. Although he submitted to this ceremony at his mother's suggestion, he expressed the opinion many years later that her churchgoing was "a sort of social gesture." If she had religious convictions, she kept them to herself and allowed August to scoff as much as he pleased.[23] Soon after being confirmed, Harry quit Sunday school, and in later years he rarely entered a church except to attend a funeral or fulfill an assignment as a newspaper reporter. Summarizing his reactions to formal religious training, he wrote

though I was . . . exposed to . . . Christian theology I was never taught to believe it. My father thought that I should learn what it was, but it apparently never occurred to him that I would accept it. He was a good psychologist. What I got in Sunday-school—beside a wide acquaintance with Christian hymnology—was simply a firm conviction that the Christian faith was full of palpable absurdities, and the Christian God preposterous.[24]

No one in his family provided Mencken with the kind of help he needed to arrive at beliefs positive enough to serve as an alternative to conventional religion. The German-American freethinkers' societies and the rationalist journals edited by German-American intellectuals might have furnished such a philosophy, but Burkhardt and August took no interest in such sources. Burkhardt may possibly have had a fairly coherent set of beliefs, but he died before Harry was old enough to begin consciously to develop a personal creed. August did not formulate his attitudes very clearly or speak about them very articu-

lately. As Harry came of age, he found the guidance he needed
not within his family, nor in German rationalism as it was im-
ported into America, but in British empiricism. "The tradition
in my family," he pointed out, "was anti-religious, but, as I recall it, it was somewhat distorted and narrow. . . . Huxley gave
order and coherence to my own doubts and converted me into
a violent agnostic."[25]

As a child of the prosperous bourgeoisie, whether German-
American or otherwise, Harry Mencken could not have avoided
becoming aware of the existence of a hierarchy of social classes
within which his own class occupied a place fairly near the top.
He accepted without question, for example, the assumption that
men like his father were socially superior to the workers they
employed. He similarly accepted the comforts and luxuries which
were the perquisites of the economically secure.

Among the Menckens, this tendency to take for granted the
prerogatives of one's own class was reinforced by strong family
pride. The earliest Menckens of whom records have survived
were wealthy merchants who flourished in Oldenburg in the
mid-seventeenth century. But the family obtained fame chiefly
in the pursuits associated with university teaching. A whole
series of Menckens, most of them professors at either Leipzig
or Wittenberg, devoted themselves to such subjects as moral
philosophy, history, and law. Through the works they wrote
or edited and through personal acquaintance and correspondence
with scholars of other countries, several of the Menckens earned
an international reputation. Through marriage, the Menckens
became allied with some of the most eminent families in Germany.

After being distinguished for more than a century for academic
achievements, most of the Menckens reverted to commercial
pursuits. The branch from which H.L. Mencken was directly
descended illustrates this process. Lüder Mencken (1658–1726),
the first of that branch to win academic renown, received his
Ph.D. at Leipzig, rose to the rank of professor in the university
law school, and served as chief judge of the Saxon High Court
of Justice. His son, Gottfried Ludwig (1683–1744), after serving
with his father on the Leipzig faculty, moved to Wittenberg,
where he became rector of the university and a judge in the local

courts. Leonhard Ludwig (1710–62), eldest son of Gottfried, was appointed associate professor of law at Wittenberg, but later left teaching to enter private practice. Johann August Ludwig (1754–1833), one of Leonhard's two sons, also had a doctorate in law but went directly into private practice. Johann Christian August (1797–1867), only son of Johann August Ludwig, apparently had no university training, but, after a period of army service, owned and operated a small farm. In 1842 he indentured his son Burkhardt Ludwig, H.L. Mencken's grandfather, to a tobacco merchant of Oschatz.[26]

As a boy separated by four generations from the record of scholarly achievement accumulated at Leipzig and Wittenberg, Harry Mencken had little precise knowledge of his family's claims to distinction. But family pride was communicated to the Mencken children as part of the atmosphere in which they grew up. Such pride was evident not only in Burkhardt's patriarchal sway, but also in his aloofness from both the wealthier and the poorer German-Americans of Baltimore. The most prosperous were merchants who traced their origins to the Hansa towns. As a Saxon, Burkhardt looked down upon them as Low Germans, even though his own ancestors, as traders in Oldenburg, had been Low Germans. With the poorer classes, he felt he had little in common. "He belonged," said H.L. Mencken, "to no organization save a lodge of Freemasons, and held himself diligently aloof from the German societies that swarmed in Baltimore in the eighties. Their singing he regarded as a public disturbance, and their *Turnerei* as insane."[27]

August Mencken, though a more genial man than his father, had his full share of family pride, and he, too, declined to join any German-American organizations. He had the Mencken coat of arms, "a linden tree between two roebucks rampant," registered as a trademark to be used on every box of cigars that left his factory. Partly because of this commercial use of the coat of arms, H.L. Mencken later regarded his father as "a curious mixture of snob and Philistine,"[28] but August's pride in his business was so great that he probably felt he was upholding the family tradition rather than demeaning it.

Family pride reinforced H.L. Mencken's class consciousness. That he himself was a member of the elite went without saying. "I inherited," he declared, "a bias against the rabble. I come of a family that has thought very well of itself for 300 years, and with some reason. My father . . . was a capitalist engaged in an active struggle with labor. It was thus only natural that I should grow up full of suspicions of democratic sentimentality." This passage shows how family pride and identification with the managerial class were fused in Mencken's thinking.

Implicit in his attitudes was the notion, later confirmed by his reading in social Darwinism, that some nationalities or races are by hereditary endowment inevitably superior to others. He was convinced early in life that bourgeois German-Americans, with few exceptions, were more competent, industrious, and honest, and therefore usually more prosperous, than Anglo-Saxons. "In the Baltimore of my early days," he observed,

most of the dead-beats and *Schnorrer* were pure Anglo-Saxons from the South or from the Southern counties of Maryland, thrown into the town by the backwash of the Civil War. My father viewed them with great contempt, as incompetent and often dishonest. The most prosperous families in my neighborhood were of foreign extraction, mainly German. The Americanos were petty shopkeepers, political jobholders, etc. To say that anything was American, in my family circle, was to hint that it was cheap and trashy.[29]

When he enrolled at Knapp's Institute, the first school he attended, Harry Mencken began a lifelong process of testing his capabilities through vigorous competition with Americans of Anglo-Saxon stock. Knapp's was a private school catering to the bourgeois German-American community, but its students included "Irish-Americans, French-Americans, Italian-Americans and even a few American-Americans." Although the mature Mencken, viewing his education in retrospect, acknowledged that old Professor Knapp, a Swabian, regarded the native Americans as "intellectually underprivileged,"[30] it apparently did not occur to him that in such an atmosphere the small Anglo-Saxon minority were at a serious disadvantage. At Baltimore Polytechnic, a public high school to which he transferred at the age of twelve, Harry's ability and his disciplined training at Knapp's put him a year ahead of other boys his age in every subject

The German-American Heritage   53

except algebra. With the assistance of a friendly teacher, he quickly caught up in algebra and was promoted one whole grade. By the time he graduated with a higher average score on the examinations than anyone else in his class, he had found no reason to alter his opinion that, generally speaking, Anglo-Saxons were an inferior group.

German-American culture focused on the family. The stable, orderly, happy family life, headed by his father, that Harry knew as a boy foreshadowed his later ideal of a stable, orderly society dominated by an elite. This later ideal also had a parallel in his interpretation of antebellum plantation life. As a grown man, Mencken believed that German-Americans achieved a secure and happy home life much more often than their Anglo-Saxon neighbors. In order to attain happiness, he concluded that a family must, like the Menckens, own their own home, have a sense of being rooted permanently in that particular place, and acquire a rich store of memories and associations that cluster about a certain house in a certain locale. The father should, like August Mencken, be competent, hard-working, and financially able to support his family in appropriate fashion. H.L. Mencken remembered that in his boyhood the German-Americans "owned their own homes and paid their own way," but the Anglo-Saxons "were renters and made a hollow show."[31] The mother should, like Anna Mencken, be primarily a homemaker. Allowing no outside interests to distract her, she should run her household smoothly and efficiently and care for her children.

In consistently refusing to hire women and children as workers at the cigar factory, August Mencken was at least in part upholding this conception of family life. It is not surprising that H.L. Mencken opposed women's suffrage and often directed his satire against women who embarked on public careers.

Many of the preferences Mencken expressed in the *Mercury* can be traced to the social habits and views of his family. Despite the standoffish attitude that Burkhardt and August maintained toward both the wealthier and the poorer classes of their own nationality, they were typically German-American in their personal traits. Much as they admired competence and punctiliousness in business matters, they frequently followed up their transactions with a session of conversation and beer drinking. Beer and German dishes appeared on the Mencken table side-by-side with southern dishes. August kept on hand a supply of locally brewed beer to serve to casual acquaintances, but for his own use and for the family councils he preferred Anheuser-Busch beer shipped in from St. Louis. While many boys of native stock were being taught that saloons were dens of vice, Harry Mencken, on his visits to them with his father, was developing a liking for "the cool, refreshing scent of a good saloon on a hot Summer day, with its delicate overtones of mint, cloves, hops, Angustura bitters, horse-radish, *Blutwurst* and *Kartoffel-salat*."[32]

Gemütlichkeit, as Mencken defined it, sums up several prejudices that were part of his inheritance. Rejecting the common American notion that Germans are either "beer-soaked boors" or "cocky strutters," he held that the really typical German qualities are "efficiency and good temper." *Gemütlichkeit,* which stands for the German ideal, "means, in the first place, comfort, ease, peace, divertisement, good eating, good drinking, a warm fire, an untroubled mind; but it also means politeness, urbanity, hospitality, friendliness, sociability, toleration, general good humor."[33] This suggests both Mencken's positive social ideal, with its stress on sensuous pleasures, and his positive ideals of honor and decency.

In their negative aspect, these ideals involved a violent re-action against threats to the way of life that sustained them. The Menckens wanted to be left free to conduct their personal lives as they saw fit, and they granted the same right to others. It was from his father, Mencken recalled, that he learned "that private conduct had better not be inquired into too closely." The chief danger to German-American values came from movements favoring various kinds of restrictive legislation, such as prohibition or Sunday-observance laws. In his heated opposition to all such movements and in his ridicule of their supporters, Mencken was in the mainstream of the German-American tradition. The following passage illustrates a typical attitude:

The Temperance Swindle is an outflow of Puritan bigotry, and comports with other of their pious pretensions, for example such a rigorous observance of the Sabbath as will reduce all sociability to the condition of a Puritan graveyard.[34]

With slight changes in phrasing, this might be one of Mencken's protests, but it actually appeared in a German-American newspaper in 1855.

The German-American cast of mind helps explain a problem which troubled some readers of the *Mercury:* why did not Mencken strive to be more objective and allow a wider range of opinions on such issues as evangelical religion and Prohibition to be presented? Gamaliel Bradford, for instance, called on him "to put up with the point of view of others, to recognize its legitimacy, to allow for their idiosyncracies and singular failures, as we should like our own allowed for." Mencken, in his reply, pointed out that his first editorial contained more signs of humility and tolerance than Bradford had recognized:

On the one hand [he wrote], I admit that I fear my own variety of truth is often not actually true, and on the other hand I offer to hear and print all proponents of antagonistic truths, so long as they are neither doctrinaire or sentimental.

Then, in a characteristic caveat, he added:

So I doubt that you will have anything to complain of, save perhaps some axe-work now and then. In that department I crave your indulgence! God hath made me so. I can withstand almost any temptation, including even that of alcohol, but when a concrete Methodist bobs up in front of me in his white choker I must simply fall upon him or bust.

In the German-American spirit, Mencken regarded tolerance and fair play as ideals to be maintained in his relations with men civilized enough to act on them and willing to live and let live. In dealing with people he encountered personally, even those he distrusted or violently disagreed with, he usually lived up to his code demanding courteous treatment of others. But in his writing he reserved the right to express himself freely and to resort to "axe-work" upon those whose views seemed to him intellectually disreputable and whose behavior struck him as uncivilized.[35]

This distinction is apparent in his editorial policies. He welcomed "the utmost freedom of opinion, and even of prejudice" in "the discussion of questions upon which educated and civilized men differ"—for example, questions as to the merits of capitalism, the composer Schönberg, or the late President Wilson. Arguing that "there are also regions in which intelligible discussion is quite impossible," he refused to print "defenses of osteopathy, chiropractic, the doctrine of total immersion, Fundamentalism, spiritualism, the New Thought, and other such imbecilities."[36] He also lashed out violently at the advocates of measures which, like Prohibition and the antievolution laws, tried to force individuals to conform to the militant moralism of the Anglo-Saxon.

Youthful Reading

In reviewing Edgar Kemler's *The Irreverent Mr. Mencken*, Edmund Wilson commented that the author failed to appreciate the sound qualities of Mencken's German heritage. Wilson is perceptive in stressing the positive values Mencken derived from the German—or, more accurately, German-American—heritage, but he is misleading when he refers to Mencken's debt to the German literary tradition.[37] During his formative years, Mencken was much more at home in the literature of England and America than in that of Germany. His lack of proficiency in German kept him from developing a home-feeling for German literature. Although he often heard his grandfathers speaking German, English was the language spoken regularly in his home. At Knapp's Institute he sang German folksongs, but frequently did not know their meaning. The teachers who tried to instruct him in German relied so heavily on sheer repetition and rote learning that they had little success. His grandfather Burkhardt described eloquently the past glories of the family, but to Harry professors at Leipzig or Wittenberg more than a century ago must have seemed as remote as the Byzantine Empire. In any case, he lacked the command of the language he would have needed to study family history or read the books written by his ancestors. Besides, his father, who was only half German, seemed to take no interest in either Germany or its people.

What first aroused Harry's interest in Germany was not the family tradition, nor his study of German in school, but his reading of Mark Twain's *A Tramp Abroad*. Much of it baffled him when he first struggled through it at the age of eight, but when he reread it at fourteen or fifteen, it had a dual effect. The text convinced him that Germany would be a fascinating place to visit, but the appendix on "The Awful German Language" confirmed his "feeling . . . that German was an irrational and even insane tongue, and not worth the sufferings of a freeborn American."

In further study at the Polytechnic, he learned to understand spoken German with some ease and to read it with effort, but he never became fluent in speaking or writing it. After the turn of the century, he developed an interest in such authors as Sudermann, Hauptmann, and, most notably, Nietzsche, but by that time his own basic assumptions were already established.

Mencken's habit of voracious reading started in his boyhood. Before he was eight, he managed, in about twenty sessions, to get through "The Moosehunters," a long story in the 1887 edition of an English annual called *The Chatterbox*. Soon afterward, he tackled an atrociously translated edition of *Grimm's Fairy Tales*, an award given him at Knapp's for his good record the previous year, but he put it back on the shelf without finishing it.

With his curiosity aroused, he began to explore the house for other reading matter. The Baltimore newspapers and his mother's files of *Godey's Lady's Book* and the *Ladies' Home Journal* had little appeal, but the books in the old-fashioned secretary in the sitting room intrigued him. His father's small library included *Chambers' Encyclopedia;* sets of Shakespeare, Byron, Dickens, George Eliot, and William Carleton; odd volumes of fiction, such as *Ben-Hur* and *Peck's Bad Boy;* a number of travel and history books; and most of the titles Mark Twain had as yet published. The first time Harry climbed on a chair to investigate this collection, he noted that the Twain volumes had much livelier illustrations than such tomes as *A History of the War for the Union* or *Adventures among Cannibals*. He took down one of the Twain books and sneaked it into his bedroom. He was embarked on his first crucial literary experience. At the age of eight, he was starting *The Adventures of Huckleberry Finn*. Stumbling quickly past unfamiliar words, he read on, entranced, to the end.

Why did he gag at *Grimm's Fairy Tales* but eagerly swallow *Huckleberry Finn?* Many years later, he thought that it was partly the bad translation that made him reject the *Fairy Tales,* but also that a temperamental aversion, the first flickering of his critical faculty, was at work. This aversion resulted from his having been born "without any natural taste for fairy tales, or, indeed, for any other writing of a fanciful and unearthly character." The same distaste, he believed, accounted for his lack of appetite for "the hortatory and incredible juvenile fiction" of Oliver Optic, Horatio Alger, and their fellows, and possibly also for his "life-long distrust of poetry."

The converse of his dislike for the "fanciful and unearthly" was a preference for what struck him as realistic and down-to-earth. That was the impression made by *Huckleberry Finn*. When August Mencken noticed what his son was reading, he told him of his own enthusiasm for Mark Twain. Soon Harry proceeded to *A Tramp Abroad, The Innocents Abroad,* and *The Gilded Age,* but he returned again to *Huckleberry Finn*. In it he found many of the qualities he later admired in fiction, among them a vivid portrayal of a specific locale, the skillful use of dialect, the creation of highly individualized characters, a probing exploration of human problems, and perceptive satire on social and religious orthodoxy. Through all his years as a literary critic, he used *Huckleberry Finn* as a touchstone of greatness, and never changed his opinion that it was the masterpiece among American novels.

At the same time Harry was developing a taste for fiction that created an illusion of reality, he also took a delight in the highly factual. Next to *Huckleberry Finn,* his favorite volume down through his early teens was *Boys' Useful Pastimes* by "Prof. Robert Griffith, A.M., principal of Newton High School." Harry was clumsy in any kind of manual work, but, following Griffith's directions, he managed to turn out a rabbit trap, a small table, and a whatnot his mother never allowed to reach its destined place in the parlor. Meanwhile, he soaked up many other kinds of specific information. He worked his way relentlessly through *Chambers' Encyclopedia,* Benson J. Lossing's *Our Country,* most of Charlotte M. Yonge's *A Pictorial History of the World's Great Nations,* and large sections of the Reverend J.G. Wood's *Our Living World,* full of colored pictures of birds and animals. He even sampled a formidable five-volume *History of Free Masonry in Maryland.*

In 1888, when the Menckens started subscribing to *Once-a-Week,* the predecessor of *Collier's,* they soon started receiving the cheap reprints in the magazine's library series. Harry could draw freely upon this new supply of titles, ranging from Tennyson's poems to Justin McCarthy's *History of Our Times.* About the same time, he was dipping into a similar series of reprints of scientific papers, including some of Herbert Spencer's essays. This was probably his first exposure to social Darwinism in print.[38]

Before entering the Polytechnic, he had acquired a larger vocabulary and greater skill in reading than most boys his age. The Polytechnic, originally called the Baltimore Manual Training School, was intended primarily to help supply the demand for skilled labor in industry. It featured subjects like mathematics, mechanical drawing, and shopwork. Although the spirit of the humanities did not thrive in that atmosphere, Harry, fortunately, encountered two English teachers who had infectious literary enthusiasms and an eye for good writing. Under their guidance, he began to read more widely and appreciatively in fiction, poetry, and the literary essay.

In explaining what these men stimulated him to read, Mencken did not mention any American titles, but selections from the standard American writers were undoubtedly part of the required work. Who some of these authors were is suggested by his listing of Irving, Lowell, and Cooper among "the unbearable bores whose 'works' are rammed into the heads of schoolboys by hunkerous pedagogues." He conceded that Poe was a major figure, but in 1913 he remarked, "And if I am cold to Poe, then blame the Poemaniacs who haunted my school-days in Poe-ridden Baltimore, mixing pifflish local pride with more pifflish literary criticism." What he stressed about his two teachers was not their routine assignments but their tips on how to organize his reading over and above school requirements. At the age of fourteen, following their suggestions, he "read the whole of Thackeray in one winter and then proceeded backward to Addison, Steele, Pope, Johnson and other magnificoes of the eighteenth century." He knew Pepys's *Diary* and Boswell's *Life of Johnson* "backward and forward."[39] Prompted by one of his teachers, he started reading Shakespeare, and then went on to Ben Jonson and Robert Herrick. Once launched on a more systematic program of study, he began to follow up fairly consistently certain lines of inquiry. After reading his father's set of Byron, he continued on to Shelley, Keats, and Swinburne. In fiction, he dipped liberally into Fielding, Smollett, and Sterne.

"Before I began to be fetched by the literary movement of the nineties," Mencken boasted, "I had read at least half of the classical English répertoire." For a boy in his middle teens, he had encompassed a remarkably wide range of reading. It is impossible to tell whether his failure to mention such writers as Richardson, Scott, Wordsworth, and Coleridge represented a gap in his reading or in his memory. He did state explicitly that he somehow missed Jane Austen and Charlotte Brontë. He also made it clear that his dislike of moralism prevented him from appreciating certain works. He could not force himself through much of Spenser or Milton. George Eliot dismayed and repelled him "as effectively as a text in Hittite." In boyhood, he regarded Carlyle as "impossible," but he was won over twenty years later by *Frederick the Great*. In time, he appreciated the genius of Dickens, but he was put off by the English writer's "sentimental view of the world, with its cardinal doctrine that all human ills are to be cured by love."[40]

Of all the British novelists, Thackeray left the most enduring impression. Much as Mark Twain had crystallized Mencken's conception of American fiction, Thackeray helped crystallize his conception of British fiction. His favorite Thackeray novel was *The Memoirs of Barry Lyndon, Esq.*, the tale of the "daring and the devilry, and the wickedness and the fall" of an eighteenth-century soldier of fortune and man about town. An epilogue reveals that the hero spent nineteen years in Fleet Prison, London, and then died of *delirium tremens*. Thackeray, contrasting Barry with "those perfect impossible heroes" of conventional romance,[41] apparently intended to portray him consistently as an unscrupulous rogue, but he frequently betrays an affectionate sympathy for his unabashed egoism, spendthrift generosity, foolhardy courage, and savoir faire.

Barry Lyndon obviously differs in many ways from *Huckleberry Finn,* yet certain similarities between the two stories suggest that Mencken was beginning to develop a pattern of literary preferences. Both novels focus on a vividly depicted hero. In each case, the hero is the narrator and presents his trials and adventures from his own point of view. As a boy, Barry, like Huck, rebels against book-learning and against many of the social conventions that restrict the lives of his elders. Both Barry and Huck observe the world about them shrewdly and perceptively; both often have to live by their wits and resort to wiles and stratagems; and both become acutely aware, at times, of man's cruelty to man. In *Barry Lyndon* and *Huckleberry Finn,* and in some other works by the same authors, Mencken discerned the traits he once attributed to Thackeray: "bitter honesty and . . . bitter wit," tempered by "genial worldliness, . . . jovial sacrilege, . . . toleration and . . . [a] broad and human philosophy."[42]

Provincial Loyalties

Mencken's loyalty to Baltimore and the border state of Maryland was so intense that he often viewed other cities and other parts of the country with a certain disdain. His provincialism was shaped primarily by his German-Americanism, but it was also affected by other local influences. As a Baltimorean, he was the heir to the traditions of the Old South and the New, both of which formed part of the intellectual climate of the city in the years following the Civil War. Two Baltimore publications voicing the spirit of the Old South were William H. Browne's *Southern Magazine* and Albert T. Bledsoe's *Southern Review.* Browne expressed the older sectionalism vigorously in 1870, when, in a letter to Paul Hamilton Hayne, he declared, "I want the new South, so far as it may be new, to be distinctly the *South,* and not a bastard New England."[43] In this spirit, both Browne and Bledsoe protested against the exploitation of the South's resources by northern capitalists and the eradication of southern-agrarian mores and values by industrialism. Although the two journals suspended publication during the 1870s, the

ideas and attitudes their editors stood for were widespread in the
South and survived into Mencken's early years.

The spokesmen for the New South, on the other hand, contended that industrialism was the best means of offsetting the
ravages of the war and revitalizing the South. Some of them
even talked openly of the need for "Yankeeizing" the region.
The Manufacturers' Record, founded in Baltimore in 1882 by
Richard H. Edmonds, a Virginian, described itself as "thoroughly identified with the New South," gloried in the progress
of southern capitalism, and gave space to the speeches and letters of northern capitalists. In 1887, in a speech before the
Maryland Institute for the Promotion of Mechanic Arts, Ferdi-
nand Latrobe, mayor of Baltimore, argued that the long-term
prosperity of the city depended on the growth of industry. As
in other parts of the country, the vogue of social Darwinism,
with its tendency to justify unrestrained economic individualism,
reinforced such traditional sanctions of capitalism as the Protestant ethic and the doctrines of the classical economists. Champions of the gospel of wealth, such as Daniel Augustus Tompkins,
North Carolina cotton miller who contributed to *The Manufacturers' Record,* echoed Herbert Spencer in asserting that "the
survival of the fittest is, has been, and will always be the law
of progress."[44]

The tradition of the Old South and that of the New were
ideologically incompatible, but in the minds of many southerners they fused emotionally about an image embodying the hope
that, somehow, the best ideals of the agrarian, antebellum South
could be maintained during the transition to the more fully
industrialized New South. Thus it was possible for men like
Walter Hines Page and Woodrow Wilson, who came to Baltimore to cross over from the Old Order to the New, to preserve
an allegiance to both traditions. In this dual allegiance, though
not in the particular form his allegiance took, Mencken was to
resemble them.

Mencken's explicit economic views, in many ways, allied him
with the spokesmen for the New South. He, too, had faith in
capitalism and admired the economic virtues it fostered. He
accepted that aspect of social Darwinism which equated economic with natural laws and justified unrestrained competition.
These assumptions and views often served as a rationale for big

as well as for small-scale industry. As consolidations, trusts, and corporations gradually absorbed many of the small manufacturing firms of Baltimore and made it hard for others to survive, the logic of Mencken's position implied that he should welcome these new and presumably more efficient forms of organization.

With regard to big industry, however, his feelings usually won out over the logical implications of his views. Although he acknowledged at times that big industry might increase production and lower prices, his feelings lingered fondly about the image of the small factory. After graduating from the Polytechnic, he had worked in the family firm and had become thoroughly familiar with the procedures developed under the paternalistic guidance of his father and his uncle Henry. The dominant spirit was that of the old tradition of handcrafts rather than that of the new more fully mechanized mass-production techniques. Although the introduction of the cigar mold in the eighties made it possible to divide cigar-making into a series of operations that could be performed by women and children, August Mencken resisted all such innovations and continued to employ only skilled male cigar-makers.[45] He personally supervised all the details of production and inspected samples of finished cigars to test their quality. After his death in 1899, his brother Henry assumed full ownership of the firm, but found it necessary to curtail its activities considerably. H.L. Mencken, undoubtedly influenced by his father's attitudes, resented the threat big industry made to the pattern of entrepreneurship and personal management established by the small manufacturer.

By threatening small business and industry, big business and industry challenged middle-class German-Americans in Baltimore to prove their ability to adapt to new conditions and still preserve their way of life. This manner of life was itself a product of a transitional stage in the development of the city, but the norms it emphasized, centering upon the home and the family, implied order, stability, permanence. For Mencken, the essential elements were the consciousness of belonging to an elite; the conception of a social system in which each class performed its proper functions and kept to its proper place; loyalty to home and family and a close circle of friends; a strong sense of personal security; a stress on competence and hard work in one's occupation; and untrammeled enjoyment of social pleas-

ures after working hours. He took pride in the ability of Baltimoreans to oppose innovations and to "change . . . their prejudices but once a generation."[46]

The superiority of Baltimore to other large American cities
was a favorite theme in Mencken's newspaper pieces after the
turn of the century. Asserting, for example, that "no sane man
would be a Pittsburger if he could help it," he summed up the
dilemma created by big industrialism by saying, "The world
needs pig iron, and it must be made, but the spot where it is
made is not fit for residence."[47] In New York City, overcrowding
had driven the average family "into unhealthful, warren-like
tenements." Mencken contrasted conditions in less fortunate
cities with those in Baltimore, where "living is an art, and not
an affliction."[48]

Even the force of coincidence encouraged Mencken to take
pride in the lore of his native city and state. In 1880, the year
of his birth, Baltimore celebrated the one hundred fiftieth an-
niversary of its founding. As a boy, he never had to go to school
on his birthday, September 12, because it was a public holiday
commemorating the victory of the embattled Baltimoreans and
their allies over an attacking British force during the War of
1812. This circumstance alone made him the Baltimore equivalent
of the "Yankee Doodle Dandy born on the Fourth of July."

His early writings reveal his interest in the local scene. In the
fall of 1899, while working as a cub reporter on the *Herald,* he
turned out the main part of the anonymous text of a copiously
illustrated piece of publicity entitled *A Monograph of the New
Baltimore Courthouse.* In sketching the rise of a court system in
Maryland and summarizing the early history of Baltimore, he
showed his enjoyment of such picturesque details as the right
of seventeenth-century justices of the peace to inquire into " 'all
manner of felonyes, witchcrafts, inchantments, sorcerys, magic,
arts, trespasses, forestallings, ingrossings and extorcons whatso-
ever.' " He devoted a whole section to the careers of such
prominent Maryland attorneys as Luther Martin, Roger Brooke
Taney, and Reverdy Johnson. His pride in the traditions of the
state comes out in passages like the following:

Maryland, from early colonial days, has furnished more than
her share of the great men of America. It is true that no Mary-

lander has ever become chief magistrate of the Republic, but it is equally true that many of her sons have attained an eminence in affairs of state. . . . Some of the nation's greatest soldiers, orators and public men have owed their allegiance to her.[49]

Mencken's provincial pride made him susceptible to an idyllic interpretation of the colonial plantation society. Many of his essays hint at this interpretation, but a striking example occurs in "Maryland, Apex of Normalcy." After describing the early planters of Maryland as leading "a life of peace, tolerance, and ease," he declared that

out of their happy estate there grew a civilization that, in its best days, must have been even more charming than that of Virginia. That civilization was aristocratic in character, and under it the bonds of all classes were loose. Even the slaves had easy work, and plenty of time for jamborees when work was done. . . . The upper classes founded their life upon that of the English country gentry, but they had more money, and, I incline to think, showed a better average of intelligence. They developed their lands to a superb productiveness, they opened mines and built wharves, they lined the Chesapeake with stately mansions—and in the hours of their leisure they chased the fox, fished the rivers, visited their neighbors, danced, flirted, ate, and drank. . . . Nor were they mere guzzlers and tipplers. Annapolis, down to Washington's presidency, was perhaps the most civilized town in America. It had the best theater, it had the best inns, and it also had the best society. . . .

This nostalgic portrait is in the tradition of those southern writers who used standards drawn from the myth of the Old South to disparage the crudities of the increasingly industrialized New South.[50] In the eighteenth-century Tidewater, especially as represented by such figures as Washington and Jefferson, Mencken found a close approximation to his ideal society. The remark that in colonial culture "the bonds of all classes were loose" suggests his belief that a firmly established aristocracy can permit more freedom to all—especially more freedom of speech—than can a democracy, threatened as it always is by the tyranny of the mob. But how much freedom did the slaves have? In the classic manner of apologists for the Old South, Mencken

evaded this issue by evoking the stereotype of the happily ir-
responsible bondsman shifting quickly from his "easy work"
to joyful "jamborees."

Nostalgia also dominated Mencken's memories of the German-
American way of life as he had known it when he was growing
up. He was convinced that the kind of prosperous burgher
typified by his own father had affinities with the colonial planter.
If, as the context clearly justifies, we take "the authentic Baltimorean" in the following passage as including—and, indeed,
emphasizing—the bourgeois German-American, such an equation
of the two patterns of life is strongly implied:

The authentic Baltimorean, . . . the Baltimorean lifted above all
brute contact and combat with the native blacks and the invading Goths and Huns . . . is a fellow who touches civilization at
more places, perhaps, than any other American. There is a simplicity about him which speaks of long habituation to his own
opinions, his own dignities, his own class. In a country so largely
dynamic and so little static that few of its people ever seem
(or are) quite at home in their own homes, he represents a
more settled and a more stately order. There yet hangs about
him some of the repose, the air, the fine superiority of the
Colonial planter, despite the pianola in his parlor and his daily
journey to a skyscraper. One sees as the setting of his ultimate
dream, not a gilded palace and a regiment of servitors . . . but
only his own vine and fig tree and the good red sun of Maryland
beating down.[51]

The true Baltimorean might work in a skyscraper or manage
a factory, but his concern with having "his own vine and fig
tree," with "the good red sun of Maryland beating down,"
had distinctly agrarian overtones. He and the colonial planter
had in common a strong sense of family and class loyalty, an
appreciation of comfort and repose, and a desire to maintain
stability in the social order. Mencken attributed to both types
such traits as competence, decency and honor, courage, a capacity
for joy, and a corresponding antipuritanism. From this composite figure of the Baltimore burgher merged with the Tidewater planter, it is not a long step to the Forgotten Man invoked
in the *Mercury*.

3
YOUNG REBEL

The Dominance of the Genteel Tradition

In the early nineties, when Harry Mencken was as yet hardly aware of the national scene, the spirit dominant in American cultural life was that of the "genteel tradition."[1] Since opposition to the genteel is one of the main themes of his mature writings, it is important to describe here the context in which his attitudes toward it developed.

Forming a social pattern as well as a critical position,[2] the genteel tradition appealed strongly to Anglo-Saxon, Protestant, middle-class Americans. Regionally, it flourished most wherever people of Anglo-Saxon stock set the cultural tone of their communities—in New England, the Middle Atlantic States, and in many parts of the South, the Middle West, and the Far West. For standards and examples of excellence in life and art, it tended to look toward Europe, particularly to England. Literature produced in America, according to this view, was a tributary of English literature, and the language spoken in America was most acceptable when it followed British norms of usage.

The genteel tradition was based on the premise that all the major issues of life and art were ethical problems to be judged and settled according to ideal standards. As a social pattern, the tradition stressed the sanctity of the home, the sacredness of the marriage ties, and strict observance of a rigid code of conduct, especially by women. The proper concerns for most men were business, breadwinning, and politics. Religion, the arts, and cultural activities were primarily the domain of ministers, college professors, and women. In sexual matters, reticence was the rule. The mother was the guardian of her family's morals; the young girl was the exemplar of purity. Ideally, she should be protected from influences which might threaten her innocence or disturb her faith in the family code. In accord with the spirit of the chief Protestant sects, at least some members of the family were likely to favor such restrictive measures as local prohibition and literary censorship. Private charity was also a popular cause among members of the genteel middle class.

This social pattern divided life into compartments. At one extreme was the divine in human beings; at the other, the animal. The church and the school flourished, but so did the saloon and the brothel. Religious precepts and democratic ideals often seemed to have little bearing on the everyday practices of business and politics. "Ideal" art, in its purity, excluded the grossness of life.[3]

This same split between the ideal and the real is evident in the prose and poetry of such major spokesmen for the genteel tradition as Thomas Bailey Aldrich, Richard Watson Gilder, Edmund Clarence Stedman, and Richard Henry Stoddard. These men did not ignore the contemporary American scene, but much of what they saw repelled them. Before the Civil War, the vulgar and commonplace aspects of the native life had often dismayed writers like Irving, Longfellow, and Lowell. Since the war, these aspects had assumed even more terrifying forms. Constantly forced upon the attention were striking extremes of wealth and poverty, industrial strife and unrest, the vulgarity of the nouveau riche, political boodling and chicanery, the spread of Darwinism and scientific materialism, and the rise of realism and naturalism in the arts. The rawness of frontier culture also troubled the genteel writers. But their awareness of these alarming realities did not prevent them from consciously cultivating an optimistic idealism.

Because of their sense of the gulf between gentility and reality, these authors did not regard the vulgar and commonplace as suitable literary material. They particularly wanted to keep poetry, which they regarded as the highest form of literary art, free from such contamination. The true poet, they believed, must lead his readers from mundane affairs to the ideal realm of the artist's creation. In quest of subjects and diction untainted by ugliness, they often chose themes remote in place and time and indulged in stock classical allusions. When they did deal with America in their own verse, it was usually to hymn a highly idealized version of their country, as Aldrich did in "Unguarded Gates" and Gilder in "The Heroic Age."[4]

Stedman, Stoddard, Aldrich, and Gilder were literary arbiters while Mencken was growing up not primarily because of their poetry, but because of their prestige as editors. Stedman exerted great influence through his extremely popular collections of poems, *A Victorian Anthology* (1895) and *An American Anthology* (1900). Stoddard was literary editor of the *New York Mail and Express* from 1880 to 1903. Aldrich edited *The Atlantic Monthly* from 1881 to 1890. Horace E. Scudder, his successor, introduced more emphasis on social issues but did not much alter the conservative literary standards Aldrich had enforced. Gilder, as editor of *The Century* between 1881 and 1909, was a leader in New York artistic, civic, and social affairs. Two other leading journals loyal to genteel criteria were *Harper's Monthly Magazine* and *Scribner's*.[5]

The views Gilder and his like-minded colleagues brought to the task of editing illustrate vividly the qualities which made the genteel tradition abhorrent to Mencken. Philosophical, personal, and practical considerations shaped their literary standards. Theoretically, these standards were grounded in a metaphysical and moral idealism. The genteel approach is well summed up in Stedman's definition: *"Criticism is the art and practice of declaring in what degree any work, character or action conforms to the Right."* "The Right," Stedman explained, applied to all matters of "verity, aesthetics and morals." In most of the genteel men of letters, a fastidious personal taste and a dislike of admitting that man has brute instincts combined to reinforce the moral scruples implicit in their literary theory. Finally, as editors of journals reaching thousands of American homes, they were practically concerned about shielding their audience from anything that might be offensive or demoralizing. Although they would not have stated the point so crudely, they shared the opinion of one of the characters in William Dean Howells's *A Hazard of New Fortunes:* "We've got to recognize that women form three-fourths of the reading public in this country, and go for their tastes and their sensibilities and their sex-piety along the whole line."[6]

Within the limits imposed by these norms, the genteel editors were in many ways able and conscientious men. They did not merely enforce taboos, but demanded a fairly high standard of literary competence. In fiction, they accepted not only the conventional romance, with its noble hero and heroine involved in passionate but bodiless love, but also the more moderate forms of realism. Ordinarily, neither the fidelity of the local colorists to regional custom and speech, nor the psychological realism of Henry James, nor the restrained social realism of Howells, nor even the humorous and satirical realism of Mark Twain seriously challenged the proprieties. Accordingly, the family magazines, in the eighties and nineties, published stories by regional authors like Sarah Orne Jewett, Mary E. Wilkins Freeman, George Washington Cable, and Joel Chandler Harris; and they serialized such novels as James's *The Bostonians,* Howells's *The Rise of Silas Lapham,* and part of Mark Twain's *Huckleberry Finn.*

The editors insisted, however, on deleting either details or language they considered offensive. Gilder, whose attitude was typical, pointed out to a correspondent that, when *The Century* ran *Huckleberry Finn* as a serial, he had obtained the author's consent to have it edited "for a miscellaneous audience." Although he defended Twain from the charge that his work had no redeeming qualities, he added, "Mr. Clemens has great faults; at times he is inartistically and indefensibly coarse." He concluded by saying that a preacher he knew, after reading Twain for several hours, had delivered "one of the most profound, moving and spiritual sermons to which I ever listened." One can imagine the disdainful snort with which Mencken would have greeted this post hoc argument intended to show that Clemens was "not a giber at religion or morality."[7]

Following the Trend of Middle-Class Taste

Mencken could not completely escape the genteel tradition any more than he could escape his middle-class assumptions. Although he did not accept the theology which, for many Americans, gave the Protestant virtues their final sanction, he retained a faith in the virtues themselves. He rejected puritanism and the glossing over of life's realities, but his basic conservatism and his conception of home and family had much in common with those of the upholders of genteel values. His reading, in part, followed the lines dictated by orthodox tastes. The sets of Victorian authors his father had accumulated had their counterparts in thousands of American homes. On the popular level, he ranged from the heart-rending tales of Mrs. E.D.E.N. Southworth to the whimsical stories of Frank R. Stockton.[8] Before 1900 he was familiar with many of the romantic novels by such authors as Stevenson, Barrie, du Maurier, Crawford, Page, and Cable.

Traces of gentility appeared in some of Mencken's early literary efforts and critical concepts. His verse and his attempts at fiction, largely imitations of the work of popular writers, deferred to genteel conventions. His contention that verse provides " a magical escape from the sordidness of metabolism and the class war"[9] suggests the actual function of much "ideal poetry." This kind of verse may well have formed the basis for his notion that poetry features lovely sound without much sense and is essentially inferior to prose. Despite the agnosticism and Darwinism which made realism and naturalism congenial to him, he enjoyed some of the genteel romances and, as a critic, gave them credit for whatever literary merit they possessed.

Even in his partial rebellion against the genteel, he was, to some extent, aligning himself with the common trend. In the nineties, a number of cultural developments worked together to expand the scope of interest and liberalize the tastes of the middle-class audience. Mencken's drive for self-education had its parallel in the eagerness of thousands of Americans to take advantage of the educational opportunities available. The spread of compulsory attendance laws, the tripling in the number of public high schools, and the rise in college and graduate-school enrollment helped create a more literate public. Cheap reprints and the proliferation of free public libraries made books available to a much wider audience. The Chautauqua system and other kinds of adult education brought instruction in the liberal arts within the range of men and women scattered through all the states of the Union. Instead of holding the line for polite standards, new magazines like *Collier's, Cosmopolitan, McClure's,* and *Munsey's* discovered and exploited the new interests and tastes of readers as they developed.

Middle-class women were changing along with the rest of the public. The young girls who were supposed to be symbols of purity were moving toward emancipation. More and more of them were getting high-school educations, and many continued on to college. Mencken had occasion to reflect on the new status of women when, as one of his news assignments in 1899, he reported on the commencement at Western Female High School in Baltimore. "In the early part of the century," he quoted the salutatorian as saying, "a girl with a degree was a kind of intellectual monstrosity, but the studiously inclined maiden of the present day may earn leave to write half the alphabet after her name without going beyond the United States." Another student speaker pointed out that the modern Baltimore girl, unlike her counterpart of Revolutionary times, was prepared to "discuss politics, law, psychology and the money question."[10]

As women became better educated, they were better able to qualify for various white-collar and professional positions. Many young girls from small towns moved to the city to get a job. Because of the independence and freedom they enjoyed, working women were less likely to marry early and raise large families. Whether married or single, many women were beginning to find the official codes of propriety irksome.

For several decades, intellectual and literary trends which challenged genteel values had been developing. From the nineties on, the American public responded to them more readily than in earlier years, but it was still slow and cautious in accepting them. Mencken, by contrast, began to follow them eagerly and sympathetically while still in high school. From Great Britain and the Continent came ideas which threatened to strip the supernatural sanctions from the Protestant theology on which the genteel code rested. The evangelical churches often assumed that the scriptures were literally God's word, but the higher criticism of the Bible, with particularly able exponents in France and Germany, challenged the whole conception of divine inspiration. Agnosticism and social Darwinism were also powerful dissolvents of Christian dogma. According to Spencer and Haeckel, man is not a divinely created being occupying the central place in the universe, but merely one among many living creatures whose struggle for survival is governed by the biological law of natural selection.

The new science seemed to vindicate the literary realists and naturalists who portrayed their characters as struggling with, and sometimes succumbing to, dynamic inner compulsions and the pressures of economic, social, and natural forces. Belonging in this category were European writers like Flaubert, Maupassant, Zola, Turgenev, Tolstoy, Ibsen, and Hardy. Most American critics viewed all of these men as too daring in their choice of themes and too extreme in their realistic method. In 1890 Maupassant's stories and Flaubert's *Madame Bovary* were usually not considered fit to be discussed in mixed company. Even though Turgenev appealed strongly to Henry James, and Tolstoy to Howells and Garland, many critics had serious reservations about both authors. At the beginning of the nineties, the postmaster-general barred Tolstoy's *The Kreutzer Sonata* from the mails. Ibsen's plays and Zola's theory and practice of naturalism were the subjects of particularly heated controversy. Eminent American men of letters argued that the society described by Continental writers was much more corrupt than that of England or the United States. Their themes and methods might be appropriate to their own culture, but had little relevance to the life led by Anglo-Saxons. Aldrich carried this attitude to an extreme by complaining,

> The mighty Zolaistic Movement now
> Engrosses us—a miasmatic breath
> Blown from the slums. . . .[11]

Hardy, of course, could not be dismissed as a Continental slum-dweller, but his somber pessimism ran counter to genteel optimism.

Nevertheless, works by Continental novelists had been attaining a fairly wide circulation in the United States. In 1881 Zola's *Nana,* in a bowdlerized translation, and in 1882 *Madame Bovary,* both published in cheap paper editions, ranked among the best-sellers. Tolstoy's *War and Peace,* competing with Frances H. Burnett's *Little Lord Fauntleroy* and H. Rider Haggard's *King Solomon's Mines,* won a place among the best-sellers of 1886. Sentimental tales like Marie Corelli's *A Romance of Two Worlds* and James M. Barrie's *The Little Minister* were favorites between 1888 and 1892, but some of Maupassant's stories published by Harper in 1889 also reached a wide audience.[12]

In the nineties, the general public continued to demand romance, but it was also enthusiastic about some works dealing with subjects previously considered sordid or vulgar. Although Mencken moved more quickly toward an acceptance of realism and naturalism than the majority of the middle-class audience, his tastes, to some extent, developed parallel to theirs. Feminine readers, for example, were defying some of the genteel taboos. Apparently much concerned about the facts of life, many women welcomed the columns of advice for girls and young mothers carried by the enterprising *Ladies' Home Journal.* The great success of George du Maurier's *Trilby* showed that women could become rapturous about fiction on morally questionable themes. In 1894, Henry Mills Alden, more venturesome than his colleagues on the other family magazines, published du Maurier's novel serially in *Harper's* with only a few discreet cuts. The story focused on the life of an artist's model in the Latin Quarter and portrayed her as less perfectly virginal than the conventional heroine. With its daring theme made palatable by liberal doses of sentiment, *Trilby*—as a serial, a book, and a play—was one of the literary sensations of the decade.

In becoming a Kipling enthusiast, Mencken joined the majority of American readers in a partial flouting of genteel norms. Because whatever was expressed through dialect was likely to be vulgar rather than ideal, the polite critics especially distrusted Kipling's use of the vernacular in poetry. Stedman, for example, recognized the virile force behind the verse, but cautioned, "It needs the British private at his best to make us tolerate the

'Gawd' and 'bloomin' ' lingo that only heroism and our poet's magic can ennoble."[13] Kipling's tales, with their emphasis on adventure in an exotic setting, had the appeal of romance and mystery, but stories like "The Man Who Was" and "The Mark of the Beast" confronted unpleasant facts so directly that they must have helped make realism more acceptable to the American public.

Joining the Avant-Garde

What most definitely set Mencken apart from the middle-class audience was his wholehearted sharing in the literary movement of the nineties. One result of this mild moral and literary rebellion was the more rapid dissemination in America of the ideas of European thinkers and men of letters of the avant-garde. In the little magazines, with cosmopolitan editors and contributors like James Huneker, Vance Thompson, and Percival Pollard, Mencken encountered comments on contemporary European authors and a bohemian revolt against orthodox social conventions and against moralism in the arts. Another phase of the movement which he followed closely was the rise of realism and naturalism in American fiction. After the turn of the century, he became a partisan of the new drama, particularly that of Ibsen and Shaw, and sometimes served as drama critic of the *Baltimore Herald.* Insofar as bohemian criticism, realistic fiction, and recent drama challenged accepted shibboleths and formulas, he saw them as part of the broad trend loosely associated with Darwinism.

Much as college students in the twenties scanned the newsstands for the *Mercury,* Mencken in the nineties scanned them for *The Chap-Book, M'lle New York, The Criterion,* and *The Lark.* More than ninety such "dinkey magazines" flashed across the literary firmament during the decade. Though influenced by *The Yellow Book* in London and the journals of the French symbolists in Paris, these reviews were not merely imitative. Usually too lighthearted and optimistic to be "decadent" in the European sense, they grew out of the response of cosmopolitan Americans to conditions at home. Gelett Burgess, founder of *The Lark,* summed up their purpose as "a revolt against the

commonplace," an effort "to overthrow the staid respectability
of the larger magazines and to open to younger writers opportunities to be heard before they had obtained recognition from
the autocratic editors."

The Chap-Book, the pioneer among the little magazines, probably gave Mencken his first inkling of Chicago's potentialities
as a cultural center that might eventually rival Boston and New
York. The World's Columbian Exposition of 1893 dramatized
the city's desire to be known as a place where the arts could
flourish. Among the authors then living there were Eugene
Field, Hamlin Garland, H.B. Fuller, George Ade, and Finley
Peter Dunne. In May 1894 Herbert S. Stone and Ingalls Kimball
started *The Chap-Book* in Cambridge, Massachusetts, where
they were Harvard undergraduates, but they moved it to Chicago
later the same year. Financial support for the handsomely
printed review came from Stone's father, originator of the
Chicago Daily News. The magazine soon outgrew its function
as a house organ for Stone & Kimball and became known as
a lively literary journal.[14]

In the early numbers, Mencken would have noticed, along
with articles on Oscar Wilde and Aubrey Beardsley, more French
than English material, including translations from Verlaine,
Mallarmé, and Anatole France. Viewing the journal in retrospect in the 1920s, he remembered it primarily not for its publicizing of foreign authors, but for its part in "the movement
against the Puritan (and especially New England) hegemony
which got under way in Chicago in the middle 90's." Letting
his enthusiasm outrun his judgment, he declared of this movement, "Once and for all time it broke the paralyzing hold of
the blue-nose upon the national literature and opened the way
for a genuine nationalism." This statement greatly exaggerates
the achievement of what, in another place, he called a "pianis-
simo revolt."[15] The suggestion that *The Chap-Book* consistently
opposed "the Puritan hegemony" is also misleading. Stone, who
acted as one of the editors, had absorbed some of Harvard's
gentility along with its mild bohemianism. He and his associates had private scruples which prevented them from being
wholly sympathetic to the greater frankness advocated by the
realists and naturalists. The need to build up a sound list for

their publishing firm also gave them a practical reason to cultivate the older, established authors as well as the younger, more adventurous ones. As a result, *The Chap-Book* published poems by Stedman and Richard Burton as well as by Stephen Crane and William Vaughn Moody, stories by conventional local colorists as well as by Garland, and criticism by Maurice Thompson and Hamilton Wright Mabie as well as by H.H. Boyeson.

Had Mencken chosen to concentrate on all the activities of Stone & Kimball rather than solely on *The Chap-Book,* he could have shown that the firm contributed significantly to the growth of native realism. Among the notable works published either by Stone & Kimball or by Herbert S. Stone & Co., its successor, were Garland's *Main-Travelled Roads* (1893), Harold Frederic's *The Damnation of Theron Ware* (1896), and Ade's *Fables in Slang* (1899). By publishing plays by Ibsen and Shaw, the Stone enterprises also helped create an American audience for the new drama.

M'lle New York, The Criterion, and *The Lark* were stimulated at least partly by *The Chap-Book's* success. Mencken especially enjoyed *M'lle New York,* for in its pages he first met Huneker's "illuminating sophistication and colorful, rapid style." This brash and gaudy review, edited by Vance Thompson, later joined by Huneker as associate editor, lasted for only fifteen issues in 1895–96 and 1898–99. In the standard periodicals for which Huneker and Thompson wrote to make a living, they constantly had to tone down their iconoclastic individualism and playful satire. But in *M'lle New York,* with the example of some of the Paris weeklies in mind, they made no effort to attract and hold a particular audience, but instead used that magazine, as Huneker remarked later, as "a safety-valve for . . . rank egotism and radicalism."[16]

The editors advocated views which, though mocking and sometimes equivocal in tone, closely parallel some of those Mencken was to express later. He was undoubtedly impressed by the review's unabashed cosmopolitanism. Here were widely travelled ambassadors of the arts, able to mention familiarly and appreciatively Ibsen, Strindberg, Hamsun, Verlaine, Wagner, Nietzsche. Already distrustful of Anglo-Saxon culture and New England influence, Mencken may have noted especially the magazine's contempt for the reigning literary set and the popular audience. Lumping Howells and Gilder together, the review denounced them outright for "intellectual priggishness" and "moral snobbishness." Thompson accused the public of "having vulgarized literature and the arts." He also argued, half-humorously, for "autolatry," a doctrine favoring extreme egoism in the artist; denounced "balletocracy" and hoped for the emergence of a new intellectual aristocracy; and ridiculed "gynolatry," or the indiscriminate idealization of women.[17]

The Lark (1895–97), though less outré than *M'lle New York*, was no less anticonformist and antiphilistine. It may have had the special value of making Mencken aware that bohemian rebels existed in remote San Francisco as well as in New York and Chicago.[18] He remembered *The Criterion,* a New York weekly, chiefly because it carried articles by four critics he admired: Thompson, Charles Henry Meltzer, Huneker, and Pollard.[19]

Of these four, Mencken much preferred Pollard and Huneker. In time, when he came to know them personally, he shared with each of them many sessions when beer and talk flowed freely. His tributes to them sum up his conception of their contribution to American letters. Pollard "worked so hard as introducer of intellectual ambassadors . . . that he never had time to write his own books." "Polyglot, catholic, generous, alert, persuasive, forever oscillating between New York and Paris, he probably covered a greater territory in the one art of letters than Huneker covered in all seven." As for Huneker, Mencken called him "the chief of all the curbers and correctors of the American Philistine; in praising the arts he has also criticized a civilization."[20]

Although Mencken's process of self-education tended to confirm his antigenteel prejudices, he did not repudiate completely either genteel conventions or the interests and tastes of the middle-class audience. From his high-school days on, his orientation toward the reading public involved many of the tensions which accounted for his constant preoccupation with American issues. As a boy of middle-class origins, he formed part of the audience for reputable magazines and standard books. At the same time, as an enthusiastic follower of the moral and literary rebellion of the nineties, he identified himself with an intellectual and aesthetic elite which prided itself on keeping considerably in advance of the main body of readers. Throughout his career, his attitudes toward the American public showed a divided allegiance. On one hand, as a member of the enlightened minority, he ridiculed the shortcomings and follies of the majority. On the other hand, he had a half-concealed affection for that majority. He reveled in its language, its humor, its occasional refusals to conform to what was expected of it. He was deeply concerned about its social, political, and literary preferences and how they developed. His success as a writer, in the end, depended on his winning over a large group of readers within the majority audience. Realizing this, he consciously perfected a style intended to capture the attention—to startle, stimulate, and entertain as well as to express a point of view. What gave this style much of its shock value was that he and his readers had a thorough awareness of the genteel tradition and partially shared its values.

While the little magazines were encouraging him to question popular standards, his skepticism and interest in science predisposed him to become a convert to Darwinism. Referring to the post-Civil War period, he once asked, "Who, indeed, will ever measure the effect of those two giants upon the young men of that era—Spencer with his inordinate meticulousness, his relentless pursuit of facts, his overpowering syllogisms, and Huxley with his devastating agnosticism, his insatiable questionings of the old axioms, above all, his brilliant style?"[21]

From the perspective of the 1970s, Spencer no longer seems so overpowering or Huxley so devastating. The many versions of social Darwinism may seem to us to be based on shaky premises and to put forward dogmas in the guise of scientific truths. Today we are likely to remember social Darwinism mainly as one source of the arguments used to justify a highly competitive industrial system and the economic inequalities existing under it. Yet Mencken and many others of his generation had no intention of becoming apologists for the gospel of wealth. Darwinism, it is true, appealed to them partly because it reinforced beliefs that were part of their heritage. In Mencken's case, these included economic and political individual-

ism, an admiration for competence and hard work, and a distaste
for conventional religion. Mencken and his contemporaries,
however, were also greatly impressed by social Darwinism because it helped explain the world about them, with the exciting
economic, social, and political changes it was undergoing. In
contrast to the genteel men of letters who lamented the ugliness
of industrial society, the popular interpreters of Darwin's biological law seemed to be developing values out of current trends
to meet current needs. The emphasis of thinkers like Spencer
and Sumner on material values, economic struggle, and the prev-
alence of human vices seemed to correspond more accurately
to the facts of an industrial age than the genteel emphasis on
spiritual values, moral striving, and man's inherent goodness.

Given Mencken's family background and the place and time
of his birth, it was only natural that before he reached twenty—
"the meditative, impressionable, speculative, iconoclastic age"[22]
—he should respond sympathetically to social Darwinism. To
blame him for not seeing at once that many of the beliefs he
adopted under supposedly "scientific" auspices had no genuine
scientific sanction would be unjust, but he can be fairly criticized for not developing that kind of insight and making the
necessary modifications in his attitudes later in life. Despite his
claim that he was skeptical about even his own views, he clung
to the assumptions and doctrines of his youth with a fixity which
inevitably impaired the quality of his thought. In his maturity,
at the same time that he flaunted his prejudices and admitted
the right of others to disagree with him, he regarded his beliefs
in the tradition of Huxley and Sumner not as articles of faith,
but as truths tested by scientific criteria. He also failed to recognize that the theoretical determinism and the dog-eat-dog ethic
he sometimes espoused were fundamentally at odds with his
code stressing the dignity and autonomy of the individual and
the importance of honor and decency.

He pondered over Huxley, Spencer, and Sumner between
1896 and 1899, the years during which he worked at the family
cigar factory. Very likely he then encountered many of the works
mentioned in his *The Philosophy of Friedrich Nietzsche* (1908),
such as J.W. Draper's *A History of the Conflict between Science
and Religion* (1874), John Fiske's *The Destiny of Man* (1884),

and Andrew D. White's *A History of the Warfare of Science with Theology* (1896).[23] From these and similar sources, he began to piece together the philosophy stated in fairly complete form in *Nietzsche* and *Men versus the Man* (1910). That philosophy, mainly a rationale for his own prejudices, was also to be affected by his experience as a newspaperman, his response to the new drama, and the studies preceding his *Nietzsche*.

4
APPRENTICE YEARS, 1899–1908

Initiation into Journalism

At the peak of his career in the 1920s, Mencken regarded himself not primarily as a literary critic but as a journalist and a critic of ideas—not as a middleman retailing the ideas of others but as an artist whose chief aim was to express himself. In explaining the motives behind his writing, he remarked, "There is in every living creature an obscure but powerful impulse to active functioning. . . . I became a writer . . . , and shall remain one until the end of the chapter, just as a cow goes on giving milk all her life, even though what appears to be her self-interest urges her to give gin."[1] The purpose of this section is to trace that "powerful impulse" as it developed through Mencken's youthful career as a newspaper reporter and editor and to show how, largely through self-education, he began to perfect a style capable of expressing vividly the whole range of the ideas and attitudes which later gained fame as his "prejudices."

Since Mencken's *Newspaper Days* gives an account of his boyhood literary aspirations and the beginning of his experience as a newspaperman, only a few key facts need to be mentioned.[2] His ambition to become a reporter developed while he was attending the Polytechnic. Arthur Hawks, a classmate who shared his literary interests, had an older brother who worked on the *Baltimore Morning Herald*. The boys discussed the possibility of applying for jobs on the *Herald* after graduation. Arthur did so and was hired, but Mencken ran up against his father's objections. His father was willing to send him to college, perhaps with a view to studying law, but, in any case, he wanted him to enter the family business. Harry vetoed the rather hazy proposals about college study. As a result, he went direct from the Polytechnic to work under his father's supervision at the cigar factory.

Like his father and grandfather before him, he started to learn the trade at the cigarmaker's bench. Already a smoker himself, he learned to appreciate the skill required in blending different kinds of leaf into a cigar. He enjoyed the aromas of the warehouse, with its tobaccos shipped in from as far away as the West Indies. What made him dissatisfied was being promoted first to the office, then to sales, then back to the office. He disliked keeping books and making out bills. Having to approach a customer to make a sale was even worse. In 1898 he summoned up the courage to tell his father how much he hated such duties, but the obvious distress this news caused made him drop the matter for the time being.

Meanwhile, he kept his other interests alive by reading widely and practicing writing. Early in 1898 he enrolled in a writing course offered by a correspondence school run in connection with *Cosmopolitan*. He read the rhetoric text and turned in the required lessons until late in the year. One of the two teachers who marked his papers complimented him on a story entitled "An Alley Case" by saying, "Your use of conversational style and colloquial expressions that prevail in the purlieus of a large city is very skillful." Mencken especially valued the advice of the second teacher, who urged him to avoid "long and pompous words" and use "simple and direct language."[3]

His dilemma—whether to submit to or defy his father's insistence that he stay on at the factory—was resolved by a sudden and unhappy eventuality. August Mencken, then only in his mid-forties, became seriously ill in December 1898, and died on Friday, January 13, 1899. Harry, as the oldest son, was now the head of his branch of the family. His uncle Henry assumed full ownership of the factory, leaving him free to continue working there or not as he pleased.

Mencken retained his job in the firm only long enough to make the transition to reporting. On the Monday evening fol-

lowing his father's death, he applied to Max Ways, city editor
of the *Morning Herald,* for a place on his staff. Ways advised
him to keep his present job, but offered to give him some trial
assignments. For several months, Mencken spent most of his
spare time reporting without pay. Finally, he was hired at a
salary of seven dollars a week, with the prospect of an early
raise to eight dollars. On July 2 he started work as the youngest
reporter on the staff, with his hours running from twelve-thirty
in the afternoon to eleven or later at night.

Thus, at the age of eighteen, he was launched on a career in
daily journalism. The city room was his classroom, Max Ways
and others served as his advisers and instructors, and the city
itself gave him "earfuls and eyefuls of instruction in a hundred
giddy arcana, none of them taught in schools." The tradition
into which he was initiated, with its emphasis on the responsibility of each reporter to write up, as well as to gather details
for, his stories, stood at the opposite extreme from the imper-
sonal assembly-line journalism of later years, when the reporter
became merely "a homunculus at the end of a telephone wire."
Mencken grew up believing in "the old-time journalist's concept
of himself as a free spirit and darling of the gods, licensed by
his high merits to ride and deride the visible universe."[4]

Mencken was only one of a whole group of important writers,
who, in the decades after the Civil War, served their apprenticeship on American newspapers. In their development as journalists, Bierce, Huneker, Hearn, Frederic, Crane, Phillips, Norris,
and Dreiser had little or no influence on each other, but, like
Mencken, they had literary ambitions and were in revolt against
the dominant mores.

The newspapers of the time drove their staffs hard and paid
niggardly wages. How was it, then, that they created an atmosphere congenial to those in whom dissent from the genteel
tradition was linked with literary interests? One reason was
that newspapers were aimed primarily at male readers and could
afford to be more outspoken than publications aimed mainly at
a genteel audience. All newspapers, of course, operated within
the restrictions imposed by local conditions, the biases of their
owners, and the editors' conception of good taste, but they often

featured some of the same brashness and iconoclasm that had fascinated Mencken in little magazines like *The Chap-Book* and in the writings of the social Darwinists. They also dealt openly with such themes as prostitution and adultery. Many editors believed that a newspaper should not merely record events but interpret metropolitan life and dramatize its human interest. They encouraged their reporters to observe the urban scene closely and to write about it in a fresh, colorful way. Sometimes they even urged their men to study the methods of Continental novelists like Flaubert and Zola and then apply them to American materials.

Looking back on the nineties from the 1920s, Mencken felt that journalism around the turn of the century did much to liberate some of the younger writers from "the so-called American tradition."[5] He himself had particularly admired the practices of the *New York Sun*, "the Bible of all the ambitious young journalists of that era."[6] With the exception of the humorists, including Mark Twain, most of the authors of the older generation, Mencken contended, took little interest in "the common, the ordinary life, and depicting things vividly was always far less their purpose than discussing them profoundly." Under Charles A. Dana, the *Sun*, by contrast, "showed a keen and unflagging interest in the everyday life of the American people—in the lowly traffic of the streets and tenements, in the tricks and devices of politicians and other zanies, in all the writhings and cavortings of the national spirit." It was largely at the hands of *Sun* men like Huneker and David Graham Phillips and the converts they made among other newspaper men "that American literature was delivered from its old formalism and hollowness."[7]

What Mencken says about the *Sun* was generally true of many other metropolitan dailies, such as the *Baltimore Herald*. No matter how much Mencken, for example, admired the *New York Sun*, he could not have used it as his model if the *Herald* policies had not encouraged him to do so. The *Herald* put more stress on human interest and the personal note than its more prosperous rival, the *Baltimore Sun*. The *Sun*, which had the best news facilities of any of the Baltimore papers, fostered reporting that stuck soberly to the facts. The *Herald*, as if to make up in color for what it might lack in solidity of detail, urged its men to pay at least as much attention to style as to accuracy.

Fortunately, it is possible to study Mencken's development as a reporter, since he preserved clippings of many of the pieces he wrote for the *Herald* and later deposited them in the Enoch Pratt Free Library in Baltimore.[8] Many of the stories he contributed while still an unpaid volunteer merely answer soberly the traditional questions: Who? What? When? Where? How? As he gained in self-confidence, guided not only by Ways's advice but also by his own reading of the *New York Sun,* he began to give a freer rein to his personal impressions and to play up whatever elements of human interest were latent in the events he covered.

Like Crane, Norris, and Dreiser before him, Mencken cultivated the ability to *see* the life about him and interpret it vividly for his readers. Sometimes, as the following lead paragraph shows, he needed only a few descriptive words to suggest the inherent picturesqueness of the subject:

W.A. Cuddy, evangelist, prophet of evil and founder of the unique Willow Tree Alley Mission, in Washington, will preach from his gospel wagon in this city today and tomorrow. He is a familiar figure at the Capital, where for three years he has preached on street corners and vacant lots from a sombre, black wagon, which bears on its sides weird warnings of the approach of the judgment day, and glaring inscriptions setting forth the articles of his doctrine.[9]

Not long after being taken on as a paid staff member, Mencken proved himself equal to the more challenging task of bringing out the local color, drama, and pathos involved in the sudden death of a Negro street preacher while conducting a service in Welcome Alley, Baltimore. Since this story illustrates his skill in organizing a narrative and giving it climactic force, it is worth quoting at length. After describing how the powerful voice of Wesley Brian, the elderly lay preacher, quickly attracted listeners, Mencken presents him in the midst of "an impassioned exhortation to the strayed and erring."

"If you are ready to go," he shouted, "buckle your armor around you and wait for the call of the Lord! Buckle on your armor, brethren and sisters! Gird yourself with the armor of the Lord!"

His voice rang out as he reached this peroration with all the earnestness of his creed and his race. He stopped, mopped his brow and stepped backward to the sidewalk. Then he "gave out" the stirring lines of an old-time camp-meeting hymn, and the outdoor congregation on the steps and curbstones and in the windows of the houses before and behind him joined in the singing with a will.

We will never say good-bye over yonder! . . .

When the hymn was over, Brian sat down on a step and gave way to a fellow preacher, then "gasped, half arose, fell, struggled slightly and . . . lay still on the sidewalk." A bigger crowd gathered, a doctor was sent for, and a police wagon took the body to Brian's home. Instead of ending the story with these details, Mencken goes on to show how the preacher's death inspired awe and a sense of foreboding in his audience. To do this, he puts into the mouth of an onlooker a fitting but probably fictitious remark:

"Dat ain't no mattah fer talk," said an old colored woman. "Dat's de Lawd's work, sho 'nuff, en you bettah let it alone. 'I'm ready to go,' sez Brother Brian, en de good Lawd call him en he went. Dat ain't no mattah fer talk, lemme tell you. Dat's de Lawd's business."[10]

Max Ways commended Mencken for this story and rewarded him with a pass to a performance of Rose Sydell's London Blondes.

During Mencken's boyhood, the dark underside of metropolitan life had been partially concealed from him, but now he had many opportunities to observe the areas in which filth, vice, disease, and death flourished. For many of its human-interest and local-color stories, the *Herald* depended on the police courts, "the Space" (Baltimore's equivalent of the Bowery), and the slums. Mencken's first regular assignments as a full-time reporter were in two of the police districts, first the southern and then the central. The central district included the busiest police court, police headquarters, the city jail, a downtown hospital, and the morgue. On this beat Mencken saw the victims of murder and suicide, witnessed hangings, and followed up leads in the toughest parts of the city. One of his chief news sources was Gene Grannan, the able and colorful magistrate of the central police court.

In an article headlined "Scenes in the Police Stations," Mencken begins with an effective pair of related metaphors: "If the police force is a mammoth drag net for the entanglement of the lawless element, the police station may be likened to the live-box in which the catch is temporarily stowed for safe keeping." In the next paragraph, he continues to use figurative language, but resorts to clichés:

The "Watch House," as it used to be called, is the place where the flotsam and jetsam of the city are cast on the beach of life. These wrong-doers first come in contact with the strong arm of the law; then violators of statute and ordinance receive the preliminary grind in the wheels of the mill of justice.

The four main types of prisoners are professional criminals, "the heroes of the dime novel"; petty thieves and streetfighters, such as the "youth with ventilated hat, rolled trousers and misanthropic air, who invests in a $1.29 'revolver' and aims to become a 'Napoleon of crime' "; respectable citizens brought in for minor breaches of the law; and habitual offenders, chiefly drunks. Probably thinking of Grannan's resourcefulness, Mencken remarks that a police magistrate, in order to cope with the varied problems that come his way, needs to know "the ethics of Aristotle, the moral code of the Meadowese, the religious rites and rights of the Russians, the construction of mule harness, the rigging of an oyster bugeye and the theory of variables." The article concludes with a matter-of-fact account of the organization of the Baltimore police force.[11]

As Crane and Dreiser had done earlier in the nineties, Mencken sometimes attempted to portray the sordid, strident life of the streets and the slums. Among the immigrants in Baltimore who were exploited as a source of cheap labor were a large number of Polish and Russian Jews, many of whom lived in tenements and worked in sweatshops in the same buildings. In 1899, after accompanying health-department inspectors on a tour of the East Baltimore sweatshops, Mencken noted particularly the stifling atmosphere created by the open grate fires used to heat irons, the smell of steaming cloth, and the intermingled odors of cooking and the gasoline used in the stoves. He explained that while the men toiled as tailors in the shops, and the younger women took work from the clothing factories to be sewn at home, the old women kept house and looked after the young children. His article contains the following vignette:

An aged and bent old woman was engaged in washing clothes in a room fronting on the porch, and the water which splashed from the tub made a large puddle on the floor. In it a phenomenally dirty urchin rolled and romped until his scanty clothing was soaked. Then he ran down the narrow steps to what was apparently the favorite playground of the children in the house—the spot where the garbage boxes of six families were piled in an ill-smelling pyramid. The old woman leaned over the rail of the porch apprehensively when he disappeared, but on seeing him playfully constructing a chain of potato peelings, returned to her work with a smile of relief.[12]

In a piece written in 1900, Mencken tries to convey some of the prevailing moods of "the Space" (Marsh Market). After an overlong introduction, he comments shrewdly on how merchants, radiating geniality and brotherly love, lure Negro workers into their shops and sell them such items as "a mandolin, a large scarfpin, a celluloid collar, a pair of gaiters and a hat." He goes on to sketch a scene in a saloon in the area on Saturday night. In the back room, shrouded in tobacco smoke, "a very tall and very awkward darky is dancing. To the rhythm of the tune played by the 'professor' at the piano he jogs up and down in a disjointed way. At the bar a double row of men, white and black, with 'schooners' in their hands, gaze at him listlessly." Now and then a sailor or a stevedore lurches in and buys everybody a drink. Finally, in the early morning hours, the profane activities of Saturday night give way to the peace of the Sabbath, as "the space dwellers climb up rickety staircases to their foul hutches and fall into a dreamless, dead-like sleep."[13]

Mencken's early newspaper writings also reflect his concern with the American vernacular. This interest antedated his career as a reporter, but newspaper work intensified it. Frequently he tried to reproduce the different dialects he heard, either as an incidental part of a local-color or human-interest story, or as a topic worthy of comment in its own right. In an article on how the Maryland blue laws were being enforced one Sunday in Baltimore, he employs dialect mainly to give a humorous effect. Since the work of messenger boys was considered necessary, they had no reason to be alarmed, but they liked to imagine that the police might try to nab them. Mencken depicts one messenger boy as putting on a great show of bravado and saying, "De peelers tries to pinch us, but dey ain't in de game. Dey can't git alongside of us. We git up too early. One of 'em chased me nine squares, but I give him de happy ho ho, 'en took to de woods. Oh, no; not on yer photygraft. De cops kin ketch de lobsters, but dey ain't got no show wid us. We're too soon."[14]

Because of his interest in the literary possibilities of American dialects, Mencken was delighted with George Ade's *Fables in Slang*, which he read soon after its publication in 1899. When put in charge of "a so-called funny column" in 1900, he printed some imitations of Ade's fables, about which he later exclaimed, "What miserable botches they were! How easy it was to imitate Ade's manner—and how impossible to imitate his matter!"[15]

Although Mencken was at first shocked by autopsies, hangings, and similar scenes, the chief effect his new experiences had on him was one of exhilaration. He felt as if he had suddenly acquired a permanent pass to a marvelous show that never lacked variety. Unlike those *Herald* reporters who were too unimaginative or too besotted to live up to Ways's demand for brisk writing, Mencken had not only the necessary talent but also the enthusiasm, energy, and capacity for hard work which enabled him to develop it. He could be relied on to stay sober during working hours and to complete an assignment left unfinished by one of his erring colleagues. He also had the ability to get along well with his superiors and with other reporters. He entered quickly into the humorously irreverent and mildly bohemian spirit that prevailed in the *Herald* office. All these qualities earned him rapid promotions and increases in pay. Between 1900 and 1906, when financial difficulties forced the *Herald* to cease publication, he served as humor columnist, drama critic, editorial writer, Sunday editor, city editor, managing editor, and finally secretary and editor.

Fledgling Satirist

In many of his early newspaper pieces, Mencken was able either to imply or express directly his agnosticism, his preference for the managerial as opposed to the working class, his feeling of belonging to a journalistic as well as an economic elite, his German-American suspicion of the dominant Anglo-Saxon culture, his opposition to prohibitionists and other reformers, and his delight in watching the cavortings of public men and pricking their pretensions to wisdom. Although his experience as a reporter and his wide reading broadened the range of his interests and activities, their chief effect was to confirm and strengthen the views he had already formed. Both the attiudes of his colleagues and his own observations tended to reinforce his prejudices and provide many examples he could cite to support them. This process can be illustrated briefly by showing the effects of his new surroundings and experiences on his religious, social, and political views.

Mencken's feeling that it was intellectually degrading to accept the doctrines of conventional religion was undoubtedly intensified by assignments requiring him to report sermons by visiting evangelists. One can imagine, for example, his private reaction to some of the prophecies he had to listen to, such as the claim that after a mighty world-wide revolution, "the multitudinous peoples of the world . . . will be ruled by God in person."[16] In *Newspaper Days,* he dramatizes his belief that religion threatened the live-and-let-live philosophy he and his associates maintained and the kinds of social pleasures they enjoyed.[17]

Mencken was already convinced, before becoming a police reporter, that the bulk of mankind was doomed by heredity to an inferior position. He was, therefore, not greatly startled by the ignorance, disease, and vice observed in the slums. He was eager to study the teeming life of those areas and report it vividly, but he did not take much stock in efforts to transform conditions there or to rescue slum-dwellers from their sins and superstitions. He was inclined to agree with Herbert Spencer that the less interference with the law of natural selection, the better. He also suspected that reformers were usually motivated not by altruism but by an urge to impose their own ideas of righteousness on others.

After about a year of police reporting, Mencken was ad-
vanced to the City Hall. This assignment gave him an intimate
knowledge of local politics, but it did not result in any basic
change in his boyhood political views. His attitude toward
American democracy was conditioned by his German-American
distrust of the dominant Yankee culture and the fear that the
majority would exert its power at the expense of dissenting
minorities. This attitude is reflected in an article he wrote in
April 1899, consisting chiefly of quotations from a letter his
Uncle Henry had received from Christian Abner, a manufacturer
from Cologne who had recently visited the United States. "The
truth is," said Abner, "that Yankees . . . have an unfounded
and absurd notion that they alone, of all the peoples of the
earth, enjoy real liberty, and that all foreigners long to share
it with them. What you call liberty, however, is, as a rule, but
a form of absolute despotism, which the dominant party exercises
over those outside of its fold. The minority in America has no
rights which the majority is bound to respect."[18] Mencken later
voiced similar sentiments.

As Mencken became familiar with the ins and outs of city
politics, he recognized that there were some honest and competent men in public office. He admired particularly Mayor
Thomas G. Hayes and his chief rival, Major Richard M. Venable, the leading member of the city council. The vociferous
disputes carried on by these two picturesque Confederate veterans always provided good copy.[19]

For the council members other than Venable and for most
other politicians down to the ward level Mencken had little
respect. Since he questioned whether they were qualified for
their positions or imbued with any sense of public service, he
often treated them satirically. In describing the inauguration
of a new city council in May 1901, for example, he points out
that, although they met ostensibly "to organize for business,"

In reality, they met to revel in the sweets of public honors, to
wear their Sunday clothes on Thursday afternoon, . . . ; to
answer to their names in loud voices; to strike attitudes in the
center of the stage; to wallow in the floral offerings of their
ward clubs; to perspire and struggle and suffocate and orate—

and all because they were city councilmen, of which there are 33 in Baltimore and 3,333,333, more or less in the civilized world.

As for the lowest political ranks, assembled in the audience, Mencken calls attention to

the slanting-browed contingent—the street corner and barber-shop politicians. . . . Some of them wore celluloid collars and some of them wore red-checked ones; others wore no collars at all. They represented the barnacles of the body politic and they were on hand to enjoy the meager pleasures with which the barnacle must be content. Theatrically considered, they were the chorus—the jolly, jolly mariners—the villagers—the tinsel brigands.[20]

Items satirizing national, as well as local, political figures and issues were a regular feature of Mencken's early humor columns. In his personal politics he was never a strict party man, and he extended his satire to leaders in both major parties. When McKinley defeated Bryan in 1900, Mencken produced "A Dirge" in doggerel verse assigning Bryan to oblivion "Till the Salt Creek stern-wheel steamer comes out of the woods again."[21] A few months later, he devoted "A Ballad of Fierce Fighters" to the prowess of the new vice-president, Theodore Roosevelt, whom he pictured hunting tigers with the Persian minister to the United States, whose first name was Isaac. The last stanza reads:

> Teddy and Ike are a fearsome pair
>   (Powder and shot and a ruby flood) ,
> Stalking the prey to its mountain lair,
> Speedy its lope and erect its hair,
> Weepful its visage with blank despair
>   (Powder and shot and a sea of blood) ,
> Blood, blood, blood, blood,
>   (Blood, blood) ,
> Blood![22]

Although Mencken's early newspaper pieces rarely approximate the skill and power of his mature style, they anticipate to a remarkable extent the mixture of common sense, humor, and satire typical of his social criticism in the twenties. They fore-

shadow not only his later treatment of American political
realities and personalities but also his later objections to righteous moralizing and to legislation intended to enforce a pre-
scribed moral code. When the Baltimore police began enforcing
the Maryland blue laws one Sunday in 1900, he wrote a number
of articles about this new policy. Since these were unsigned
news reports, he did not voice his own opinions directly but
managed to ridicule the blue laws nevertheless. In one article,
for example, he quoted the statute forbidding anyone "to profane the Lord's Day." Then he remarked that this law "was
passed by the Legislature of the State in 1723, when Baltimore
was a straggling hamlet of seven houses and a windmill," and
quoted a sign in the window of a pharmacy that remained open
but was allowed to sell only drugs:

Ask not for the baneful cigar nor yet for the sportive cigarette;
lest they bring you to the ashes of repentance.
Avoid the sparkling soda water—Satan lurks within every irri-
descent bubble. . . .
For it is decreed that man was made for the Sabbath.[23]

Mencken's humor column demonstrates that many of the types
upon which he heaped ridicule in the 1920s were arousing his
ire in 1900. He was already attacking the "prophets" who were
full of what he later called the "messianic delusion." Taking
as his text a line from Pope's *The Dunciad*—"O! born to see
what none can see awake"—he denounced "calamity-howlers,
religious prognosticators of the millenium, peach-crop prevarica-
tors, phrenologists and college professors of the kind that discover that the inoffensive Dutchmen of Pennsylvania are becoming Indians." The manner in which he would have liked
to dispose of them suggests his contention in the 1920s that
physical violence had its utility. When the "ready-made laws
of the land" are set aside, he said in 1900, then "The peach-
crop fabricator will be stoned to death with 'blighted' peaches;
the phrenologist will have his adamantine skull fractured by
a stone-crusher; the calamity-howlers will be sent to the work-
house; the religious prognosticators will be taught the use of
the razor; the college professors will be tarred like vinegar
barrels and feathered like Pennsylvania Dutch Indians."[24]

As a fledgling satirist, Mencken worked consciously in the tradition of Mark Twain as well as that of daily journalism. As a boy, he had sensed instinctively the artistic power in *Huckleberry Finn*. In the second by-lined column he printed as a newspaper humorist, he seized the chance to protest against the popular tendency to classify Mark Twain as a mere entertainer. "Someday," he declared, "the critics will awaken to the fact that . . . 'Huckleberry Finn' is the greatest novel yet produced by an American writer. At present it seems to be regarded as a cross between the 'Elsie' books and the 'Fables in Slang.' The penalty of humor is a cruel one."[25] This comment anticipates Mencken's assertion in *The Smart Set* that "the average man is far too stupid to make a joke" and therefore looks with suspicion upon those who can.[26] A truly intelligent man, by contrast, can create humor because he perceives the incongruities caused by the discrepancy between truth and illusion, performance and pretence.[27] Mencken showed the close affinity he felt for Twain by attributing to him a view of life similar to his own:

What a sharp eye he [Mark Twain] had for the bogus, in religion, politics, art, literature, patriotism, virtue! What contempt he emptied upon shams of all sorts—and what pity! . . . He regarded all men as humbugs, but as humbugs to be dealt with gently, as humbugs too often taken in and swindled by their own humbuggery. He saw how false reasoning, false assumptions, false gods had entered into . . . their thinking; how impossible it was for them to attack honestly the problems of being; how helpless they were in the face of life's emergencies. And seeing all this, he laughed at them, but not often with malice. What genuine indignation he was capable of was leveled at life itself and not at its victims.[28]

Finally, Mencken's clippings from the *Herald* show how his literary ambitions and strong urge toward self-expression made him strive to attain a vivid style. Stimulated by writers as diverse as Thomas Huxley, Mark Twain, Bierce, Ade, Hearn, Huneker, and Kipling, he sought to achieve lucidity combined with a verve and color that expressed his individuality. Frequently, he fell short of this ideal. Among the least successful of his youthful efforts are a series of thirty-three "Untold Tales"

printed in 1901–2. Most of these sketches ridicule some form
of political chicanery, but they are too sophomoric, cynical,
and heavy-handed to be effective.[29] Some of Mencken's apprentice work, however, makes its point aptly and concisely. This
is especially true of the pieces written when some flagrant example of "humbuggery" had aroused his iconoclastic zeal. Articles like the one on the city-council inauguration anticipate
the rhetorical resourcefulness and sustained gusto with which,
in his first contributions to *The Smart Set* seven years later,
he was able to dramatize his personality and create a mood,
an attitude, an insight that would capture the reader's imagination and often win his assent.

Experiments in Verse and Fiction

Despite the long hours demanded by his job on the *Herald*,
Mencken had the energy and self-discipline to do much writing
in addition to his regular assignments. By 1900 he was contributing occasional articles to out-of-town newspapers, either by direct
negotiation or through a syndicate. He also tried writing advertising copy, but his literary ambitions made him concentrate
particularly on verse and fiction.

In 1900 he commented in one of his columns on "these days
. . . when editors really pay minted coin for hexameters, and
triolets have a market value; when good verse distends the
lithographed hides of every magazine . . . and fairly rational
doggerel yells at one from every issue of every daily newspaper."[30]
He had begun to respond to this fad in his early teens. His first
writing to appear in print was "a satirical poem on a baseball
theme" which he sent into the *Baltimore American* unsigned.[31]
An apostrophe to Kipling, submitted anonymously, was published in *The Bookman* for December 1899. Other journals that
accepted his poetic efforts were *Life,* the *New England Magazine,*
and the *National Magazine.*

In 1900 and 1901 Mencken's drawerful of verses in manuscript,
dating from his teens, provided much of the copy for his humor
column. It was chiefly these which formed the contents of his
first book, *Ventures into Verse* (1903). This small volume, hand-

set in Caslon type and elaborately decorated, was a by-product
of the phase of the literary movement of the nineties concerned
with typography and book design. Marshall, Beek & Gordon, a
firm just founded by three of Mencken's friends, issued the
book as a sample intended to attract prospective customers.
Charles S. Gordon and John Siegel, both staff artists on the
Herald, did the illustrations. Mencken protested that most of
his verse "was poor newspaper stuff,"[32] but the urgings of his
friends and the prospect of having a book of his own printed
broke down his resistance. The complete title gives an adequate
and appropriately modest account of the contents: *Ventures into
Verse, Being Various Ballads, Ballades, Rondeaux, Triolets,
Songs, Quatrains, Odes and Roundels All rescued from the Pot-
ters' Field of Old Files and here Given Decent Burial [Peace to
Their Ashes].*

When *Ventures into Verse* appeared, Mencken had lost interest in versifying and was absorbed in writing fiction. *H.L.M.:
The Mencken Bibliography* lists fifteen of his stories published
in popular magazines between 1900 and 1906. Among the Menck-
en papers in the Enoch Pratt Free Library in Baltimore is the
typescript of an unfinished, untitled novel, probably begun in
1901. Intending to exploit the current vogue of historical romance, Mencken set his story in Elizabethan England and introduced Shakespeare as a main character. Handicapped by his
limited knowledge of his subject, he abandoned the project
after completing only fifty pages.

Although his fiction constitutes a considerable body of work,
it has largely been ignored or given only passing notice by his
biographers and critics. A study of the fragment of a novel
and of ten of the published stories shows that none of them
have much literary merit. Some of the stories are competent
enough to be plausible and entertaining; others are mediocre.
They are all apprentice work. They are valuable mainly for the
insight they give into Mencken's literary attitudes and concerns
during an important transitional period in his career. The experience of writing them provided Mencken with much of that
intimate knowledge of the craft of fiction later evident in his
work as a literary critic and magazine editor. As he commented
in a review of Montague Glass's *Abe and Mawruss,* "It seems

easy to spin such droll colloquies, to devise such simple plots.
But those of us who have poured out our sweat upon the making
of short stories know just how much careful planning, just how
much hard effort goes into every one of them."[33]

The themes and settings of Mencken's tales reflect both his
own experiences and his reading. His trip to Jamaica in 1900
explains his fairly frequent use of West Indian locales. "The
Cook's Victory" (*Short Stories,* August 1900), his first story to
be printed, dramatizes a conflict of will and wit between the
captain of a Chesapeake Bay oyster boat and his Negro cook.
The hero of "The Woman and the Girl" (*Short Stories,* February 1901) is a newspaper boy, in an unnamed American city,
who achieves his ambition to become a buck-and-wing dancer
in a burlesque troupe. Of two stories dealing with newspapermen, "The Flight of the Victor" (*Frank Leslie's Popular Magazine,* September 1901) takes place in Kingston, Jamaica, and "The
Bend in the Tube" (*Red Book Magazine,* February 1905) in
an unidentified American city. "The King and Tommy Cripps"
(*Red Book Magazine,* July 1906) is about an American boy
visiting a kind of musical-comedy European kingdom. The five
remaining stories are all tales of adventure, two of them set in
Central or South America and the other three in the West Indies.

The stories dealing with South and Central America, places
Mencken had never visited, were inspired by the tales O. Henry
was publishing in magazines and later collected in *Cabbages and
Kings.* They are only moderately successful in approximating
the stereotyped characters, humorous overtones, and surprise
endings of their models. In "Firing and a Watering, an Episode
of a South American Revolution" (*Short Stories,* August 1902),
two American engineers defeat the plan of some revolutionaries
to raid the supply of rifles at an American-owned mine. In "The
Passing of a Profit, the Story of a Losing Venture" (*Short
Stories,* January 1903), a man who is both chief of police and
American consul in a Central American town recovers his losses
from two American adventurers who have broken the bank at
his casino.

The marked influence Kipling's themes and manner had on
Mencken is apparent in such stories as "Hurra Lal, Peacemaker"
(*Short Stories,* May 1902). Its hero is the small son of Moffut

Lal, a laborer who had emigrated from India to Jamaica, where he works as a mule-driver on a banana plantation. Moffut explains to Hurra that the Queen is "a great white memsahib, with a gold crown on her head, and that she lived in a place called England, far beyond the sea." Hurra comes to associate the song "God Save the Queen" with the soldiers he once saw in Kingston, and he senses vaguely that they are defenders of her empire. Moffut is forced against his will to take part in a rebellion of workers against heavy taxes. Mencken's imitation of Kipling's style becomes especially obvious when he describes the Indian as knowing "that the devils of battle were loose and that there would be no reason until blood had been shed and houses burned, for when the devils of battle enter into the hearts of men—unless something marvelous happens—it is past time to talk to them. Blood alone will appease them."

Through Hurra's agency, the "something marvelous" happens which prevents a bloody conflict. Stealing out early in the morning, he sees the Negro soldiers of Her Majesty's West India Regiment marching down the road. As he scrambles up the mountain toward the rampart built by the rebels, he falls into a ditch just as the workers begin firing on the troops. When he sees a soldier crawling toward him, he jumps up and cries "God Save the Queen." Yelling "Spare the child!," Moffut leaps over the barricade. The other rebels, alarmed for their own safety as well as Hurra's, take the opportunity to surrender. Hurra's intervention has pleased and amused the Negro soldiers and their white officers. As the rebels march off, prisoners of war, Hurra rides "on a palanquin made of crossed guns, shouting 'God Save the Queen!' "[34]

Such traces of genteel sentimentality occur in a number of Mencken's efforts at fiction. It is impossible to tell to what extent he took these saccharine touches seriously, or to what extent he inserted them with tongue in cheek to cater to a popular audience. A passage from his attempted novel may represent a sincere effort to imagine how an Elizabethan boy would respond to his mother's love, or it may be merely an attempt to exploit a convention of romantic fiction. In one scene, Mencken shows the mother of the hero and narrator, George Wailes, reading to him

some story of the martyrs and the saints. The tale and her manner of telling were ofttimes so romantic that I would sit spell-
bound until rudely awakened by the loud sounding supper bell.
In my career as a man of fortune . . . I have more than once
thought of those glorious evenings of holy thought and heavenly
contemplation, and whatever I may have done in this life that
deserves to be called good or noble . . . found its inspiration, I
know, in my mother's angelic example and influence.[35]

"The Woman and the Girl" is a curious mixture of realistic
and sentimental elements. In its stress on the drabness of life
in a burlesque troupe and in its ironic conclusion, it reminds
the reader of some of Stephen Crane's *Bowery Tales*. Whitey,
the newsboy hero distinguished by his ability as a buck-and-wing
dancer, haunts the gallery at the theater and dreams of becoming
a performer. Once he achieves this goal, he quickly becomes
disillusioned:

He saw the life of those behind the scenes in all its naked ghastli-
ness and prosaic commonplace, and he knew the pang which
comes with the destruction of an ideal. As face to face he met the
soubrette whose loveliness had enchanted him when he was yet
an unsophisticated gallery god the greasy red of her erstwhile
fair complexion sickened him. As man to man he met the comedian whose wit had once been charming he knew him for what
he was—a hard-working mechanic, given to drink and the display of artificial diamonds.

The potential realism, however, soon becomes bogged down in
implausible situations and sentimental dialogue. Mencken does
not depict the process through which Whitey falls in love with
the nine-year-old daughter of the comedian, and the reader is
likely to sniff at the notion that a tough ex-newsboy, only ten
years old, would fall in love at first sight. The girl, billed as
"Eloise, the Infant Phenom," sings and dances and strums a
dummy guitar. Her parents force her to rehearse regularly and
appear in every show, no matter how ill or worn out she feels.
She and Whitey express their reactions to the villainy of her
parents in the language of stage melodrama. When Whitey
learns that her father has booked her to appear three times
a day and twice on Sunday at a summer resort, he runs to her
with the news:

"He signed you for the summer!" exclaimed Whitey excitedly. He was hardly able to keep the lump from his throat. "He signed you for the summer," he said again, "three performances a day! He's a beast—a beast! That's what he is!"

Lizzie took no notice of this slander of her parent, for the tears were coming unbidden to her eyes and soon she was crying softly. Her head found rest on Whitey's shoulder.

"I can't do it," she sobbed with her arms around his neck. "I can't do it! It'll kill me! Oh, I'm so tired, Whitey"—she clung to him despairingly—"I'm so tired, so tired!"

Whitey's face grew hot and his muscles swelled in strain.

"You shan't do it!" he exclaimed. "You shan't do no such work. You can't stand it!"[36]

After this rather awkward resort to the trite devices of popular fiction, Mencken developed a conclusion in keeping with the realistic tone of the first part of the story. Determined to help Lizzie escape, Whitey commands her to follow him, and they emerge into the crowded streets. Suddenly, the one person in the world of whom Whitey is deathly afraid confronts them. In a Kiplingesque phrase, Mencken describes her as "the woman who had borne him."[37] The veteran of many a drunken brawl, she is tough and unrelenting. Forgetting his concern for his companion, Whitey darts into the crowd. Lizzie breaks into tears.

Several marked contrasts between "The Cook's Victory" and "The Woman and the Girl" illustrate how Mencken's stories vary in quality. The point of view in both stories is that of the omniscient author, but in "The Cook's Victory" Mencken uses more varied and subtle methods of character portrayal. He not only describes Captain Johnson and Windmill, his Negro cook, but also depicts them through skillful dialogue. The controversy starts when the captain objects to the charred pancakes served by the cook. The captain's heated questioning begins on the first page and quickly arouses the reader's interest. Infuriated by what he mistakenly takes to be the cook's defiant attitude, Johnson orders the other crew members, both shanghaied men, to put Windmill in irons. He then delivers the following verdict:

"You're a dead nigger." The cook shuddered, and the captain went on: "Yes, you're a goner. You're a mutiner, by Jupiter, a rank, howlin' mutiner. Article two twenty-one, chapter thirteen, verse seven, of the Acts of the Legislature of Maryland in Congress assembled covers you all right. 'And if any man shall commit mutiny aboard any vessel in the Ches'peake Bay or tributaries thereof, he shall be taken to the jail from whence he come, and be there hanged by the neck 'till he be dead. And may God have mercy on his soul.' That's the law—chapter and verse."[38]

This ominous, yet humorous, version of the law of Maryland which Mencken puts into the captain's mouth vividly suggests the implications of the situation.

"The Woman and the Girl" is marred by inconsistencies in tone and by characters too stereotyped to be convincing, but "The Cook's Victory" creates a unified impression. The world aboard the *Sally* is a man's world, and Mencken appropriately combines realism with grim humor. Because of the lack of oysters in Maryland waters, the captain decides to risk crossing the Virginia line, even though he knows that if a patrol boat catches him he may get as much as five years in prison. He releases Windmill from his irons so that he can keep a lookout from the bow. Not long after crossing the line, the boat becomes embedded in floating ice which gradually freezes solid on the shore side. After quarreling with Johnson, the two shanghaied men leap out of the boat and escape across the ice. Windmill helps the captain work the pungy out into the channel again, but, when a police boat bears down on them and starts firing, he refuses to lend a hand. He knows the captain fears five years in jail as much as he fears death by hanging. The captain cannot hoist the mainsail without his help. In a hasty exchange, the captain reduces his "sentence" first to life imprisonment, then to ten years, and so on, until he finally pardons him altogether. Then Windmill falls to with alacrity. With some well-aimed rifle shots, the captain manages to disable the police sloop, and the *Sally* is safe once more.

When Mencken achieved both clarity and liveliness, as he does in "The Cook's Victory," Thomas Huxley was often the model he had in mind. "Huxley," he declared in his posthumously published *Minority Report,* "greatly influenced my early short stories, though he never wrote any fiction himself. I well recall how pleased I was when Ellery Sedgwick, then editor of *Frank Leslie's Popular Monthly,* praised the directness, simplicity and vividness of a story of mine, 'The Flight of the Victor.' "[39]

In their themes and opening situations, their trend toward realism tempered by humor, and their patches of vivid writing, Mencken's stories show promise. In bringing out the implications of the theme and in developing characters, they are usually less successful. At their worst, as in "Like a Thief in the Night" (*Short Stories,* August 1901), they are merely inflated anecdotes. Even at their best, they lack depth. Mencken's remark about a story by Rowland Thomas applies equally well, say, to "The Cook's Victory." "The incidents," Mencken wrote, "are well imagined and the whole tale is well managed, but only the externals are laid before us." Contrasting Thomas's treatment of a white man's reversion to savagery with Conrad's *Heart of Darkness,* he concluded that "the difference between the two writers is that which separates a promising apprentice from a superb master workman."[40] Similarly, Mencken's own efforts as a writer of fiction are fairly promising, but they fall far short of artistry.

A number of reasons account for the defects of his stories. They were, after all, youthful experiments modeled chiefly on the work of writers who had gained wide popularity. Like O. Henry and other authors competing for space in the popular magazines, he consciously sought to produce fiction suitable for a mass audience. This aim directed his stories into fairly conventional patterns. The haste with which he tossed off his stories in moments snatched from his heavy newspaper schedule helps explain why most of them lacked consistency and polish. Although he might have made considerable progress if he had continued to write fiction, he was probably right in deciding that other literary forms suited him better. Except for some concoctions he later used as fillers in *The Smart Set,* and a few tall tales like "Christmas Story" written in the thirties and forties, he virtually abandoned short-story writing in 1905, when he was twenty-four. "Then it suddenly dawned upon me," he declared twenty years later, "that I had no talent for them. Those that I wrote sold readily enough but they were hollow things, imitative and feeble."[41]

Ellery Sedgwick helped bring about this decision by urging Mencken to try his hand at articles and by accepting several for publication. Between 1903 and 1905, the *Popular Monthly* printed four pieces by Mencken under the pseudonym John F. Brownell—one on "Marketing Wild Animals" and three on prominent Baltimore personalities. Sedgwick was so favorably impressed that he offered him a job as his assistant in New York at more than twice the salary the *Herald* paid him. Loyal to his family and his duties as head of the house, Mencken declined the offer, but Sedgwick's faith in his abilities increased his self-confidence.

Meanwhile, as a reader and an embryonic literary critic, he moved toward the acceptance of literary realism and naturalism faster than anyone would have guessed from reading his stories. His attempted novel showed his response to the vogue of the historical romance, but several experiences confirmed the temperamental preference for realism which had been whetted by his early reading of Mark Twain and Thackeray. These experiences, which have already been discussed, included his interest in the literary movement of the nineties, with its partial rebellion against genteel standards, and his adapting to his own needs the views of the social Darwinists. His newspaper experience made him eager to see novelists record all facets of American life as faithfully as the best reporters did.

Although he decided early that writing fiction was not his own forte, he resembled Dreiser in finding in European as well as American novels examples of what might be done. In the early nineties, Dreiser had admired the vivid portrayal of life in Tolstoy's *The Death of Ivan Ilyitch* and *The Kreutzer Sonata* and had undergone "a literary revolution" in reading Balzac. In his later teens, Mencken read these same authors, but much more decisive for him were his discoveries of Crane, Zola, Dreiser, and Conrad. "I am old enough," he wrote in the twenties,

to remember the blast *The Red Badge of Courage* made in 1895. . . . [It] came like a flash of lightning out of a clear winter sky; it was at once unprecedented and irresistible. . . . The miracle lifted newspaper reporting to the level of a romantic craft, alongside counterfeiting and mining in the Klondike.

More, it gave the whole movement of the nineties a sudden direction and a powerful impulse forward.

About 1900, when he started to read the Vizetelly translations of Zola, he was excited to find at last a novelist who recognized the relevance of Darwinism to literature. What Zola "introduced . . . ," Mencken asserted in 1912, "was the conception of man as a mammal—man swayed and fashioned, not by the fiats and conspiracies of a mysterious camorra of arbitrary gods, but by natural laws, by food and drink, by blood and environment." In addition to being a philosopher of literary naturalism, Zola was also "a creator of vivid and memorable characters, an accomplished workman in large forms." Late in 1900, Mencken borrowed from a friend one of the few copies of *Sister Carrie* to get into circulation. "It made a colossal impression upon me," he recalled, "and I became a Dreiserista at once."[42] In 1903 he was equally enthusiastic about the much different kind of artistry in Conrad's *Youth*. He could appreciate Conrad's selective, impressionistic method as well as Dreiser's massive piling up of details. Thus, by 1903 his literary enthusiasms were already moving beyond the preference for O. Henry and Kipling revealed in his short stories and were preparing the way for the essays on Dreiser and Conrad that appeared fourteen years later in *A Book of Prefaces*.

The Darwinian Tradition and Drama Criticism

From about 1902 to 1908, the drama appealed to Mencken even more strongly than the novel. In the little magazines, he had come across intriguing references to such controversial playwrights as Ibsen, Sudermann, and Hauptmann. In 1900, when he returned from Jamaica on a Norwegian tramp steamer, he had heard a good deal more about Ibsen from the young captain and his wife. When he began reviewing plays for the *Herald* in 1901–2, Robert I. Carter, a seasoned drama critic who joined the staff as managing editor, wrote the leading notice himself. At first Mencken was satisfied with concentrating on the lighter and frothier productions, but Carter's enthusiasm

for serious drama was infectious. Another impetus came from
Will A. Page, a former dramatic editor of the *Washington Post*
who moved to Baltimore in 1901 to be press agent for a newly
organized stock company.[43] From Page, Mencken first heard of
George Bernard Shaw and also learned much about the current
state of drama in the United States. Within the next few years,
he reviewed a whole series of recent plays, including works by
Ibsen, Shaw, Pinero, Hauptmann, and Sudermann. He began
to study plays in print and read drama criticism by Huneker,
Shaw, William Archer, and A.B. Walkeley.

Through his own drama criticism, Mencken found his métier
as a critic of ideas. As his interest in writing fiction declined,
his interest in writing drama criticism mounted. He was impressed not only by the literary merits of the new drama and its
effectiveness on stage, but also by its potentialities as a vehicle
for iconoclasm in a broadly Darwinian vein. In men like Darwin, Huxley, White, and Haeckel he had discovered one elite
with which he could identify himself, and in the aesthetic elite
favored by the bohemian critics he had discovered another.
Dedication to truth-seeking and iconoclasm was the common
quality shared by these two groups. Since dramatists like Ibsen
and Shaw were both artists and iconoclasts, they had links with
both elites. What suggested most directly to Mencken the proper
use of his own talents was the literature on the trail blazers
in various fields. As the following comment shows, he felt that
some of this literature had permanent importance:

> Shaw's pair of critical pamphlets—"The Perfect Wagnerite"
> and "The Quintessence of Ibsenism"—will go down into history
> beside Robert Schumann's early reviews of the compositions of
> Chopin and Huxley's opening broadsides for Darwin. Each
> paved the way for better knowledge and better understanding.[44]

In 1905, eager to be the first to publish a book on Shaw,
Mencken outlined a short study of the playwright modeled on
The Quintessence of Ibsenism. Brentano's, the firm which had
just started printing Shaw's plays, rejected the proposal, but
John W. Luce & Co. of Boston, which had recently issued Shaw's
essay, "On Going to Church," expressed interest. In April,
Mencken submitted his manuscript to Harrison Hale Schaff,

editor and partner in the company. After some revision, *George Bernard Shaw*, which Mencken always considered his first real book, was printed and put on the market the following autumn.[45]

In the introduction to *Shaw*, Mencken insists that the playwright should be an artist, not a preacher. He should dramatize conflicting points of view accurately and understandingly, without pointing a moral. "In other words, it is not his business to decide the matter for his audience, but to make those who see his play think it out for themselves."[46] Except for this proviso, Mencken was more interested in the themes of the new drama than in the finer points of technique. The theater appealed to him, as it did to Shaw, as a powerful medium for propagating not so much specific beliefs or disbeliefs, but a general attitude subjecting all taboos and conventions to a searching scrutiny. Insofar as the drama conveyed this general attitude, he regarded it as derivative from the broad movement of late nineteenth-century scientific thought. Although he found that this attitude originated chiefly in Darwin's research in biology, many of the assumptions he fitted loosely under Darwinism owed as much to the new discoveries in astronomy, physics, and geology as they did to Darwin's work.

According to the analysis in *Shaw*, the Darwinian epoch made possible an unprecedented reversal of attitudes which, at last, put orthodoxy on the defensive. It had also produced the dramatists, the scientists, the social scientists, and the philosophers who were the chief agents in bringing about that reversal.

From him [Darwin], through Huxley, we have appendicitis, the seedless orange, and our affable indifference to hell. Through Spencer, in like manner, we have Nietzsche, Sudermann, Hauptmann, Ibsen, our annual carnivals of catechetical revision, and the aforesaid George Bernard Shaw.[47]

That "all of these men and things . . . might have appeared if Darwin were yet unborn . . . is . . . overwhelmingly improbable."

Why? Simply because before Darwin gave the world "The Origin of Species" the fight against orthodoxy, custom, and authority was perennially and necessarily a losing one. On the side of the defense were ignorance, antiquity, piety, organization, and respectability—twelve-inch, wire-wound, rapid-fire guns, all of

them. In the hands of the scattered, half-hearted, unorganized
attacking parties there were but two weapons—the blowpipe of
impious doubt and the bludgeon of sacrilege. . . . Voltaire, who
tried both, scared the defenders a bit . . . , but when the smoke
cleared away the walls were just as strong as before and the
drawbridge was still up. One had to believe or be damned. There
was no compromise and no middle ground.

And so, when Darwin bobbed up, armed with a newfangled
dynamite gun that hurled shells charged with a new shrapnel—
facts—the defenders laughed at the novel weapon and looked
forward to slaying its bearer. Spencer, because he ventured to
question Genesis, lost his best friend. Huxley, for an incautious
utterance, was barred from the University of Oxford. And then
of a sudden, there was a deafening roar and a blinding flash—
and down went the walls. Ramparts of authority that had resisted doubts fell like hedge-rows before facts, and there began
an intellectual reign of terror that swept like a whirlwind
through Europe, America, Asia, Africa, and Oceania. For six
thousand years it had been necessary, in defending a doctrine,
to show only that it was respectable or sacred. Since 1859, it has
been needful to prove its truth.[48]

This version of how Darwinism brought the walls of orthodoxy
tumbling down, whatever its shortcomings as sober history, is
crucial to an understanding of Mencken. On one hand, it sums
up a long process of exposure to scientific and Darwinian thought
beginning with his childhood. On the other, it anticipates the
more thorough statement of his attitudes in *The Philosophy of
Friedrich Nietzsche* and *Men versus the Man*. The small minority
of fearless truth-seekers, he asserted in these later volumes, constituted the highest caste produced in human society by natural
selection. He disputed the contention of Sumner and other
apologists for the gospel of wealth that the captains of industry
necessarily represented the highest caste.[49] Industrial magnates
might at times qualify as true iconoclasts, but they were less
likely to do so than scientists, artists, and philosophers. Actually,
the field in which the iconoclast worked was of little moment.
The proper test was to determine the extent to which, without
regard to the consequences, he pursued the truth by the standards of the Darwinian dispensation. So long as he remained
true to the revelation of 1859, he belonged to the saving minority.

Upon the efforts of that minority depended whatever slow and halting progress could be made in the painful process of social evolution. Whether the iconoclastic campaign was artistic, polemical, or philosophical, it had two main aims. One was to dislodge the pseudoaristocracy, the genteel guardians of orthodoxy. The other was to get the sluggish, convention-ridden masses to glimpse the vision and move upward toward the light.

If Shaw had deigned to comment upon Mencken's little book,[50] he might have protested that "ignorance, antiquity, piety, organization, and respectability" were much more resistant to Darwinian shrapnel than Mencken's enthusiastic metaphor implied. Shaw was also more critical than Mencken of some of the concepts popularly associated with Darwinism. Shaw, as he himself says of Ibsen, "seems to have welcomed" natural selection "for the mortal blow it dealt to the current travesties of Christianity," but he also stressed that a too exclusive faith in Darwinian rationalism could put a mind in blinders just as surely as a too literal faith in Christian dogma. Mencken called Shaw, among other things, "a socialist, a cart-tail orator, a journeyman reformer," all labels which suggest the side of Shaw with which Mencken had little sympathy. Speaking in these capacities, Shaw was much more concerned than Mencken with the use that conservatives made of Darwinian "facts" to justify existing social and economic inequalities as the inevitable result of natural selection.[51]

Mencken derived his whole approach to the drama chiefly from Shaw's critical essays and the prefaces to his plays. From the very first chapter of "The Quintessence," for example, Mencken took over the concept of the two classes of "pioneers" who further human progress. Mencken's belief in the power of the theater to mold attitudes has a parallel in Shaw's claim that "Bad theatres are as mischievous as bad schools or bad churches; for modern civilization is rapidly multiplying the class to which the theatre is both school and church." When Mencken says that the main function of the new drama is to challenge the audience to think for themselves, he may have had in mind Shaw's statement that "my plays are built to induce, not voluptuous reverie but intellectual interest, not romantic rhapsody but humane concern."[52]

Mencken also echoed Shaw in maintaining that progress involves the repudiation of outmoded ideals and institutions. Mencken had declared in the *Herald* that Ibsen contributed to progress by making "us more honest with ourselves and more tolerant of our neighbors. As he has spitted, one after another, the Eminent Citizen, the Patriot, the Saintly Wife and other familiar shams, he has put us into the mood for a sane, commonsense cross-examination of the whole hypocritical company." Finally, Mencken's fearless truth-seeker, although originally modeled on Huxley, had a counterpart in Shaw's "pioneer." Shaw and his young American critic agreed upon the need for the iconoclast who, in Shaw's words, "repudiates duties, tramples on ideals, profanes what was sacred, sanctifies what was infamous, . . . everywhere proclaiming that 'the old beauty is no longer beautiful, the new truth no longer true.' "53

Mencken could appreciate the "wonderfully illuminative and searching passages" in "The Quintessence," but he was too immature and inexperienced to emulate Shaw's brilliant performance. Shaw was thirty-five and at the height of his career as a London critic when he completed his essay, and he aimed at no less an objective than "to distil the quintessence of Ibsen's message to his age." Mencken, in dealing with Shaw, wisely confined himself to the much more modest intention of producing "a little handbook."54 Except for a brief "Preface," the enthusiastically Darwinian "By Way of Introduction," and three concluding chapters on Shaw's life and his nondramatic writings, the book simply summarizes and comments on fifteen of Shaw's plays. A separate chapter is devoted to each drama.

Mencken's treatment of *Mrs. Warren's Profession* is typical. Apparently because he adjudges this to be "Shaw's most remarkable play," he discusses it first. He begins by explaining the paradoxical conflict between Mrs. Warren and her daughter, Vivie, through which the theme is brought out. Using allusions illustrating some of his literary interests at the time, Mencken terms Mrs. Warren "a successful practitioner of what Kipling calls the oldest profession. . . . She is no betrayed milkmaid or cajoled governess, . . . but a wide-awake and deliberate sinner, who has studied the problem thoroughly and come to the conclusion, like Huckleberry Finn, that it is better . . . to sin and be damned than to remain virtuous and suffer." Yet, "despite all her elaborate defense of herself and her bitter arraignment of the social conditions that have made her what she is, she is a worshiper of respectability." Vivie, recently returned from study at Cambridge, turns out to be the real iconoclast. She admits the force of the arguments her mother uses to defend her means of livelihood, but she objects to her mother's hypocritical deference to convention. After summarizing the action of the play, Mencken seconds favorable judgments by William Archer and Cunninghame Graham and objects to unfavorable judgments by Huneker and Max Beerbohm. "Taken as a play," Mencken declares, "the drama is wellnigh faultness. It might well serve, indeed, as a model to all who aspire to place upon the stage plausible records of human transactions."[55]

At the time Mencken's little volume appeared, it must have proved useful to the small audience it reached. Its summaries of the plays are lucid and entertaining. It cites opinions by critics who had written perceptively about Shaw. Mencken's own judgments, though not supported by much analysis, are concise and pointed. For *The Devil's Disciple, Caesar and Cleopatra, A Man of Destiny, Candida,* and *You Never Can Tell,* as for *Mrs. Warren's Profession,* he has little but praise, but he detects certain faults in other plays. *Arms and the Man* has a weak second act. *Widowers' Houses* is "rather elemental" in its portrayal of character. The first act of *Captain Brassbound's Conversion* contains "an immense amount of talk without action." *Man and Superman* is too unwieldy for stage presentation to a modern audience.[56]

Mencken's modest handbook, however, quickly and inevitably became dated. After 1905, as Shaw continued to write plays, more ambitious and more carefully analytical studies gradually superseded it. Today the volume is more important for what it reveals about Mencken than for what it reveals about Shaw. The rudiments of Mencken's mature style, for example, are evident in passages like this one:

Measured with rule, plumb-line or hay-scales, "Man and Superman" is easily Shaw's *magnum opus.* . . . Like a full-rigged ship before a spanking breeze, it cleaves deep into the waves, sending

ripples far to port and starboard, and its giant canvases rise
half way to the clouds. . . . It has a preface as long as a campaign speech; an interlude in three scenes, with music and red
fire; and a complete digest of the German philosophers as an
appendix. . . . It is a three-ring circus, with Ibsen doing running
high jumps; Schopenhauer playing the calliope and Nietzsche
selling peanuts in the reserved seats.

In a final burst of metaphor, Mencken concludes that *Man and
Superman* is a "colossal effort to make a dent in the cosmos
with a slapstick." He was justified in deciding, twenty years
afterward, that his *Shaw* "turns out to be very fair work for a
man of twenty-four. . . . It contains some acute criticism and
some very amusing writing."[57]

When the proofs of *Shaw* arrived in Baltimore, Mencken was
city editor of the *Herald* and was soon to be promoted; but
while he was rising through the editorial hierarchy, the *Herald*
itself was financially on the decline. For several years, the political ambitions of its owner, Wesley M. Oler, a Republican trying to breast strongly Democratic currents, had damaged its
reputation. The business manager Oler appointed—a Canadian
named Peard—was unable to obtain enough advertising to meet
expenses. The *Herald* building was destroyed in the great fire
which swept through downtown Baltimore in February 1904.
Taking pride in the youthful stamina which kept him going
for sixty-four hours without sleep, Mencken recorded in *Newspaper Days* that after the fire "the *Herald* was printed in three
different cities, and I was present at all its accouchements, herd-
ing dispersed and bewildered reporters at long distance and
cavorting gloriously in strange composing-rooms."[58] When the
Herald resumed publication in Baltimore, its circulation and
advertising increased for a time, but by early summer it was
again in financial difficulties. As a morning paper, it had to compete with both the *Sun* and the *American,* but the only important evening paper was Charles H. Grasty's *Evening News.*
In an effort to get more advertising, Peard decided to switch
from morning to evening, but without more skillful management,
this change alone was not enough to prevent disaster. In 1905
Lynn R. Meekins, who had replaced Carter, became editor-in-
chief, and Mencken was promoted to managing editor. After

Peard resigned in January 1906, Meekins was listed as president and publisher and Mencken as secretary and editor. Mencken tumbled from this shaky eminence when Meekins was unable to meet the deficits. In June the *Herald* ceased publication.

All three of the larger Baltimore dailies offered Mencken jobs. He accepted a post as news editor of the *Evening News,* but he was beginning to resent the executive and supervisory duties which deprived him of time for his own writing. Within a few weeks, he transferred to "a more leisurely and literary job" as Sunday editor of the *Sun.*[59] Thus began his long association with the various editions of the *Sun*—morning, evening, and Sunday—which lasted with only an occasional break until 1941. Soon he was writing editorials and serving as the *Sun's* drama editor.

A Little Night Music

During Mencken's first few years of newspaper work, music had become one of his main sources of enjoyment and diversion. Joining the *Herald* staff had put him in touch with men who greatly expanded his musical knowledge and encouraged him to make use of his musical talent and training. Carter, whom he admired, was a music lover. W.G. Owst, the paper's music critic, prevailed on him to review some minor concerts and recitals and set him to reading a text in harmony. When he became city editor, his assistant was Joe Callahan, an enthusiastic but inept amateur violinist. Among their acquaintances were Samuel Hamburger, a pants salesman who played the violin with considerable skill, and Al Hildebrandt, a violin dealer who was a competent cellist. The four of them began meeting together to play trios and quartets. By 1904, other amateurs and some professionals had joined them and formed a club which met regularly on Saturday nights. At these gatherings, two hours of music-making were followed by two hours of talk and beer-drinking. In the music sessions, the emphasis was always on the fun of playing, not on the finer points of execution. The few nonperforming members were forbidden to comment on any false starts or sour notes.

Through his experiences in this club, Mencken gained a wide knowledge of classical music. When the group performed, he usually played the second piano part. He and the other members ranged through the whole standard orchestral repertory, tackling everything from waltzes to symphonies. He began to collect and study scores, and he made some of the arrangements used by the club. As the years passed and the membership underwent many changes, he remained a seemingly permanent fixture. By the late 1940s he was the only survivor from the era of his own admission.[60]

His love of music was colored by his frustration at having neither the talent nor the training which would have enabled him to become a successful composer. In his boyhood, he had turned out waltzes, marches, and other piano pieces, harmonizing them by trial and error. In later life, he maintained that his best ideas came to him in musical form, but he acknowledged that he lacked the ability to embody them in a string quartet or a symphony. Yet he could not express such concepts in writing, the art to which he had devoted himself. Music, he felt, was the one art that could be made wholly pure and was therefore wholly satisfying. The topics of his articles rarely appealed to him as much as musical ideas. "I'd rather have written any symphony of Brahms'," he declared "than any play of Ibsen's. I'd rather have written the first movement of Beethoven's Eroica than the Song of Solomon; it is not only far more beautiful, it is also far more profound. . . . In music a man can let himself go. In words he always remains a bit stiff and unconvincing."

Mencken's writings on music reveal a surge of emotion which only rarely emerges to the surface of his social and literary criticism. The emotions sustaining his articles on nonmusical subjects varied from sheer good humor to indignation and even horror, but he rarely stated his feelings baldly and directly. His restraint resulted partly from his fear of sentimentality and his belief that one of the marks of a superior man is the ability to control one's emotions. Such control was also an aspect of his literary strategy. He so disguised and modified his feelings that they became part of the persona he adopted for a particular literary purpose. When, for example, he appeared in the guise of a cynic, he was motivated not by true cynicism, but by his conviction that the majority of men would continue to violate or ignore the standards he cherished. He once complained that reviewers showed little sign of understanding, or even suspecting, his feelings. "Many of them," he remarked, "actually set up the doctrine that I have none, which is an imbecility. Every man has feelings. Mine chiefly revolve around a conception of honor."[61]

Mencken's comments on great composers and great music, on the other hand, ordinarily leave no doubt as to the source and the strength of the emotion behind them. He was most enthusiastic about orchestral music, especially chamber music and symphonies by Mozart, Schubert, Beethoven, and Brahms. He professed to dislike most vocal music, but he was deeply moved by certain operas and choral works. Apropos of Wagner's *Tristan und Isolde,* he wrote, "The love-song in the second act is full of plain defects, and they are made ten times worse by the presence of fat and puffing singers. Nevertheless, who ever encountered a love song in mere words that was one half so eloquent and poignant?" He was also captivated by Wagner's *Die Meistersinger,* Richard Strauss's *Elektra* and the first act of *Der Rosenkavalier,* and, to a lesser extent, Puccini's *La Bohème.* In the front rank of choral works he placed Bach's Mass in B Minor and Brahms's *German Requiem.* The latter work, he said, is "irresistibly moving . . . because a man of the highest intellectual dignity, a man of exalted feelings, a man of brains, put into it his love .for and pride in his country." A short piece titled "Masters of Tone" sums up Mencken's reactions to a number of his favorite composers:

Wagner—The rape of the Sabines . . . a *kommers* in Olympus.
Beethoven—The glory that was Greece . . . the grandeur that was Rome . . . a laugh.
Haydn—A seidel on the table . . . a girl on your knee . . . another and different girl in your heart.
Chopin—Two embalmers at work upon a minor poet . . . the scent of tuberoses . . . Autumn rain.
Richard Strauss—Old Home Week in Gomorrah.
Johann Strauss—Forty couples dancing . . . one by one they slip from the hall . . . the sounds of kisses . . . the lights go out.
Puccini—Silver macaroni, exquisitely tangled.

Debussy—A pretty girl with one blue eye and one brown one.
Bach—Genesis I, 1.[62]

When writing in a serious mood, Mencken conceived of music
as the supreme art and of the great composers as the supreme
artists. This attitude reflected his sense of how far he had fallen
short of his own aspirations to be a composer; it also found
support in his reading of critics like Pater and Huneker. His
glorification of the individual composer is in the vein of nineteenth-century romanticism. In one unrestrained outburst of
feeling, he described Beethoven as

a lonely wanderer from some fallen Olympus. . . .
There he stands upon his mountain top, the voice of all the
ages, the heir of the great captains and heroes of the race, the
messenger of the gods. There he stands in his supreme and
tragic loneliness, his agonies turned into beauty by the alchemy
of his incomparable art, . . . his greatness shining into the eyes
of all of us. Nearly a century dead, he speaks forever as one
living and near and much loved.

This passage, published anonymously in *The Smart Set* in 1915,
is too extreme to be typical, but the same note of awe and homage
recurs in Mencken's later music criticism.[63]

Mencken often made analogies between music and literature.
The highest compliment he could pay a writer was to compare
his work with that of a great composer. In Conrad's *Heart of
Darkness,* for instance, he found

a perfection of design which one encounters only rarely and
miraculously in prose fiction: it belongs rather to music. I can't
imagine taking a single sentence out of that stupendous tale
without leaving a visible gap; it is as thoroughly *durch com-
poniert* as a fugue. And I can't imagine adding anything to it,
even so little as a word, without doing it damage. As it stands
it is austerely and beautifully perfect, just as the slow movement of the Unfinished Symphony is perfect.[64]

A Selective Portrait of Nietzsche

In 1906, after joining the staff of the *Baltimore Sun,* Mencken
completed plans for his next book. His *Shaw* had been widely,

and for the most part favorably, noticed by newspaper reviewers around the country, and it "enjoyed a very fair and steady
sale." He was eager to follow it up with another volume. The
idea of devoting it to Nietzsche grew out of his correspondence
with Harrison Hale Schaff. In reply to Mencken's first letter
proposing the Shaw book, Schaff had mentioned that his firm
hoped to publish a study of Nietzsche, but Mencken had declined to undertake such a project because of lack of time and
the inadequacy of his German. He referred to Nietzsche occasionally in *Shaw* and used a quotation from him as an epi-
graph, but his knowledge of Nietzsche at that time came mainly
from secondary sources. After the publication of *Shaw,* when
Mencken proposed a book digesting and criticizing the current
drama, Schaff countered by repeating his suggestion about
Nietzsche. With increased confidence in his own powers, Mencken
agreed to the proposal[65] at a time when only a few volumes of
an eleven-volume English translation of Nietzsche had been
published. Undaunted, he began to wade through the complete
set in German available in the Enoch Pratt Library. He also
used the English translations and read everything he could find
on Nietzsche in English. By 1907 he was submitting copy to
Schaff. After a series of revisions discussed through correspondence, *The Philosophy of Friedrich Nietzsche* was printed early
in 1908.

"In my own mind," Mencken wrote in 1937, "my debt to
Nietzsche seems very slight, though I confess that other people
seem to have put a larger value on it." Among these "other
people" are the biographers and critics who have greatly exaggerated the extent to which Mencken's views stemmed from
Nietzsche. Edgar Kemler, for example, asserted that Mencken
"explored the iconoclastic movement both in breadth and depth,
until he traced it to its ultimate source in the philosophy of . . .
Nietzsche." Kemler fails to mention that the book on Nietzsche
was not a labor of love, but the result of Schaff's timely suggestion. He also overlooks the basic importance of the habits of
dissent produced by Mencken's boyhood experiences in Baltimore. As the "By Way of Introduction" in *Shaw* tells us, Mencken
believed that the "ultimate source" was not Nietzsche, but Darwin. Although Mencken probably first met Nietzsche in the

essays of the bohemian critics, especially Huneker, and in Shaw's prefaces, he soon recognized the landmarks that led from Darwin through Spencer and Huxley to Nietzsche. In a letter to Schaff, he remarked that "Nietzsche himself was merely the successor of Spencer," and he reiterated this judgment in *Shaw*. When he began to read Nietzsche in his own right, he became more convinced than ever that the German thinker was "a thorough Darwinian" whose philosophy would have been impossible without Darwin's work.[66]

If Mencken eventually discovered more arguments congenial to his prejudices in Nietzsche than in any other single source, it was because of his conviction that he, more fully than anyone else, had laid bare the implications of the movement set going by *The Origin of Species*. Mencken's pride in his own German descent also helps account for his eagerness to familiarize English and American readers with the ideas of an important German philosopher. The point of view which determines the pattern of his interpretation is well summed up in the "Introduction": "It is high time for the race of Darwin and Huxley to know Nietzsche better."[67]

Viewing his subject in the perspective of evolutionism and scientific naturalism, Mencken stressed the philosopher's empiricism and iconoclasm and ignored or minimized his idealism and mysticism. Nietzsche's arguments appealed to him not as unique revelations, but as the most incisive statements of ideas with which he was already familiar. He called Nietzsche "the high priest of the actual," "the king of all axiom smashers and the arch dissenter of the age." He sought to show how Nietzsche's teaching "leads to a rejection of Christianity and democracy; how it points out a possible evolution of the human race through the immoralist to the superman; how it combats the majority of the ideas held holy and impeccable by mankind today."[68]

With a bias which was probably largely unconscious, Mencken interpreted Nietzsche in ways that reflected his own attitudes toward economic, social, political, and religious matters.[69] Stressing Nietzsche's social Darwinism to the exclusion of corrective elements in the philosopher's thought, he characterized him as a "biological monist" uncompromising in his belief "that the struggle for existence went on among human beings exactly as it went on among the lions in the jungle and the protozoa in the sea ooze, and that the law of natural selection ruled all of animated nature—mind and matter—alike."[70] Mencken's equation of biologic evolution with economic competition is, however, more in keeping with William Graham Sumner's doctrines than with Nietzsche's. Poverty is the brand of unfitness, "a symptom of . . . neglect, license, ignorance, and inefficiency—if not in the individual, at least in his family." Since giving paupers charity cannot alter their innate unfitness, it does positive harm by allowing them to survive, have children, and through them pass on their unfitness and its attendant sufferings.[71]

With natural selection the ruling principle, a caste-system social structure is inevitable. Mencken, of course, identified himself with the "dionysian individualist" of the highest of Nietzsche's castes—"a small, alert, iconoclastic, immoral, progressive master class." Some first-caste men may conceivably appear in either an established social aristocracy or an industrial plutocracy, but Mencken carefully distinguished Nietzsche's first caste from the other two groups. In the middle is a military-judicial caste, " 'guardians and keepers of order and security.' " At the bottom is "a vast, inert, religious, moral slave class."[72] Mencken concerned himself mainly with the highest and lowest castes.

Many of the themes to which he later returned again and again are present in his *Nietzsche*. The account of Nietzsche's opposition to Christianity, for example, clearly implies Mencken's agnostic faith in the methods of science. His antipuritanism found support in Nietzsche's conclusion that the "universal tendency to submit to moral codes" is "a curse to the human race and the chief cause of its degeneration, inefficiency and unhappiness."[73]

Nietzsche's opinions on the war of the sexes also appealed to Mencken. The fellow-feeling of one bachelor for another is shown in Mencken's statement that "'celibacy tempered by polygamy" is the "ideal state for a philosopher." Nietzsche, Mencken explained, "saw that womanly guile was as useful, in its place, as masculine truth; that man, to retain those faculties which made him master of the earth, needed a persistent and resourceful opponent to stimulate them and so preserve and develop them." But, he added, Nietzsche "was far from exalting mere women into goddesses, after the sentimental fashion of those virtuosi of illusion who pass for law-givers in the United States," especially those who cling to the old southern code of chivalry. As to women's suffrage, it "could lead to but one result: the contamination of the masculine ideals of justice, honor and truth by the feminine ideals of dissimulation, equivocation and intrigue."[74] These views later formed the framework for Mencken's ironically titled *In Defense of Women* (1918).

Also apparent in *Nietzsche* are the tensions which marked Mencken's political attitudes in the twenties. These attitudes swung between conservative suspicion of democracy and socialism, at one extreme, and an anarchic individualism, at the other. As a conservative, Mencken saw the central problem of government as that of keeping the masses within bounds. "Wherever universal suffrage, or some close approach to it, is the primary axiom of government," he declared, "the thing known in the United States as 'freak legislation' is a constant evil." Arguing that the doctrine of equal rights runs counter to the workings of natural selection, he objected to any kind of popular sovereignty. A democratic or socialist government results in a leveling upward of the weak but a leveling downward of the strong—overall retrogression, since "the only progress worthwhile is . . . at the top." The "saving grace" of these systems is that their ideals of equality and brotherhood are impossible of attainment. In England and Germany, "the two upper castes have solved the problem of keeping the proletariat, despite its theoretical sovereignty, in proper leash and bounds." Even in America, the upper castes usually manage to assert their authority, as in the southern states, where "the educated white class . . . has found it easy to take from the black masses their very right to vote, despite the fact that they are everywhere in a great majority numerically, and so, by the theory of democracy, represent whatever power lies in the state."[75] Here Mencken was so eager to make his point that he overlooked the fact that, contrary to his assertion, the whites outnumbered the Negroes in many parts of the South.

Despite this antidemocratic bias, Mencken was a zealous libertarian. His heroes, the iconoclasts, had to be individualists; and their liberty to experiment was the prerequisite to progress.

No form of government could escape the evil tendency "toward permanence and against change" which made it "opposed to all increase in knowledge." Mencken sympathized with Nietzsche's view "that a sort of glorified anarchy" would prove most suitable for the highest caste, but, unlike Nietzsche, he did not advocate an oppressive regime which would act under orders from the highest caste and keep the mob in check. For, he asked, if there is no opposition to stimulate and sustain the high-caste man, how can there be any progress? Nietzsche, he maintained, forgot "that, without enemies, there can be no heroes—that without abuses, there can be no reforms." The "one ineradicable fault" in Nietzsche's philosophy, he concluded in his final chapter, is that "he showed the strong man's need for an enemy and yet argued that all enemies should be enchained."[76] These words are prophetic of Mencken's later staunchness in defending the right of every person to freedom of thought and speech.

Certain passages in *Nietzsche* reveal the ambivalent attitude toward the common people which helps account for Mencken's being fascinated by popular culture. In some moods he felt that the lowest caste had at least a glimmer of the vision of a fully emancipated society. After describing the dionysian as "a being capable of facing the horrors of life unafraid, . . . of gazing down upon the earth in pride and scorn," he found traces of these aims in

the profane folk-philosophy of every healthy and vigorous people. . . . "Let us so live day by day," says a distinguished American statesman, "that we can look any man in the eye and tell him to go to hell!" We get a subtle sort of joy out of this saying because it voices our racial advance toward individualism and away from revelation and rabbinism. We believe, at heart, in freedom, in toleration, in moral anarchy. We have put this notion into innumerable homely forms.

> Things have come to a hell of a pass
> When a man can't wallop his own jackass!

At other points in the book, the outlook is pessimistic. The majority, tenacious of its comforting illusions, never initiates change; every step upward in the slow and painful process of social evolution originates with the high-caste, error-fighting, truth-seeking minority. The common denominator of men like Pasteur, Huxley, Lincoln, Bismarck, Darwin, Virchow, Haeckel, Hobbes, Macchiavelli, Harvey, and Jenner is that they went "violently counter to the view of the herd." While acknowledging that the iconoclast needs opposition, Mencken was inclined to ridicule the masses for not responding more quickly.

The masses are always a century or two behind. They have made a virtue of their obtuseness and call it by various fine names: conservatism, piety, respectability, faith. The nineteenth century witnessed greater human progress than all the centuries before it . . . , but the majority of white men . . . still believe in ghosts, still fear the devil, still hold that the number 13 is unlucky and still picture the deity as a patriarch in a white beard, surrounded by a choir of resplendent amateur musicians.[77]

Mencken's Darwinian premises gave him no logical reason for speaking as if the incompetence of the masses was the result of deliberate choice, rather than being innate. The dogmatism of his belief in heredity as opposed to environmentalism is evident in his discussion of "the futile and fatuous effort to improve the negroes of the Southern United States by education." The white man, Mencken asserted, is so far ahead in the scale of evolution that the Negro can never catch up. Attempts to educate the Negro serve only to deprive him of his contentment and peace of mind. This point of view, resting on the assumption that race and heredity account for the inferiority of the masses, is consistent with one set of characteristics Mencken attributed to the dionysian individualist—the forerunner of the superman. Practicing "prudent and intelligent selfishness, . . . absolute and utter individualism," the dionysian regards "the proletariat merely as a conglomeration of draft animals made to be driven, enslaved and exploited."[78]

But, as an iconoclast, the dionysian has another and conflicting set of characteristics. His fervent dedication to truth-seeking transcends, or even defies, the overruling drive of self-interest, even if we grant Mencken's inclusion in the latter of the interests of one's descendants. The iconoclast's mission was "the most noble and sublime task possible to mere human beings: the overthrow of superstition and unreasoning faith, with their long train of fears, horrors, doubts, frauds, injustice and suffering." Justifying Nietzsche's greatness as an iconoclast, Mencken wrote, "It is a fine thing to face machine guns for immortality and a medal, but isn't it a fine thing, too, to face calumny, injustice and loneliness for the truth which makes man free?"[79] It is the religious quality of Mencken's enthusiasm for the ideal of truth-seeking which helps account for his impatience with the mob. He conceived of the scientific method as, potentially, a highly effective guide to progress, but he found that most men are all but incapable of responding to it. When his sense of the gulf between proletarian reality and his ideal of a society totally converted to truth-seeking became most acute, he lashed out at the mob, even though his logic, based on the premise that heredity has primacy over environment, told him that the mob could not help itself.

As measured both by the response of critics and by sales, Mencken's *Nietzsche* met with considerable success. It had to be reprinted before the end of the year, and it was published in a British edition by T. Fisher Unwin. In 1912 Mencken rewrote parts of it for a new edition issued the next year.

Early in 1908, meanwhile, with the book on Shaw behind him and the one on Nietzsche in preparation, he felt that he was finding his real métier. He was eager to reach an audience beyond the bounds of Baltimore not only through his books but through regular contributions to magazines. The needed opportunity came in 1908 when he was unexpectedly offered a post as literary critic of *The Smart Set,* with the understanding that he could continue to live in Baltimore and work for the *Sun.* He accepted at once. Thus he embarked on a new phase of his career, one which would lead through the troubled days of World War I to his emergence as a major spokesman for "the civilized minority" in the 1920s.

5

SMART SET CRITIC, 1908–1914

Finding Freedom within the *Smart Set* Formula

Two friends that Mencken had made in his *Herald* days influenced his appointment to a post on *The Smart Set,* but he probably owed the job mainly to a new acquaintance, Theodore Dreiser. As the editor of the Butterick Publications, including *The Delineator,* Dreiser was on the lookout for new talent. He first heard about Mencken from George Bronson Howard, the Baltimore writer who had loaned Mencken a copy of *Sister Carrie* back in 1900. On August 23, 1907, Dreiser wrote to Mencken, repeating Howard's suggestion that he might be "just the person to get out a popular edition of a German Philosopher or Dramatist." Dreiser had not pursued this possibility very far when he learned that Mencken could meet one of the immediate needs of *The Delineator* by supplying popular articles on medical subjects. A few years before, when Sedgwick had asked Mencken to find someone to do a series of such articles for *Leslie's,* he arranged to write them himself in collaboration with a physician named Leonard K. Hirshberg. At Dreiser's request, Hirshberg and Mencken began a series of articles on the care and feeding of babies. Hirshberg, under whose name the articles were published, supplied the data; Mencken did most of the writing and editing. In October, Dreiser, well pleased with the results, urged Mencken to come to see him whenever he visited New York.[1]

When Mencken appeared in the *Delineator* office in March 1908, Dreiser was so struck by his young visitor's impish and self-confident manner that he laughed and exclaimed, "Well, well, if it isn't Anheuser's own brightest boy out to see the town."

Mencken quickly retorted, "Certainly, my father is the richest brewer in Baltimore, and he makes the best beer in the world. See this gaudy tie and these yellow shoes? Every jack-dandy and rowdy-dow in Baltimore wears them. What else do you expect from me?"

The "palaver and yoo-hoo" that followed resulted in "an understanding based on a mutual liking." From then on, Dreiser recalled, he counted Mencken "among those I most prized—temperamentally as well as intellectually."[2]

Not long after this first meeting between Dreiser and Mencken, the editorial staff of *The Smart Set* underwent a reorganization. Fred Splint, formerly one of Dreiser's subordinates on the Butterick Publications, was the new editor. Splint's assistant was Norman Boyer, who had known Mencken when they were both reporters in Baltimore. Channing Pollock, the magazine's drama critic, had become well acquainted with Mencken during his visits to Baltimore as a theatrical press agent. When Splint asked Dreiser to recommend someone for the job of reviewing books for *The Smart Set,* Dreiser advised him to sound out Mencken.[3] With Splint's help, Boyer composed a letter asking Mencken to come to see him on his next visit to New York. In May, when Mencken appeared, Boyer introduced him to Splint, and Splint offered him the position as book reviewer, "with the rank and pay of a sergeant of artillery."[4] Pollock's drama department had appeared during the two preceding theatrical seasons, but the book section was an innovation. Mencken's first contribution was printed in November 1908. He did not meet George Jean Nathan until the following spring, when Nathan was taken on to replace Pollock.[5]

The Smart Set had its origin in the commercial success of its raffish sister publication, *Town Topics,* which Colonel William D'Alton Mann had taken over in 1891. The success of *Town Topics* resulted primarily from its stress on gossip and scandal-mongering about high society, but it also carried lively departments on literature, drama, and music. From 1897 on, Pollard was in charge of the section headed "The Literary Show" and signed "The Ringmaster." For a number of years, Huneker and Charles F. Nirdlinger—George Jean Nathan's uncle—were the music and drama critics. In 1900, when the circulation approached 100,000, Colonel Mann poured some of his profits into a new venture. He apparently intended *The Smart Set* to appeal to much the same audience as *Town Topics,* but to feature fiction and verse rather than titillating nonfiction. He wanted the magazine to live up to its name and authentically reflect the tastes, views, and activities of New York society. He even hoped that its chief contributors could be recruited from the social elite.[6] The editors soon discovered, however, that they could not obtain enough literate copy from that source to meet their needs. As an alternative, they began to accept manuscripts from aspiring authors whose work was too unorthodox in content or point of view to win them an entry into established journals like *Harper's, The Atlantic,* or *The Century.* Among the young American writers encouraged by having their work accepted during the first five years of *The Smart Set* were Gelett Burgess, James Branch Cabell, Zona Gale, O. Henry, and Jack London.

When Mencken joined *The Smart Set,* some of these writers were still contributing, but the issues for 1908 and 1909 reveal many names of authors who remained obscure. A typical number contained one complete novelette, a dozen short stories, and eight or ten poems, with a short drama or an essay sometimes included for variety. Each issue usually carried at least one play, story, or poem in French. The original sub-title, *Magazine of Cleverness,* was still in use. As the announcements of the contents of forthcoming issues suggest, the fiction was not predominantly realistic, but catered to the popular taste for love, adventure, and intrigue. The November 1908 number, for example, describes a story by George Bronson Howard as "a delicious eerie little thing to be told around an open fire-place with shaded lights." The "complete novel" for May 1909 is "a story of the post-bellum South, of the charming ward of a governor and the dashing scion of an old and proud but war-stricken family." In Harriet Prescott Spofford's "The Countess de Chassepierre," "An ambitious mamma schemes to marry off her daughter to a visiting count." *Therese,* a novelette by Helen Talbot Kummer, takes the reader to "Paris studios and drawing-rooms and wild, Albanian frontiers under the rule of the Turk,"[7] but is only one of many stories with exotic settings.[8]

Despite the conventionality of much *Smart Set* fiction, the new editors continued the policy of allowing authors greater freedom of expression than they normally had in the older, conservative magazines. Sometimes *The Smart Set* even satirized the trite situations common in popular fiction. In an article published in 1909, John Kendrick Bangs identified such formulas as those characteristic of "mortuary fiction" and the "Eastern-made Western story." He explained that most editors preferred stories with a significant theme and some literary merit, but that meeting a press deadline often forced them to accept "mere sheaves of words" instead. Other contributors also poked fun at popular tastes. The twelve endings Carl Van Vechten proposed as appropriate for best-selling novels included this one: "The woman still wore her hyacinths, but the man had lost his soul." Louis Baury parodied the styles of such popular favorites as Rudyard Kipling, Elinor Glyn, and Arthur Conan Doyle.[9]

When Splint, with no apparent hesitation, accepted him as a qualified book reviewer, and Boyer handed him an armful of books,[10] Mencken must have had some misgivings. Had he made the right decision? He had reviewed plays for the *Herald* and was now doing so for the *Sun,* but only occasionally had he tried to review books. He was preparing a study of Nietzsche and had already published a handbook on Shaw, but to what extent did these accomplishments justify his assuming the role of literary critic? On the *Sun,* in addition to his drama criticism, he was turning out editorials on a wide range of subjects, most of them nonliterary. Would book reviewing allow him to express his views on religious, social, economic, and political topics as well as on literary matters? He had developed the habit of reading widely, and the ability to write quickly, but would he enjoy producing reviews month after month?

Fortunately for Mencken, he was free to give his literary section the content and form that suited his aims and temperament. Since he had no predecessors, he did not have to conform to a pattern set by someone else. Publishers constantly supplied him with more volumes than he could possibly review. Splint and Boyer left him the responsibility of deciding which works to emphasize. They also allowed him to state his opinions as candidly and vigorously as he saw fit. Accordingly, his criticism did not need to be "literary" in any narrow sense. In considering fiction, drama, or poetry, he was not obligated to concentrate on its form and style, but could bring out its underlying philosophy, evaluate its social implications, or examine its relationships to the author's life and background. Whenever he wanted to, he could turn to books on religion, science, philosophy, history, or a multitude of other subjects, including cooking and bar-tending. Since he was not expected to defer to *Smart Set* contributors and authors whose works were advertised in the magazine, he could decide for himself which writers to praise and which to ridicule and denounce.

It was probably because he anticipated having almost sole responsibility for the book section that Mencken felt the *Smart Set* offer too promising to be rejected. This new position would allow him to reach regularly an audience outside of Baltimore. Since he could determine the shape his reviews would take, they would help satisfy his powerful urge to express his prejudices and dramatize his personality. They would also give him a better chance to speak out against the prevailing "complacency and conformity."[11]

Bohemian Truth-Seeker

When Mencken started reviewing for *The Smart Set,* the tone of American literary criticism had once again become cautious and conservative. In 1923 he singled out the suppression of *Sister Carrie* in 1900 as a sign that the defenders of "the old tradition" had successfully reasserted themselves. When the revolt of the nineties had spent itself, he maintained, "the Presbyterians marched in and took possession of the works. Most of the erstwhile *revoltés* boldly took the veil—notably Hamlin Garland."[12] *The Chap-Book, The Lark,* and the other little magazines that had intrigued Mencken during his boyhood had all but died out. *The Criterion* survived until 1906, but had gradually become converted into a conventional middle-class periodical. In *Everybody's, McClure's,* and *Collier's,* Ida Tarbell, Lincoln Steffens, and other muckrakers were exposing economic and political corruption and demanding reforms, but no such concerted effort was being made to challenge either literary commercialism or literary snobbery. Ranged on the side of gentility were powerful academic critics like Hamilton Wright Mabie and George Edward Woodberry. Paul Elmer More extended the sway of academic influence when he took over the editorship of *The Nation* in 1909.

More and Mabie deplored the more obvious kinds of poetic and fictional pot-boiling, but the chief literary journals often combined gentility with a practical acceptance of works written for the market. In Mencken's opinion, *The Bookman, The Dial,* and the *New York Times* Literary Supplement fell short of their responsibilities on two main counts. On one hand, they discouraged writers who wanted to make innovations either in materials or methods. On the other, by hailing many of the best-sellers, they gave a certain literary status to works which were primarily commercial products. The same attitudes prevailed within the chief publishing houses and on the older journals like *Harper's* and *The Century*. Because of the watchful propriety of most editors and critics, "the young man or woman who came to New York with a manuscript which violated in any way the pruderies and prejudices of the professors had a very hard time getting it printed." Because of the dominance of commercial criteria, the writers who attained the greatest vogue were of the second and third rank. In the nineties it had been possible for *The Red Badge of Courage* to become a best-seller, but, between 1904 and 1910, booksellers invested heavily in such titles as Gene Stratton Porter's *Freckles,* John Fox, Jr.'s *The Trail of the Lonesome Pine,* and Harold Bell Wright's *The Calling of Dan Matthews*. To Mencken, the popularity of such stories proved only that their authors were "assiduous and diverting manufacturers of best sellers," not that they were to be taken seriously as novelists.[13]

During this comparatively stagnant period in American literature, Mencken's chief accomplishment in his *Smart Set* reviews was to help keep alive the fin de siècle spirit of moral and literary revolt. His book section carried on the tradition of the more iconoclastic little magazines of the nineties. Although Mencken did not consciously adopt a creed or a program, his reviews show that from the beginning he had definite aims. These aims embodied the whole range of his prejudices. They reflected, for example, his preoccupation with American life and his curiosity about all its facets. Like his prejudices, his aims had both negative and positive aspects.

On the negative side, he struck out against the attitudes and conditions which he felt prevented many young American writers from making the best use of their talents. At one extreme, he opposed the genteel tradition as it manifested itself in the conservatism and timidity of academic criticism, the stress on manner rather than matter, the distaste for the everyday realities of American life, and the use of censorship to curb realism and naturalism. At the other extreme, he spoke out against the literary commercialism which gave financial success to writers who stuck to the accepted formulas but made survival difficult for those who tried to break away from them.

On the positive side, he fought with great gusto on behalf of a vigorous native literature. In poetry, he was satisfied with genteel verse, providing it was skillfully done, but he helped some young poets who were stressing American materials and breaking away from traditional forms. In the drama and the novel, he called for a realistic or naturalistic treatment of American themes, but he also welcomed romance, fantasy, or burlesque provided that they showed an honest talent at work.

The conception of criticism he carried over to *The Smart Set* embodies the same two apparently contradictory views of the critic's task evident in his writings in *The American Mercury* sixteen years later. The critic is an iconoclast, engaged in a kind of error-blasting and truth-seeking operation, but he is also an artist, properly concerned neither with preaching nor even with presenting accurate data and cogent arguments, but with dramatizing his own personality in a vivid, entertaining way. How Mencken's close identification of the iconoclastic and artistic impulses reconciles these two views is discussed at the end of chapter 1. They are reconciled in the same way in *The Smart Set*. There, as in the *Mercury*, Mencken's usual strategy is not to prove his case by logical demonstration, or to exhort his audience to repent and reform, but rather to use all his stylistic resources to create a mood, an attitude, an insight which will capture the reader's imagination.

Mencken's approach and manner were basically the expression of his prejudices, temperament, and talent, but his newspaper experience helped determine the particular form they took. As a literary critic, Mencken aligned himself most closely with the bohemians, notably Poe, Bierce, Pollard, and Huneker. By comparing and contrasting him with these men, we can see that he worked partly within and partly outside the bohemian tradition. In this respect, he resembled William Marion Reedy, an older survivor from the era of the nineties who edited *Reedy's Mirror* in St. Louis. Reedy and Mencken were never personally on very friendly terms, but they were similar in having tastes broad enough to encompass a naturalistic as well as an aesthetic vision of life.

Since Mencken grew up resenting the hero worship of Poe which prevailed in Baltimore, it is not suprising that his attitudes toward him were ambivalent. He attacked Poe as "ignorant and pretentious" and disparaged his short stories and poetry, but also called attention to "his underestimated virtues as a critic." He credited Poe with making no concessions either to "the dominant English taste" of his time or "to the maudlin emotions that passed for ideas in America." He especially enjoyed the wit and mastery of epithet with which Poe disposed of second-rate authors.[14]

Bierce, with his love of the macabre and his command of invective, continued the Poe tradition in both the short story and criticism. Although Mencken admired Bierce's war stories, his scorn of sham and pretence, and his skill in epigram and satire, the recent biographers of Bierce are mistaken when they imply that as an iconoclast the younger man was merely aping the older one. Mencken rejected Bierce's narrow purism in matters of grammar and style and recognized the wrongheadedness and unevenness which made his *Collected Works* "a depressing assemblage of worn-out and fly-blown stuff, much of it quite unreadable." He had no intention of following his friend Pollard into the "small band of disciples" who hymned the crusty Californian "in a passionate, voluptuous, inordinate way."[15]

Despite such reservations, Mencken appreciated Bierce as a worthy predecessor and profited from his example. His friendship with Pollard intensified his interest in Bierce, and the two men met in December 1911 when attending Pollard's funeral in Baltimore. Prior to Bierce's mysterious disappearance in Mexico in 1913, they carried on a friendly correspondence, with Bierce complimenting Mencken on his articles and Mencken urging Bierce to contribute to *The Smart Set.* Mencken ranked the "devastating epigrams" in Bierce's *The Devil's Dictionary* with those of Oscar Wilde and liked to quote, for example, "Ah, that we could fall into women's arms without falling into their hands," or "Husband: one who, having dined, is charged with the care of the plate." These invite comparison with Mencken's similar efforts, such as "Love is the delusion that one woman differs from another," or "Husband—One who played safe and is now played safely." In reviewing *The Cambridge History of American Literature,* Mencken criticized the editors for failing to recognize that "in the post-Harte-and-Twain literary movement in California . . . the Bierce tradition . . . is almost as vivid as the Emerson tradition in New England." In later years he remembered Bierce as a "magnificently decent" man who "fell upon the current mountebanks, great and small, in a Berserker fury."[16]

Huneker and Pollard, who were closer to Mencken in age and interests than Bierce was, also had a more direct influence. Mencken's youthful reading of their articles and reviews helped stimulate his wholehearted response to the revolt of the nineties. He admired their cosmopolitanism, their wide knowledge, their skill as popularizers of European artists and ideas. As a literary journalist, he felt the same need to cultivate a vivid style in order to capture the attention of a large middle-class audience. Later his reviews attracted the two older critics, and he became a good friend of both.

Yet it considerably oversimplifies matters to conclude that he was their disciple. The bohemians were not a critical school, with common principles, a common aim, a common program. Their basic premise—given its classic statement in the essays of Walter Pater and Oscar Wilde—was that much of the value of a work of art lies in the response of the temperament that confronts it. Since each temperament is unique, it follows that the aims and style of each critic are unique. Faithful to this logic, Mencken did not hesitate, on occasion, to react unfavorably to some of the assumptions and judgments of Pollard and Huneker.[17]

Furthermore, the kind of union between iconoclasm and artistry that he liked was not confined to the bohemian critics. He observed it in certain British drama critics, like A.B. Walkeley and William Archer. It also leavened the work of his favorite dramatists and novelists, including Ibsen, Shaw, Hauptmann, Zola, Arnold Bennett, H.G. Wells, Mark Twain, Crane, and Norris. Although the social Darwinists were not always artists, some of them, especially Thomas Huxley and Nietzsche, appealed to him as much because of their style as because of their unorthodox views.

In several important respects, Mencken differed considerably from Huneker and Pollard. In developing his style, he emulated rather than imitated them. He learned to be more concise and colorful than Pollard and more aggressively and humorously iconoclastic than Huneker. He was much less the aesthete than they. He shared their love of music, but not their enthusiasm for the other nonliterary arts. The chief purpose of the bohemian critics was to popularize the ideas and works of European thinkers and artists, but Mencken, although he sometimes performed that function, regarded it as subordinate to his other aims. In addition to being a bohemian, he was a truth-seeker in the Huxley manner who kept his eye focused primarily on the American scene. His reviews were a vehicle not only for literary comment, but also for his reactions to the American people, their language, their culture, their institutions, their politics. In his determination to free the United States from literary colonialism and in his insistence that the best hope for a representative native literature lay in realism and naturalism, he revived aspects of the rebellion of the nineties which Huneker largely neglected and which Pollard viewed in a different way. Looked at in broader perspective, Mencken's demand for a literature embodying all aspects of American life links him with a tradition going back to Emerson and Whitman.

Like Huneker and Pollard, Mencken thought of himself as part of an elite, but in his case this assumption was the outgrowth of the German-American tradition as transmitted to him through his family. He slipped naturally into the habit of thinking of himself as separate from both "the mob," which he tended to denounce as stupid, bigoted, or philistine, and "the plutocracy," whose claims to being a genuine aristocracy he rejected. His concept of an elite was, however, given a more definite aesthetic dimension by his boyhood reading of *M'lle New York*, *The Criterion*, *The Chap-Book*, and *The Lark*. Although such reviews were either very short-lived or became converted into conventional periodicals, the bohemian spirit survived in many newspaper offices. Editors and reporters, especially those with literary aspirations, easily assumed that they were superior to most of the people whose activities and views they recorded and commented on. Having observed that no social class had a monopoly on ignorance, stupidity, hypocrisy, greed, and lust, they were skeptical about the notion that wealth was necessarily a sign of intelligence or cultural accomplishment, or that the common people were the repository of wisdom.

Considering oneself part of a superior group was, therefore, a characteristic Mencken shared with many other journalists. The form this tendency took varied from writer to writer, but its presence in any form created a problem. In theory, critics like Huneker, Pollard, and Mencken were as ready to "set their private cogitations against the jurisprudence of the world"[18] as any of the European "anarchs of art" they admired. In practice, they earned their livelihood by pleasing a middle-class audience which, to an extent not easily defined, formed part of the despised "mob." Huneker and Mencken depended for their living almost entirely on the income from writings directed to that audience. Pollard had a private income, but he continued his career as a journalist until his death in 1911.

The fact that the bohemian rebels of the nineties had to satisfy the editors and readers of established periodicals helps account for the brevity and relative mildness of their revolt. The little magazines of the time were rarely self-supporting. Huneker and Thompson, for example, paid for their youthful fling on *M'lle New York* with money earned writing for more conventional journals. When they toned down their views and presented them entertainingly, they found a ready market for them. Many middle-class readers enjoyed the kind of artistic gossip and comment that made them feel distinctive from their fellows. The cynicism and amoralism professed by some European artists intrigued them, but they doubted whether such attitudes were appropriate in America. They appreciated satire not only when directed against other groups, but also when directed against their own class, because they could ordinarily assume that it did not apply to themselves. But they were not ready for the rank egotism and open defiance of convention featured by *M'lle New York*. *The Chap-Book* and *The Criterion* survived longer partly because they had adequate subsidies, and partly because they compromised with the reigning taste.

The career of Walter Blackburn Harte, with whose work Mencken was familiar, illustrates what was likely to happen to the journalist lacking the talent or the will to adapt his views to the tastes of middle-class readers. Harte, who had once been befriended by Walter Pater, had emigrated to America in 1887 to better his literary fortunes, but he was poor and obscure when he died prematurely in 1899. According to Pollard, Harte failed because he refused to compromise. "After a few years in the masked service of journalism," Harte asserted, "even the most robust talent is crippled and deformed; and for men who are lacking in vanity, doggedness of character and the most intense . . . tenacity of purpose, a year or two as a journalistic cut-throat is enough to wholly currupt and falsify their talent forever."[19]

Harte apparently possessed his full share of vanity and determination. So did Huneker, Pollard, and Mencken, but they were more successful because they learned how to bend without breaking. As professional journalists, they recognized that they must adapt their writing to the needs of a particular periodical, have a specific audience in mind, keep the length of their copy within the assigned limits, and occasionally defer to the opinions of editors. They could not avow their iconoclasm and defy prudery so baldly in their articles as they might in personal letters, but they did not need to abandon their individualistic creeds. They discovered that audience reactions were determined not so much by what was said, but by the "what" and the "how" working together. As a result, each writer consciously developed a style intended to be so individual, zestful, and colorful, that it would attract many readers and perhaps even win them over to views which would otherwise seem too extreme.

The approaches worked out by Huneker and Pollard typify those of the more successful literary journalists. Although Huneker's criticism reflects his knowledge of the classical tradition and his thorough grounding in music theory, he thought of himself as a journalist first and a critic of the arts second. This attitude helps explain his concern with capturing and holding his readers' attention. "It doesn't matter what you gossip about," he declared, "whether it be the stars or clam-chowder. The important matter lies in the manner of gossiping." When he started up in the eighties, there was a growing interest in serious music, literature, and painting, but none of these subjects had a wide popular appeal. To attract as many readers as possible, he developed a polychromatic style which communicated his gusto for the arts. In his youth he had gone to Paris to seek Bohemia, but his mature judgment was that "there is only one way to become a perfect Bohemian; lead the existence of a sober sedentary bourgeois, with cobbler's wax on your chair, grease on your elbow, sweat on your brow, and, what the metaphysicians call the Will-to-Sit-Still."[20]

Pollard, like Huneker, sought to discuss art like a well-informed but not infallible critic eager to make the subject interesting and comprehensible to laymen. "If you cannot get yourself read," he asked, "of what value is your lore, your idea, your truth?"[21]

Mencken's approach was similar to Huneker's and Pollard's chiefly because he had to cope with much the same conditions. Since his first efforts to capture some of the atmosphere of the Baltimore slums, he had been cultivating the ability to express his sensations and opinions colorfully. In the fall of 1901, when first called upon to write reviews of musical shows and plays for the *Herald*, he received expert advice from Robert I. Carter, the new managing editor. A reviewer, Carter insisted, must constantly keep his readers in mind and appeal to them in a lively, entertaining style. He should trust his own impressions and adopt an aggressive manner, expressing unfavorable judgments with appropriate humor, ridicule, or ferocity. "You must give a good show to get a crowd," said Carter, "and a good show means one with slaughter in it."[22]

Carter's principles, with their assertion of the critic's individuality, fitted not only Mencken's immediate needs as a beginning critic, but also his temperament and personality. As Mencken gained more experience, he felt increasingly justified in asserting his own opinions, however heretical. At the same time, he realized the need for phrasing these views so strikingly that they would appeal to a wide audience. As he pondered Carter's advice and reviewed more plays, he examined more carefully his own aims and methods as a writer. He studied the assumptions and techniques of some of the major writers of fiction as well as of dramatists and drama critics. By 1908 he had developed an impressionistic approach to dramatic criticism which he carried over, with some modifications, to the much more varied reviewing he was to do on *The Smart Set*.

Although this critical self-reliance was most directly a product of Mencken's experience as a journalist, he found much support for it in the writings of the bohemian critics. "Perhaps," W.B. Harte ventured, "with all the mountains of literature behind us, all the originality possible for us moderns lies in our prejudices." Huneker, in similar vein, liked to quote Whitman's saying, "I find no sweeter fat than sticks to my own bones." In 1905 Mencken showed his sympathy with this philosophy by citing approvingly Huneker's statement that "the chiefest malady of our age is that of the will enfeebled by lack of exercise." In commenting on *Their Day in Court,* Mencken revealed his liking for Pollard's individualistic creed. "In a country . . . which regards Hamilton Wright Mabie as a serious critic and James Whitcomb Riley as a great poet," he remarked, "a man of Mr. Pollard's assertive masculinity stands forth like a truth seeker in the Baptist college of cardinals."[23]

The concept that criticism is primarily an act of self-expression implies that the best critics are artists in their own right. In W.B. Harte's words, they are "essentially creators, and not mere commentators and cataloguers." The belief of Huneker, Pollard, and Mencken that they themselves were artists reinforced their sense of belonging to a cultural elite, but it also helped justify their resistance to the pressures threatening their independence of judgment. As reviewers, they were overwhelmed by contemporary books, the majority of which had little merit. From 1908 through 1914, Mencken commented on a total of 1,831 volumes, including 289 briefly noted—an average of more than twenty-five a month.[24] In dealing with the novels forming the bulk of the new books, Mencken and his bohemian colleagues rarely felt that their souls were adventuring among masterpieces. Mencken estimated that the American output of "first class, full length novels" between 1900 and 1910 was about one and a half a year. The others, at best, were "entertaining trifles." He complained about "the cheapness, the childishness, the unspeakable trashiness of most of the so-called fiction that we . . . try to wade through each month."[25] Like the bohemian critics, however, he knew that his reactions to such books might stimulate some of his best efforts as a critic. His feeling that he was free to condemn inferior books forthrightly and that his commentary had an artistic value of its own helps account for the zestful spirit of many of his reviews.

In addition to sympathizing with the general attitudes toward criticism held by Huneker and Pollard, Mencken greatly appreciated the contribution each of them made as "an introducer of aesthetic and philosophical ambassadors." In 1909 he credited Huneker with leading the fight in America for Ibsen, Shaw, Sudermann, Strindberg, and Nietzsche. Huneker's knowledge, gusto, and persistence did much to dispel American complacency and philistinism. "If a merciful Providence had not sent . . . Huneker into the world," Mencken asserted, "we Americans would still be shipping union suits to the heathen, reading Emerson, sweating at Chautauquas and applauding the plays of Bronson Howard."[26] Pollard performed a function similar to Huneker's in his columns in *Town Topics* and in his *Masks and Minstrels of New Germany*. From the latter volume and from his talks with Pollard, Mencken derived much of his knowledge of such innovators in recent German literature as Otto Julius Bierbaum, Ludwig Thoma, and Franz Wedekind.

In *Shaw* and in *Nietzsche,* Mencken had the same general aim as Pollard and Huneker. Between 1909 and 1913 he continued in the same vein in five books which he edited or to which he contributed introductions. Three volumes reflected his interests as a drama critic; the other two showed his undiminished enthusiasm for Nietzsche. After hearing several actors and actresses complain about the stiffness of William Archer's translations of Ibsen, Mencken persuaded Holger A. Koppel, the Danish consul in Baltimore, to collaborate with him in putting a series of Ibsen plays into idiomatic English. Versions of *A Doll's House* and *Little Eyolf,* with the editing credited to Mencken alone, appeared under the John W. Luce imprint in 1909. In 1913 Mencken wrote the preface for the Luce edition of English translations of Eugene Brieux's dramas, *Blanchette* and *The Escape.*[27] The same company published *The Gist of Nietzsche* (1910), a compilation of excerpts, and a revised edition of *Nietzsche* (1913).

In *The Smart Set,* publicizing European artists and thinkers was one of Mencken's subsidiary aims. In a passage on Strindberg, Mencken showed his awareness of his role as a popularizer by saying, "I myself had the honor of being one of his first whoopers up in this fair land; I wrote about him at great length so long ago . . . as 1901."[28] The playwrights he commented on included not only Ibsen, Shaw, Brieux, and Strindberg, but also Wedekind, Hauptmann, Sudermann, Andreyev, and Synge. As for Nietzsche, Mencken frequently used new translations and studies as the occasion for calling attention to the philosopher's increasing vogue and for summarizing his doctrines.

Mencken's discussions of such authors as Ibsen, Shaw, and Nietzsche, however, usually differed from those of Huneker and Pollard in both point of view and tone. The latter critics, in the tradition of art for art's sake, stressed the need for discarding outmoded artistic conventions and supplanting them with an expressive individual style. They viewed the leading European artists as primarily "anarchs of art." Mencken, at times, wrote in the same spirit,[29] but he was much more concerned than Huneker and Pollard with religious, moral, scientific, economic, social, and political issues. His thought on these subjects, unlike theirs, was strongly impregnated with social Darwinism. Nietzsche may serve as a test case to illustrate these differences. Huneker agreed with Pollard that Nietzsche was significant chiefly for his "literary leadership." Mencken, on the other hand, stressed Nietzsche's Darwinian heritage as much in *The Smart Set* as in *The Philosophy of Friedrich Nietzsche,* insisting that the law of selection was the German thinker's "one supreme mandate and revelation." Mencken's heroes were not confined to artists, but included all "those men who make the most successful war upon the forces and conditions that work against the race—disease, climate, distance, time, terrestrial catastrophes, religions, superstitions, handicapping customs and laws."[30]

This statement helps explain Mencken's belief that literary artists should embody in their work a protest against certain of the institutions and values of their society. Mencken admired writers as different as Shaw, Ibsen, Nietzsche, Zola, and Mark Twain partly because in each of them the iconoclastic, truth-seeking impulse was indissolubly linked with the artistic impulse. As early as 1904, he implied this point by quoting Thomas Huxley:

"I believe," said Huxley in his old age—and Huxley was an artist, if the creation was the universe's supreme work of art— "that the only lasting happiness in life, aside from a few human affections, comes from fighting shams and seeking out the truth for the truth's sake, day in and day out, month in and month out, year after year."

"And, after all," Mencken declared in 1905, "it is the truth that every man worthy of the name is seeking, in science and in faith, and none the less in art."[31]

But was truth in the arts truth to fact, or truth to insight? Huxley, in his dual role as scientist and artist, dealt with two different kinds of truth. In his biological research, he sought to find objective truth in the data he collected and interpreted. As an essayist expressing himself with charm and persuasiveness, he often advocated controversial social, moral, and religious "truths" which were not capable of scientific demonstration. In handling this latter category of truths, he benefited from the prestige which his reputation as a scientist gave him, but he was nevertheless functioning as an artist. The values he championed were part of his personal vision. They rested ultimately on his agnosticism and Darwinism.

Huxley appealed to Mencken not so much because of his strictly scientific accomplishments, but because of his agnostic vision, his dogged pursuit of the insights it afforded him, and his ability to record and defend them in lucid and forceful prose. It was largely the Huxley tradition which suggested to Mencken that the artist's prejudices and impressions should have a Darwinian orientation and should result in iconoclasm. As a bohemian truth-seeker, Mencken intended to speak out on a much wider range of topics than either Pollard or Huneker.

A Short Way with Poetry

Mencken's evaluations of poetry reveal him at his most inept. Beginning in 1912, Harriet Monroe's *Poetry: A Magazine of Verse* formed a rallying point for the "new poets," but neither Mencken's sensibility nor his conception of verse equipped him to guide the "renaissance" that followed. Among American poets, Mencken preferred minor lyrists like Robert Loveman and Lizette Woodworth Reese. Without any ironical intention, he asserted that Loveman's "April Rain" ("It isn't raining rain to me,/It's raining daffodils.") was composed of "the ultimate corpuscles of music, . . . embodying all there is of song in next to nothing." "It floats around in my mind," he continued, "with half a dozen other such fragments of sheer delight—Eve Gore-Booth's 'The Roads of Cloonagh,' William Watson's 'April,' Miss Reese's 'Tears,' Kipling's 'Dirge of Dead Sisters,' broken reminiscences of Henley, Kingsley, and Christina Rossetti."[32] This list suggests Mencken's liking for the conventional short lyric. He disliked long poems and poems which were intellectual or philosophical in content.

His reactions to Miss Reese's sonnet, "Tears," illustrate the handicaps his limited conception of poetry placed on him. After depicting the brevity of human life and the suffering that accompanies it, the sonnet ends on this optimistic note:

> Loose me from tears, and make me see aright
> How each hath back what once he stayed to weep:
> Homer his sight, David his little lad!

When Mencken considered why "Tears" strongly appealed to him despite his lack of sympathy with its main idea, he theorized "that the overpowering impressiveness of certain . . . poetry depends largely . . . upon the very fact that it is incredible." This "gorgeous unveracity," temporarily dulling the reader's sense of "the sour facts of life," lifted him above mundane reality.[33] Thus poetry is essentially an escape from life, not a means of insight into it.

Reedy was a discriminating judge of poetry, and his *Mirror* encouraged young poets and printed samples of their work much more frequently than *The Smart Set*. But Mencken, within his limits, assisted in clearing the way. He ridiculed "the pious poets of . . . the God-Help-Us School—poets who see the world as a place of sin and sorrow and look forward to death as to a glad release." He denounced "the gentlemanly strophes of Richard Watson Gilder . . . , the somnambulistic rhapsodies of Dr. S. Weir Mitchell, the passionate stanzas of Professor Woodberry, and the pompous piffle of a horde of other pundits." Although the intellectual bent of Moody and E.A. Robinson alienated him, he recognized the merits of the work Ezra Pound and William Rose Benét had produced by 1912. He helped Edgar Lee Masters, Sara Teasdale, and Louis Untermeyer get published in *The Smart Set*. When confronted by Masters's *Spoon River Anthology* or Sandburg's "Chicago" and "Cool Tombs," he even abandoned temporarily his view that poetry is an escape mechanism. Such poets, he observed, replaced "ancient conventionality" with "an eager curiosity in life as men and women are actually living it—a spirit of daring experimentation that has made poetry vivid and full of human interest, as it was in the days of Elizabeth."[34]

The "Failure" of American Drama

Since Nathan reviewed performances of plays for *The Smart Set*, Mencken confined his comments to plays in print, but until 1912 he continued to see many performances as drama critic of the *Baltimore Sun*. The new drama, he noted in 1911, "is more closely in contact with life than the old drama it combats, and in consequence of greater interest and value as a criticism of life." Between 1908 and 1914 he did not lose faith in the new drama as such, but he gradually downgraded such favorites of his youth as Shaw and Strindberg. Shaw, he discovered, had no consistent philosophy; his formula was "putting the obvious into terms of the scandalous." Worst of all, Shaw had begun to take himself too seriously—in "becoming a wholesale reformer he has also become a bore." Mencken still regarded Strindberg's *The Father* as a masterpiece, but he felt that recent English translations showed the playwright's "frequent blunders in construction" and "the general looseness and absurdity of his more serious thinking."[35] He reserved his greatest enthusiasm for Ibsen, Hauptmann, Sudermann, Wedekind, Andreyev, and Synge.

Mencken was acutely conscious of the difficulties facing any playwright who wished to adapt the tradition of the European drama to American needs. One major force discouraging change was the audience itself, with its deference to puritanism and its love of melodrama. As early as 1905, Mencken had complained that in Baltimore, musical shows like *Floradora* and dramas with "some moral well rubbed in" played to crowded houses, but *Hedda Gabler* and *The Second Mrs. Tanqueray* were poorly attended. Drawing upon such observations, he concluded that most American theatergoers wished only to be entertained or edified, not to be challenged to think seriously about human problems. They wanted the kind of emotional shock caused by "conflict—between dastardly villain and pure heroine, honest State's attorney and rascally trust magnate, Eliza and the bloodhounds."[36]

Mencken became disillusioned not only with the American play-going audience, but also with the American theater system. During twelve years as a drama critic, he had the opportunity to see only five of Ibsen's social dramas, two plays by Sudermann, and one play by Brieux. The best plays were rarely performed because the theater system stressed the safe, money-making formulas and kept novelty and experimentation at a minimum. Mencken sympathized with the Baltimore theater managers because the New York syndicate gave them little choice of either plays or casts, but he felt obligated to inform the public by giving his honest opinion of each drama and its performance.

He was convinced "that Pinero is a better dramatist than Charles Klein, that 'Strife' is a better play than 'Ben-Hur,' that Eleanora Duse is a better performer than Chauncey Olcott," but a manager, knowing that Klein, *Ben-Hur,* and Olcott pay better, might easily assume that they *are* better. Because of his hard-hitting reviews, Mencken often came into conflict with local theater managers, and he reported that on three occasions they had brought pressure on his employers to discharge him.[37]

Another reason for his growing dislike of the theater system was his low opinion of most directors and actors. The influence of both these groups, he argued, was generally "against good plays, against good acting and against sound art." While admitting that the urge to act may be "something high and noble—an irresistible yearning for self-expression," he claimed that usually 'it is merely a yearning for self-exhibition" which is "proof . . . of the actor's inherent stupidity and overmastering vanity." Directors and actors tended to preserve the outmoded stock characters, soliloquies, and asides the new dramatists were trying to eliminate. Richard Mansfield's "two prime faults as a producing manager," for example, were "his persistent confusion, natural enough to an actor, of theatrical effectiveness with dramatic value, and his curious detachment from the great movement toward naturalness which marked his time."[38]

After resigning as drama critic of the *Sun* in 1912, Mencken rarely attended performances of plays. "The truth is," he declared, "that complete satisfaction in the theater is little more than a dream, a will-o'-the-wisp, an ideal never realized. Its attainment depends upon a collocation of talents and opportunities . . . virtually impossible, save perhaps as a rare miracle." The solution to this problem was for readers to *"read* plays and imagine the scene and action for themselves, helped by the more extensive stage directions that have come into vogue."[39] To make this possible, Mencken urged publishers to print reasonably priced editions of a wide selection of plays.

Although American plays had improved remarkably since the 1890s, Mencken knew of none that compared with the best work of the European dramatists. This was not surprising considering the many obstacles that the more adventurous American playwrights had to overcome. Romantic melodramas, social comedies, and period plays far outnumbered such realistic dramas of character as Clyde Fitch's *The Truth* (1907) and Augustus Thomas's *The Harvest Moon* (1909). About 1910, Mencken cited the efforts of Eugene Walter, Edward Sheldon, and Charles Klein as well as those of Fitch and Thomas to show that "our native dramatists, however clumsily they stumble along, are at least headed in the right direction." "Around the corner," he concluded optimistically, "the first really great American play may be waiting."[40]

It was disappointing to find that no American Ibsen appeared to carry the revolution to its completion. William Vaughn Moody might have developed into "the pioneer of real daring" Mencken was looking for, but his premature death in 1910 destined him to be remembered chiefly for one play. This was *The Great Divide,* the only American drama Mencken found "worthy to be ranked with 'A Doll's House' or 'Hedda Gabler.'" By 1916, when the Provincetown Players' production of Eugene O'Neill's *Bound East for Cardiff* finally opened a new era, Mencken made only occasional forays into dramatic criticism. He did help O'Neill by agreeing with Nathan to accept three of the young playwright's one-acters for publication in *The Smart Set.*[41] But Nathan, not Mencken, became O'Neill's friend and champion.

For Mencken, the main trend toward a distinctive literature lay in fiction rather than drama. Consequently, his reviews of fiction provide the best source for a study of the negative and positive aspects of his literary criticism.

"Sanitary" Demolition

In evaluating the huge output of novels and short stories, Mencken's chief negative aim was to expose and ridicule the groups and conditions that prevented promising young writers from fulfilling their potentialities as artists. Among his main targets were the mass audience and its mediocre tastes, the spinelessness of most critics, and the commercialism of many publishers and authors.

In his eagerness to attack not only the ideas odious to him, but also the men behind the ideas, Mencken was more like

Pollard than like Huneker. Huneker, Mencken observed, "detested what he called the tripe-sellers of the market-place . . . ,
but he seldom attacked them head on. His method was the
indirect one of crying up the sellers of honest red herring. He
disliked combat, and was no hand at sanitary tearing down."
Pollard and Mencken, however, shared the kind of "fine bellicosity" Mencken attributed to Shaw. Pollard argued that the
gate of American letters "stands wide open, and all the fools
may enter. What is needed at the gate is a club."[42] Mencken,
as if he had anticipated this call, was already swinging a club
in *The Smart Set.*

Mencken agreed with Pollard that a collusion between "the
publisher and the petticoat" accounted for many of the shortcomings of American fiction. "Nine-tenths of our readers of
books are women," Mencken commented, "and nine-tenths of
our women get their literary standards from the *Ladies' Home
Journal.* As a result, their literary deities are Hopkinson Smith,
Mary E. Wilkins, Dr. Henry van Dyke, and Mrs. Burton Harrison." When the "harmless virtue" featured by such writers
palls, "the great human yearning to be devilish . . . asserts itself."
Then

we arrive at "The Yoke," "Sir Richard Calmady," "The Awaken-
ing" and other such putrid stuff, beloved of high school girls and
discussed in hoarse whispers by the woman's clubs.

In this way feminine prudery and eroticism produce two classes
of books, the one made up of incredible love making in the
open air, and the other made up of indecent love making on
the hearth rug. . . . For novels that deal seriously with life as
it is actually lived . . . , putting love making in its proper
place—which is to say, far down the scale, above eating, perhaps,
but well below dying—there is no profitable audience in our
fair republic. That field, indeed, is entirely forbidden to the
author. If he would see his portrait in the "literary section" and
know the taste of truffles, he must keep out.[43]

Another influence which, in Mencken's opinion, corrupted
the audience was the vogue of the New Thought, with its
branches ranging "from psychical research to anti-vaccination,
from vegetarianism to the Emmanuel Movement, and from

zoöphilism to New Buddhism." "Books upon the occult and the incredible," Mencken remarked, "seem to be driving the great American novel to the wall." He directed his strongest ridicule at spiritualism and Christian Science. As an example of the literature on spiritualism, he cited Hamlin Garland's *The Shadow World,* commenting sarcastically on the credulity involved in the author's "personal dalliance with the spooks." Mencken opposed Christian Science because it encouraged attitudes running counter to the efforts of heroes like Vesalius, Jenner, Pasteur, Haeckel, and Huxley "to free the science of medicine from the clutches of superstition and magic." Just as plague after plague was yielding to exact knowledge and the span of life was lengthening, there arose "crusaders who call upon us . . . to place medicine within the clutches of the theologians once more, to put our faith again in cabalistic formulas, empty affirmations and idle dreams."[44]

The pressures inducing most writers to follow the established formulas were, Mencken believed, moral as well as financial. Because of the "ferocious intolerance" and the "snouting Puritanism" that prevailed in America, noncomformity either in one's private life or in one's writing was risky. As Dreiser discovered in 1916 when the New York Society for the Suppression of Vice proceeded against his *The "Genius,"* censorship was a threat which any author who defied the accepted taboos had to face. Two years before, considering the effects of moral pressures and the imminence of censorship, Mencken had declared that the so-called Comstock law enacted by Congress in 1873 rested "on American letters like a millstone on the midriff of a medieval heretic." "Our national literature . . . ," he added, "no more represents the lusty and barbarous life around us than it represents the life of the Periclean Greeks."[45]

Like Pollard, Mencken accused most critics writing for American periodicals of abrogating their responsibilities as "guardians of the gate." The standards of these critics reflected the prevailing gentility. A "majority of all the professional critics . . . ," observed Mencken, "are women, and many of the men in the minority are tenors." If the reviewers were not "ladies" enough to prefer Dr. Elwood Worcester and Robert W. Chambers to

Havelock Ellis and Conrad, commercial pressures nevertheless often forced them into the role of press agents for the best-sellers.[46]

As for academic critics like Mabie and More, Mencken scored both their genteel standards and their staid conservatism. "How long," he asked, "does it take a new idea to gain lodgment in the professorial mind?" The slowness with which the academic critics had recognized the artistry of Mark Twain was his chief case in point. He hoped that someday a statistician would "measure for us . . . the hiatus between the appearance of 'Huckleberry Finn' and its acceptance by any reputable professor . . . as a work of art of the first rank." Mencken guessed that the interval lasted exactly twenty-five years, from the publication of the novel on March 15, 1885, to the delivery of William Lyons Phelps's *Essays on Modern Novelists* to his door on March 15, 1910.[47] If the "professors" were reluctant to admit Mark Twain's genius even at the end of his life, what help could they be expected to give to the younger men of great talent just starting their careers?

When Mencken considered the various forms of popular fiction he did not reject them en masse—not even all romances. As shown by his liking for the romantic elements in the stories of Kipling and Conrad, and later those of Cabell and Hergesheimer, he did not object to the romance as such. He was willing to praise a popular novel which had some literary merit, as he did when he called Maurice Hewlett's *The Song of Renny* "a picaresque romance to warm the cockles of your heart." He acknowledged that "the entertaining trifles, designed frankly for the department store book counters," might serve as "anesthetics . . . to deaden the little pains of life."[48] He did not deplore occasional indulgence in this kind of reading. What angered him was that the outpouring of popular fiction threatened to overwhelm the authors who tried to stem the current.

The bulk of "machine-made American fiction," as Mencken defined it, constituted "a literature vast, gaudy and rich in usufructs, which outrages all sense and probability without descending to actual vulgarity, and so manages to impinge agreeably upon that vast and money-in-pocket public which takes instinctively a safe, middle course." In this category belonged Frances Hodgson Burnett's *Little Lord Fauntleroy*, Bertha

Runkle's *The Helmet of Navarre,* and Gene Stratton Porter's *Freckles* and *Laddie.* In criticizing such works, Mencken assumed that a novel, "whatever its play of humor," should "deal earnestly with the human beings it presumes to depict." Rather than creat-ing convincing characters, popular novelists turned out "mere dummies, with the sawdust of the theater in their arteries." Instead of concentrating on ordinary individuals, they often depicted "the soul struggles of the opulent minority." Most Americans could only marvel, for example, at the good fortune of the "songstress-heroine" of Francis Marion Crawford's *The Diva's Ruby,* among whose wedding presents are " 'two luxurious private cars of entirely different patterns, one for America and one for Europe,' and a ruby worth, at the current rate of ex-change, $68,040."[49]

Mencken also complained that popular novels embodied false and misleading values. Speaking of the typical best-sellers, he said, "The essence of this literature is sentiment, and the essence of sentiment is hope. Its aim is to fill the breast with soothing and optimistic emotions—to make the fat woman forget that she is fat, to purge the tired business man of his bile, to con-vince the flapper that Douglas Fairbanks may yet learn to love her." In a detailed analysis, Mencken pointed out how sentimen-tality ruined a potentially promising novel, William Allen White's *A Certain Rich Man.* The significant theme of John Barclay's rise from poverty to wealth and industrial power is spoiled by the "banal philosophy" that the desire to marry is "the most . . . honorable and godlike impulse native to the human con-sciousness." White "esteems yielding above victory, sentiment above reality, piety above progress. Of the gorgeous drama which lies in the ruthless struggle for existence he seems to have no no-tion whatever." He is, indeed, the last Victorian, whose work breathes "Honest Poverty, Chaste Affection and Manly Tears."[50]

Mencken justified his use of ridicule by saying that "when we ourselves indulge in titters and cat calls, it is only because we hope thus to punish trifling by the novelist himself." The capsule reviews appearing at the end of his book section illustrate vividly his strafing of specific novels. James Lane Allen's *Enter-ing the Kingdom,* for example, was "A dissertation on virtue, with a road map of Heaven. Good reading for the chemically

pure." Upton Sinclair's *Prince Hagan* was "An amateurish fable
by a perennial bore." So fascinating was the badness of Thomas
Dixon's *Comrades* that the reader "felt the thrill of the astronomer
with his eye glued upon some new and inconceivable star—of
the pathologist face to face with some novel and horrible *coc-
cus.*"[51]

"Crying Up the Sellers of Honest Red Herring"

The negative aims of Mencken's destructive criticism imply his
chief positive aim in *The Smart Set:* to encourage writers to
portray the common life of Americans honestly and vividly. He
wanted them to "consider the problems and passions of that
average American who makes up the nether millions—that average American to whom the struggle for existence is a very real
thing, because his average annual income, as the census reports
tell us, is less than six hundred dollars." He urged young authors
to study the methods of certain European novelists in order to
learn how to deal with American materials. In one such suggestion, he recommended "a careful reading of George Moore,
Émile Zola, Joseph Conrad, and William Makepeace Thackeray,
and particularly . . . of 'Evelyn Innes,' 'Germinal,' 'Lord Jim' and
"Barry Lyndon.' " He also emphasized the "master idea" behind
the works of each of these authors:

In the books of George Moore the basic motive is always the
eternal strife between faith and facts, the spirit and the flesh.
In the books of Joseph Conrad it is the utter meaninglessness
of life, the remoteness of first causes, the inexplicable vagaries
of fate. Again, in Thackeray, it is the deep rooted human impulse to play a part, to pretend, to dissemble, to wear a mask.

Although Mencken criticized Zola for his "ardent pursuit of
scientific half-truths, . . . his air of an anatomist dismembering
a corpse," he nevertheless regarded the French novelist as a great
artist-iconoclast in the Darwinian tradition. As an artist, Zola
produced at least four masterpieces—*Germinal, L'Assommoir,
Nana,* and *La Débâcle.* Furthermore, "his propaganda, as novelist
and critic, did more than any other one thing to give naturalism
direction and coherence and to break down its antithesis, the

sentimental romanticism of the middle Nineteenth Century—
'Uncle Tom's Cabin,' 'David Copperfield,' 'La Dame aux Came-
lias.' " Much of Zola's spirit, though not necessarily his direct
influence, pervaded the works of "Wells and Bennett in England,
Sudermann and Wedekind in Germany, Norris and Dreiser in
America, Gorki and Andrieff in Russia, a whole school of writers
in Scandinavia."[52]

The phrase, "the meaninglessness of life," runs like a refrain
through Mencken's discussion of serious modern fiction. He called
it "the central fact of human existence . . . —the capital discovery
of our day and generation—the one supreme truth that must
eventually revise and condition every other truth." At first glance,
one might assume that Mencken believed life is "meaningless"
because human beings are so completely the victims of heredity
and environment that they are reduced to impotence. One might
expect him to prefer the work of the "naturalist," who professes
to conceive of his characters as determined by forces within and
without, to that of the "realist," who does not necessarily accept
a deterministic philosophy. In fact, although Mencken held that
men and women are part of nature and subject to natural laws,
he recognized that "determinism, like free will, is only a half
truth." "Most of the things I do," he continued, "are forced on
me: I couldn't avoid doing them if I tried. But over the *way* in
which I do them I seem to have some control."[53] Rather than
insisting on any rigid interpretation of life, he tried to judge
each piece of fiction on its individual merits. He appreciated the
kind of realism which allows Huck Finn to assert his moral
responsibility as well as the naturalism which makes McTeague
a victim of his bad heredity.

Mencken's concept of "meaninglessness" can best be understood as part of his agnostic vision. It is closely related to his
view of the artist as a Darwinian iconoclast. The ultimate problems of human life, Mencken suggested, are beyond human
comprehension, and the traditional answers, such as those of
conventional religion, are inadequate and stultifying. In a comment inspired by Conrad's stories, he declared:

We may describe an event, but we can never hope to explain it;
the mystery of birth, the fact of death, the infinite chains of
causation which lead a man to choose this woman for his wife

and that color for his necktie; which make him a fat man in a stuffy office, or a thin man in a tattered tennis coat, fighting a rhinoceros in some African mudhole.

The artist who questions and rejects the orthodox explanations of such problems helps achieve what Mencken later called "the central purpose of a genuinely significant native literature"— "the criticism of the current cultural theory."[54]

Mencken, then, did not accept Zola's doctrinaire theory that a novelist can study human beings as objectively as a scientist making a laboratory demonstration. According to Zola, the novelist, after observing the necessary facts, "introduces an experiment, that is to say, sets his characters going in a certain story so as to show that the succession of facts will be such as the requirements of the determinism of the phenomena under examination call for." This view, if literally carried out, could easily result in a focus on the "facts" of heredity and environment which dwarf the individual, not on the individual himself. Mencken, on the other hand, saw the creation of character as the central task of the novelist, and he would have said that Zola was a better artist when he ignored such "scientific half-truths" as his own critical theory. A true novel, Mencken explained, is a

book which tells, with insight, imagination and conviction, the story of some one man's struggle with his fate—which shows us, like a vast fever chart, the ebb and flow of his ideas and ideals, and the multitude of forces shaping them—which gives us, in brief, a veritable, moving chronicle of a human being driven, tortured and fashioned by the blood within him and the world without—a chronicle with a beginning, a middle and an end, and some reasonable theory of existence over all.[55]

For Mencken, as for Norris and Dreiser, realism and naturalism are not incompatible with a sense of the intrinsic significance of human life and of the romance and mystery that encompass it. When Mencken wrote in *The Smart Set* that Conrad gives us "romance set free from sentimentality," he anticipated his later conclusion that

No such thing as a pure method is possible in the novel. Plain realism, as in Gorky's "Nachtasyl" and the war stories of Ambrose Bierce, simply wearies us by its vacuity; plain romance, if we ever get beyond our nonage, makes us laugh. It is their artistic combination, as in life itself, that fetches us—the subtle projection of the concrete muddle that is living against the ideal orderliness which we reach out for—the eternal war of experience and aspiration—the contrast between the world as it is and the world as it might be or ought to be.

Life is "meaningless" because men can never completely surmount the obstacles it puts in their way nor triumph over death, yet the pitting of human aspirations and ideals against "the over-whelming sweep and devastation of universal forces" does have meaning. As illustrated in Conrad's stories, it is "a gallant and a gorgeous adventure, a game uproariously worth the playing, an enterprise 'inscrutable . . . and excessively romantic.' "[56]

Out of "the eternal war of experience and aspiration" come the materials of both tragedy and comedy. Mencken drew a parallel between Greek tragedy and Dreiser's novels, but he did not really come to grips with the problem of whether the tradi-tional Aristotelian conception of tragedy can be reconciled with Dreiser's philosophy. According to Aristotle, tragedy results when an essentially noble character of heroic stature, through an effort of will, transgresses an unchanging moral law and suffers the appropriate punishment. Greek tragedy presupposes, then, a uni-versal moral order and a sphere of action in which man's will is free to make significant choices. Although Mencken does not comment specifically on these two main premises of the older definition of tragedy, he emphasized that Dreiser finds "no moral (or even dramatic) plan in the order of the universe" and looks upon man as being in the grip of forces he cannot understand. Mencken did not outline his own notion of tragedy very clearly, but he implied that Dreiser's characters, although theoretically the playthings of fortune, at least *act* as if they possessed free will. The life of Eugene Witla, hero of *The "Genius,"* is "a bitter conflict between the animal in him and the aspiring soul, between the flesh and the spirit, . . . between what is base and what is noble." Jennie Gerhardt, a character Mencken regarded as much more convincing than Witla, is "of the nobler, finer metal," with "a great capacity for service, a great capacity for love, a great capacity for happiness." Because of her inability to win

from life more than "the mere license to live," Mencken found
Jennie "more tragic . . . than Lear on his wild heath or Prome-
theus on his rock."[57]

Jennie's dilemma corresponds to Dreiser's "vision of life as
a seeking without a finding." Mencken suggested that Dreiser
might well take as his motto these lines from *Oedipus Rex:* "O
ye deathward-going tribes of man,/What do your lives mean except that they go to nothingness?" Dreiser achieves tragedy because "the thing he exposes is not the empty event and act, but
the endless mystery out of which it springs"; because he portrays
vividly how forces within and without his characters distort
and frustrate their ideals and aspirations; and because he com-
municates to his readers the "passionate compassion" with which
he contemplates human strivings and sufferings.[58]

Mencken's own ebullient humor explains better than any sober
argument why he could appreciate a humorous as well as a tragic
attitude toward life. "Imagine the Creator as a low comedian,"
he wrote to a friend, "& at once the world becomes explicable.
Rabelais was far nearer God than Xst." Enlarging on this view
in *The Smart Set,* he speculated that "in some high and merry
heaven, there is an angel who diverts himself by chuckling over
my puerile agonies, just as I myself, on my lower, lowlier plane,
get a subtle joy out of the furious leapings and sweatings of a
cockroach pursued by my bludgeon, of a vice crusader trying to
repeal and re-enact with amendments the way of a man with a
maid." To show why he could appreciate Montague Glass's
Abe and Mawruss as well as Edith Wharton's *Ethan Frome,* he
commented, "I am not one who perceives any inherent virtue in
tragedy, or any inherent vice in comedy."[59]

At the head of the native tradition in fiction which Mencken
wanted to encourage were several favorites of his youth, with
Huckleberry Finn taking precedence over the others. In a rebuke
directed at G.K. Chesterton, he protested: "Let us alone, O Fat
Mullah. . . . We are happy in our wallow. We are even beginning
to produce a literature exalting its charms. You will find the
germs of that literature . . . in the scene in *Huckleberry Finn*
wherein Huck wrestles with his conscience."[60] In its realism and
its tragic overtones, *Huckleberry Finn* anticipated the more somber explorations of "the meaninglessness of life" in those other

favorites of Mencken's youth: *The Red Badge of Courage, Mc-Teague,* and *Sister Carrie.* Mencken regarded the trend represented by these volumes as the most important in American fiction. As a vehicle for comedy and satire conveyed through dialect, *Huckleberry Finn* forecast another development Mencken valued highly. Although he discovered no other American writer with Mark Twain's comic genius, he felt that authors like George Ade and Montague Glass deserved to be recognized as artists with a keen eye for sham and a good command of the vernacular.

Since Crane died prematurely in 1900, and Norris in 1902, neither produced as much work of lasting value as their talent and industry seemed to promise. Another author whose realistic novels Mencken admired was Henry B. Fuller, whose *The Cliff-Dwellers* and *With the Procession* appeared in the nineties. Fuller survived Norris and Crane by many years, but he did not consistently use American materials as his subject. In a review of Fuller's *Waldo Trench and Others,* a collection of short stories, Mencken had little sympathy with its chief characters—"those queer, dreaming, unhappy Americans who haunt the *pensions* of Florence and Pisa and try to convince themselves that home is not sweet." In *A Book of Prefaces,* Mencken mentioned Fuller as a forerunner of Dreiser, but found *Jennie Gerhardt* superior to *The Cliff-Dwellers* in portraying the "Chicago of those great days of feverish money-grabbing and crazy aspiration."[61]

Between the death of Norris and the appearance of *Jennie Gerhardt,* Upton Sinclair, Jack London, and David Graham Phillips worked partly in the tradition of naturalism, but their novels had serious faults. While praising these writers for their occasional achievements, Mencken condemned their failure to make the most of their talents. His basic complaint about all three was that their novels tended to degenerate into propaganda. Sinclair, when he started out, seemed to have "something of the vigor of Frank Harris, even of Zola, in him," but, after the success of *The Jungle* (1906), he started down "the road of Walt Whitman, of Edwin Markham, of the later Zola, all of whom began as artists and ended as mad mullahs." Sinclair's *The Money-changers* showed that he must "choose between crusading and writing." As illustrated by the Alaskan tales in *Lost Face,* London could achieve "good form, dramatic movement, and interesting

personages," but his novels too often became tracts for socialism
or prohibition. His *Martin Eden* was "a combination of incredible
biography and undigested philosophy." Phillips engaged in "the
vain trade of manufacturing best sellers" and, as a muckraker,
preached against "the Crimes of the Affluent." But in some of
his later novels he had begun to overcome these restrictions,
particularly in depicting the American woman "as he saw her,
with her essential faults painted boldly." The wife in *The Hungry
Heart,* for example, "is as real as Evelyn Innes or Sister Carrie,"
with "exactly that combination of formless aspiration and vague
discontent which marks the average American woman of the middle class."[62]

Early in 1911 Phillips was murdered by a lunatic who imagined
that his family had been maligned in the novelist's books. In
a newspaper article printed March 22, Mencken observed that
"Phillips, stricken down at forty-four, was the hope of American
fiction, just as Frank Norris had been a decade before." As possible
candidates to succeed Phillips, Mencken passed in review Robert
Herrick, Jack London, Winston Churchill, Robert W. Chambers,
and William Allen White, but he dismissed them all as being
comparatively unpromising. At this time he was eagerly awaiting
the manuscript of *Jennie Gerhardt,* which Dreiser had asked
him to criticize. Mencken certainly had this in mind when he
concluded, "Dreiser, perhaps, will be the man of tomorrow."[63]

After reading the manuscript of *Jennie Gerhardt,* which reached
him on April 19, Mencken hastened to congratulate Dreiser.
"The story," he said,

comes upon me with great force; it touches my own experience
of life in a hundred places; it preaches (or perhaps I had better
say exhibits) a philosophy of life that seems to me to be sound;
altogether I get a powerful effect of reality, stark and unashamed.
It is drab and gloomy, but so is the struggle for existence. It is
without humor, but so are the jests of that great comedian who
shoots at our heels and makes us do our grotesque dancing.

"You strained (or perhaps even broke) the back of *Sister Carrie,"*
Mencken told Dreiser, "when you let Hurstwood lead you away
from Carrie"; *Jennie Gerhardt's* "obvious superiority lies in its
better form." In *The Smart Set,* Mencken called *Jennie* "the best
American novel I have ever read, with the lonesome but Himala-

yan exception of 'Huckleberry Finn.'" *Jennie* is "assertively American in its scene and its human material," yet it is "so European in its method, its point of view, its almost reverential seriousness, that one can scarcely imagine an American writing it." Its simplicity and sincerity reminded Mencken of *Germinal, Anna Karenina,* and *Lord Jim.*[64]

From 1911 on, Mencken became one of Dreiser's main champions. As Dreiser turned out *The Financier, A Traveler at Forty, The Titan,* and other books, he submitted the manuscripts or the proof-sheets to Mencken. Mencken read them carefully and returned them with critical comment, often including suggestions for cuts and revisions. As each volume was printed, Mencken reviewed it in the *Sun, The Smart Set,* and any other publication which opened its pages to him.

Since Mencken's admiration for Dreiser never amounted to adulation, both his letters to Dreiser and his reviews contain some unfavorable judgments. Mencken doubted whether all the details in *Jennie, The Financier,* and *The Titan* were relevant, and he saw no sign of a "painful groping for the inevitable word" in Dreiser's commonplace phrases like "helpless poor" and "untutored mind." He regretted that Dreiser had not picked up from his reading of Thomas Huxley "a talent for that dazzling style, so sweet to the ear, so damnably persuasive, so crystal-clear." "If H.G. Wells," Mencken noted, "had as firm a grip upon character and situation as Theodore Dreiser, . . . ; and if Theodore Dreiser . . . had half the humor and a third of the feeling for phrase and climax of H.G. Wells, . . . then we should have a very excellent novelist indeed." At times, Dreiser, failing to achieve artistic detachment, "vacillates perilously between a moral sentimentalism and a somewhat extravagant revolt." This, Mencken felt, was particularly true of *"The "Genius,"* a novel which he condemned outright.[65]

On the whole, however, Mencken remained faithful to his conviction that Dreiser was "a great instinctive artist." In his letters, he tried to allay Dreiser's fears and urged him to complete quickly whatever project he had underway. In 1913, for example, he assured Dreiser that he was winning acceptance as "the leading American novelist," citing as evidence the fact that serious new novels were no longer compared to *Silas Lapham* and

McTeague, but to *Sister Carrie* and *Jennie Gerhardt.* When Mencken read page proofs of *A Traveler at Forty,* he called on Dreiser to follow it up at once with the novels he was then working on, *The Titan* and *The "Genius."* "You ought to have seven or eight volumes on the shelves," Mencken advised, "instead of only three. Once you get them there, you will be discussed more, and also read more."[66]

In his preference for the tradition of Zola and Dreiser, Mencken parted company with both Huneker and Pollard. Huneker preferred the "daylight clearness of Flaubert," "the delicate arabesques of the De Goncourts," and the restrained artistry of Henry James to "the sooty extravagances and violent melodrama of Zola and his disciples." Contending that "Zola was not a realist merely because he dealt with certain unpleasant facts," Huneker called him "a myopic romanticist writing in a style both violent and tumefied, the history of his soul in the latrines of life." As for Dreiser, Huneker recalled that he had read *Jennie Gerhardt* "in Ms. and sweated blood in the corrections—to no purpose. He is without an ear for prose, or an eye for form." To offset the "appalling exposition of our average culture" in the novel, Pollard asked for less deference to "quantity, to story, to realism" and more emphasis on preciosity, "the artist's fairest mask." Preciosity meant not "pedantry and profusion," but "reticence, music and simplicity." Among contemporary writers of English, he found that only Pater, Maurice Hewlett, Henry Harland, the earlier Edgar Saltus, H.B. Fuller, and James had approximated this ideal of a "precious" style. Mencken, in his review of *Their Day,* chided Pollard for failing to mention, "in a book plainly designed to be comprehensive," such writers as Conrad, H.G. Wells, Norris, and Dreiser.[67]

Although Mencken believed that the chief hope for American fiction lay with men like Dreiser, he recognized the merits of many stories in the older tradition of social and psychological realism. He expressed his feelings about the "genteel and well-made books" in this tradition while commenting on Edith Wharton's *The Hermit and the Wild Woman.* "I have read Conrad and Kipling," he said, "on the deck of a smelly tramp steamer, with my attire confined to a simple suit of pajamas . . . ; but after I had passed the first story in Mrs. Wharton's book, I began to long for a velvet smoking jacket and a genuine Havana substitute for my corncob pipe." He admired the craftsmanship of Mrs. Wharton, Howells, and Willa Cather, but he felt that Henry James carried "that painful striving, that elaborate effort to avoid the commonplace" too far. Despite his likening of the "Jacobin syntax" to "the façades of Polish churches in mining towns," he was pleased by some of James's novelettes, calling *What Maisie Knew*, for instance, "a riotous and delightful piece of Olympian foolery—and happily free from Mr. James's more recondite snarls of speech."[68]

In general, from among all the stories produced by "the School of Plot," Mencken enjoyed most those which dealt convincingly with American types usually neglected in fiction. He had reservations about most of the novels by "the venerable and consummate Howells," but he commended *New Leaf Mills* for reminding us that besides the successful pioneer there was a "vast company of dreamers and impossibilists who hung at his heels—founders of empires that come to nothing, . . . believers in brummagem milleniums, the grotesque white crows and black swans of the humdrum East." Mencken gave only moderate praise to Willa Cather's first novel, *Alexander's Bridge,* but later, when she chose Nebraska farmers and villagers for her subjects, he gave her firm critical support. His highest praise, significantly enough, went to Mrs. Wharton's venture into naturalism, *Ethan Frome.* "Frome, the lorn New England farmer . . . ," Mencken declared, "is the archetype of an American we have been forgetting, in our eagerness to follow the doings of more . . . spectacular fellows." With "the poignancy of true tragedy," his story conveys "the unutterable desolation of those Northern valleys, the meaningless horror of life in those lonely farmhouses."[69]

In its positive aspects, then, Mencken's criticism sought to encourage either a realistic, naturalistic, humorous, or satirical portrayal of everyday American life. When his judgments about a book were largely favorable, Mencken did not usually support them with a detailed analysis. When a really superior novel came along, he argued, the critic's "customary vocabulary . . . fails him, for it is made up almost entirely of terms derogatory and infuriate, and when he seeks to make use of the ordinary phrases of praise he finds them flat to his taste." "When a book is a good one and worth the price asked for it . . . ," he asserted, "the best thing for the reviewer to do is to say so in plain words and have done."[70] This procedure was consistent with his impressionistic method and allowed him to crowd a larger number of reviews into a limited space.

In 1913, when Wilbur Huntington Wright, a young protégé of Mencken's, became editor, *The Smart Set* began to take on the pattern maintained, with some modifications, by Mencken and Nathan when they succeeded him as editors the following year. Wright, promising to defy "some of the holiest conventions of the 'family periodical,'" aimed to make the magazine "fearless and independent enough" to become the "outlet . . . needed to prove that American writers are capable of meeting European writers on an equal footing." Declaring war on "effeminacy and formalism," he made room for writers ranging from Wedekind and Strindberg through Moore, Conrad, D.H. Lawrence, and Yeats to Frank Harris and Dreiser.[71]

Although *The Smart Set* was still chronically handicapped by its meager budget when Mencken became editor, he could now encourage promising authors not merely by praising them in his reviews but by inviting them to contribute stories and articles. As his editorial correspondence increased, he gradually acquired the wide acquaintance among writers which served him well in his later editing of the *Mercury*. But first he had, like other German-Americans, to face the crisis of World War I. The anguish he felt and the trials he experienced helped prepare him for the important role he was to play in the revolt of the twenties.

6

WARTIME TRIALS
AND HOPES

Before 1914: Friendly Rivalry with Anglo-Saxons

Between 1908 and 1914, Mencken—as an advocate of rebellion
in literature, manners, morals, and religion—was a comparatively
isolated figure. Through his books and reviews, he had gained
some national recognition, but the ideas and values he upheld
did not triumph until the twenties. To understand how and
why this postwar victory occurred, it is necessary to consider
the effects the conflict had on him and the movement he represented, on one hand, and on American public opinion, on
the other.

Before the outbreak of war in 1914, he lived and worked
side-by-side with Americans of other nationalities without being
particularly self-conscious about his German heritage. He had
frequently noted how quickly the descendants of immigrants
became Americanized. The average member of an immigrant
family, he contended, had little chance to preserve the traditions
of his forefathers:

A few whirls in the machine and he emerges wrapped in the
Star-Spangled Banner, with American slang in his mouth, American sentimentality in his heart. . . . He may hold to his national
customs for a generation, but no longer. Ridicule makes him
ashamed of them; ambition makes him abandon them.

Only where many families of one nationality had settled in the same city were they able to make some headway against the demands for conformity.[1]

This account of how rapidly immigrants were assimilated is substantially accurate. Among German-Americans, the increasing stress put on the "American" rather than the "German" side of the hyphen before the war illustrates the process. Many German-Americans, especially those of the first generation, supported newspapers and organizations they hoped would keep alive their language and their cultural heritage. They took an understandable pride in the great progress made by imperial Germany, especially after 1870.[2] Nevertheless, America was their real home. Most members of the first generation, though still maintaining many traditional attitudes and customs, became American citizens. The second and third generations grew further and further away from the German cultural heritage. The large community of German-Americans in Baltimore were cohesive enough to resist the efforts of native "uplifters" to interfere with their social freedoms, but their language and many of their economic and political views were hardly distinguishable from those of Anglo-Saxons of roughly the same occupational and class interests.

To his friends and associates, H.L. Mencken must have seemed much more American than German. Like August Mencken before him, he declined to join any of the German-American societies. His German, though better than his father's, was imperfect. Yet, in certain ways, the Germanic tradition was more vital to him than it had been to his father. Like his grandfather Burkhardt, he was proud of the accomplishments of the Menckens in Europe during the Age of the Enlightenment and of their alliance by marriage with the family of Prince Otto von Bismarck in the nineteenth century. It was one of his duties as a newspaperman to keep informed about European affairs, and he had followed developments in Germany with particular interest. He had written editorials and articles on such topics as Germany's military preparedness and Kaiser Wilhelm's personality and policies. His study of Nietzsche and other German authors, his liking for composers like Brahms and Richard Strauss, and his admiration for scientists like Rudolf Virchow and Wilhelm Koch all contributed to his feeling that modern Germany was undergoing a cultural as well as a political renaissance. His vacation trips to Europe in 1908, 1912, and 1914, each including a visit to Germany, strengthened that impression.

For a journalist of Mencken's background, especially when writing for a Baltimore audience, it was natural to exploit the conflicts between the native culture, on one side, and the German-American culture and the survivals of the culture of the Old South, on the other. His "The Free Lance" column in the *Baltimore Evening Sun* illustrates his skill in stirring up controversy and thus attracting large numbers of readers. In this column, which appeared daily on the editorial page from May 8, 1911, to October 23, 1915, his iconoclasm on nonliterary subjects ranges much more widely than in his *Smart Set* reviews. Mencken also edited two adjoining columns devoted to letters from readers, and he saw to it that all the most violent attacks on himself were printed.

Much as the *Mercury* later appealed to the enlightened minority, "The Free Lance" calls for "a rising of the civilized and intelligent people of this town" to combat "a plague of bad advisers, of moral, political and economic charlatans." Perhaps a thousand such citizens, Mencken estimates, stand out from the "abnormally large proportion of ciphers—darkies, foreigners, invading yokels, professional loafers and so on." The values and practices he attacks are chiefly those typical of the dominant native culture but not of the German-American community or of the Old South. Accordingly, his ideal audience consisted mainly of German-Americans and unreconstructed southerners.[3]

In "The Free Lance," Mencken constantly appeals—at first usually by implication but after the outbreak of war directly and openly—to German-American standards. He also cites approvingly the example of "that alert and daring New Germany which has scarcely a trait in common with the traditional Germany of abysmal learning and beery tears." To illustrate this new German spirit, he quotes his own translation of Otto Julius Bierbaum's *"Gott sei Dank!,"* including these stanzas:

> Show me worth—and I'll bow to it,
> Hallelujah!
> Show me sham—and sham will rue it,
> Hallelujah!

. . . .

In myself I put my trust,
　　Hallelujah!
I will pay my way—or bust!
　　Hallelujah!

All my friends are on the square,
　　Hallelujah!
By their friendship I can swear,
　　Hallelujah!

Foes have I—the devil take 'em!
　　Hallelujah!
Shake 'em, break 'em, rake 'em, bake 'em!
　　Hallelujah!

Mencken's allegiance to the tradition of the Old South is shown in his condemnation of "the South of 1914" by the standards of "the South that Jefferson knew."

The latter boasted a civilization which . . . performed admirably the capital function of producing first-rate men. The South of today, with all governmental powers transferred to what the old South called the "poor white trash," produces no such men. . . . Politically, at least, it is stupid, unimaginative, credulous, emotional, suspicious, vulgar, "moral." Imagine . . . prohibition and the blind pig in the Virginia of Washington and Randolph![4]

Because of his German-American heritage, Mencken deplored the condescension with which many Americans regarded Europeans. "The . . . average American," he declared, "is . . . densely ignorant of other peoples, even those who have immigrated to his shores, and . . . his ignorance commonly reveals itself as contempt." To dispel American notions that the Germans were "beer-soaked boors" or "cocky strutters" Mencken reminisced about having dinner with twenty or thirty salesmen in a commercial hotel in Leipzig.

You know, of course, what such a crowd of American drummers would have talked about: sales, hotels, railroads, baseball, poker, women. But not these Germans. They talked about a Beethoven sonata! . . .—how it should be played, and what public performer played it best.

Another contrast that struck Mencken forcibly was that between the genial social attitudes of the Germans and the moralistic and often intolerant views of native Americans. He pointed out, for example, that the uplifters, moral crusades, and blue laws that plagued Baltimore were unknown in Munich. The same contrast was implied in his statement that "The Bavarians have no false pruderies, no nasty little nicenesses. There is, indeed, no race in Europe more innocent, more frank, more clean-minded."[5]

Before the outbreak of war in Europe, Mencken could defend German culture and German-American social customs without much risk of being accused of subverting American values. In Baltimore, as in other cities with a large German-American population, the rivalry between the native majority and the German-American minority was not usually openly hostile. When Mencken dramatized this rivalry in "The Free Lance," he assumed that his readers would acknowledge that Americans of German descent were just as loyal and had just as much right to express their opinions as citizens of any other nationality. His own views bore traces of their German-American and semi-southern origins, but he did not profess to be a spokesman for any group or party. He appeared before the public as an American newspaperman voicing and assuming responsibility for his own opinions.

After 1914: Championing German-Americans and the New Germany

By interrupting the gradual fusion between Americans of German descent and those of other nationalities, the war created a crisis for Mencken and most German-Americans. A large part of the American public sympathized with the enemies of Germany from the start. "The nerve of the war-feeling," observed Randolph Bourne, "centered . . . in the richer and older classes of the Atlantic seaboard, and was keenest where there were French or English business and particularly social connections." The most influential newspapers, either purposely or because most of the news channels to Germany had been closed, presented the war news from the Allied point of view. Even while the country was ostensibly dedicated to the policy of strict neutrality

proclaimed by President Wilson, the normal activities of German-American clubs, churches, schools, and newspapers were
often denounced as part of an organized German propaganda
effort. American citizens of German descent as well as Germans
abroad were labeled "Huns." Men and women whose integrity
and loyalty had never been questioned suddenly had to defend
themselves against the accusations of fellow citizens with whom
they had previously been on good terms.[6]

After America's entry into the war in 1917, the anti-German
feeling became even more intense. The Committee on Public
Information, headed by George Creel, was formed to present
the Allied case and to keep public opinion alerted to oppose
any kind of disloyalty. The Espionage Act, passed by Congress
in June 1917, penalized any incitement to disloyalty or interference with recruiting and forbade any false statement which
might injure the prosecution of the war. The much more severe
Sedition Act, passed in May 1918, made punishable all statements which were scornful or strongly critical of the Constitution, our form of government, the armed forces, the flag, or the
military uniform. German-American publications were subjected
to an official censorship. In many localities, self-appointed patriots brought about the abolition of the teaching of German
in the public schools, and even brought German cooking and
German music into disrepute. Under these circumstances, the
more than eight million persons of German background in
America became much more self-conscious about their status
as a minority group. For them, the war initiated a period of
emotional crisis, divided loyalties, misunderstandings, and per-
secutions.

"How do you stand on this war?" Mencken asked Dreiser in
November 1914. "As for me, I am for the hellish Deutsche until
Hell freezes over." "The Free Lance" remained iconoclastic,
satirical, and humorously combative in tone, but Mencken now
devoted less space to local issues and more to the cause of Germany. For the benefit of readers who might assume that he was
a native German, he carefully explained his position in regard
to the English as well as the German tradition. He was, he pointed
out, born in Baltimore of Baltimore-born parents, and he had
English and Irish blood as well as German. He had no close rela-

tives or friends in Germany, had only a partial command of
German, and had not visited Germany until he was twenty-
eight. "What is more," he added,

the most massive influences of my life have all been unmistakably
English. I know Kinglake's "Crimea" and Steevens' "With Kitchener to Khartoum" a great deal better than I know any history
of the American Revolution or Civil War; I make a living writing the language of Thackeray and Huxley, and devote a good
deal of time to studying it; I believe thoroughly in the imperialism for which England has always stood; . . . I regard the net
English contribution to civilization as enormously greater than
the German contribution.

But, Mencken argued, the great England he admired had de-
generated into a caricature of its former self. "The old governing class, with its honorable traditions, its tenacity to order, its
sturdy common sense, its steadiness in great emergencies," he asserted, "is now practically an outlaw class." It has gradually
yielded to "a camorra of pecksniffs and time-servers, a breed of
professional job-holders and mob-orators." "The slimy 'morality'
of the unleashed rabble," he concluded, "has conquered the
clean and masculine ideals of the old ruling caste."[7]

According to Mencken, the real cause of England's hostility
to Germany was jealousy. The "new might and consequence of
Germany," including its growing sea-power and its competition
in world markets, had challenged Great Britain's position as
"the boss of Europe, and with Europe, of the world." Eager "to
crush and dispose of Germany before it is too late," the English
"wooed the French day in and day out, and inflamed their old
thirst for *revanche*," and "stirred up the Russian bear with
promises of help." Instead of frankly admitting its rivalry with
Germany, England "artfully dissembled, her mouth full of
pieties, until Germany was beset by enemies in front and behind,
and then she suddenly threw her gigantic strength into the
unequal contest." And still "this new, this saponaceous, this
superbrummagem England" did not admit the truth, but "went
into battle with a false cry upon her lips, seeking to make her
rage against a rival appear as a frenzy for righteousness." Her
claim that she was fighting for democracy was hardly consistent

with her previous roles as "the throttler of the Boer republics, the persecutor of Ireland, the ruthless foe of Egyptian nationality."[8] For these reasons, Mencken came out unequivocally on the German side.

In peacetime, both before and after World War I, Mencken occasionally judged America by German (or other European) standards, but normally he invoked the standards clustering about his nostalgic images of German-American life in Baltimore and of life in the Old South. The war made him temporarily a partisan of the new Germany. The favorable conception of the German Reich he featured in "The Free Lance" can best be understood as part of his reaction as a German-American to the unfavorable conception stressed in the American press. With his belligerence thoroughly aroused, he now praised Germany's economy and government as well as her social customs and her accomplishments in the arts. When Ellery Sedgwick, editor of the *Atlantic,* invited him to submit an essay about the effects of Nietzsche's teachings on the German bureaucracy, he had an opportunity to state his case for the new Germany at some length.

This article, "The Prophet of the Mailed Fist," oversimplifies Nietzsche's philosophy and over-idealizes imperial Germany. Mencken begins by pointing out that Nietzsche had been a bitter critic of the old German culture. Throughout the seventies and eighties, he had denounced its boorishness and its superstitions, its supine yieldings to a clumsy and unintelligent government, its addiction to the two great narcotics, alcohol and Christianity. But meanwhile, a new Germany was springing up. As "the old aristocracy of the barracks and the court" gave way to "a new aristocracy of the laboratory, the study, and the shop," there began an era of productiveness and prosperity marked by the rising influence of the universities, the growth of the sciences, the development of industries, the expansion of trade in world markets, and the establishment of colonies. In the early nineties, Nietzsche's *Thus Spake Zarathustra* provided just the doctrines the new ruling caste needed to help them oppose "the petty ideals of the rising proletariat" embodied in socialistic and democratic theories. From Nietzsche, "the young intellectuals, the rulers of the morrow," learned to look out on the world proudly and disdainfully, to preach the will to power, to glory in nationalism, to argue that " 'a good war hallows every cause.' "9

Mencken's arguments do not adequately support his thesis that Nietzsche was "The Prophet of the Mailed Fist." Mencken makes only a passing reference to the concept of the "good European" Nietzsche often stressed as a corrective to German nationalism. He also completely ignores the complexities and ambiguities of Nietzsche's thought as expressed by the seer Zarathustra. He quotes a few passages justifying the "Be hard!" philosophy, but neglects those which might be used to favor mystic contemplation rather than militant efficiency. He neither proves that Nietzsche had a wide following among members of the German ruling caste, nor considers the relationship of Nietzsche's teachings to the many other influences affecting German opinion. His oversimplification is typified by the statement that with the war, which was bringing "at last the great test of the gospel of strength, of great daring, of efficiency," "Germany becomes Nietzsche; Nietzsche becomes Germany."10

To the popular view that the German government was a tyrannical regime dominated by a ruthless military clique, Mencken opposed his claim that it was "a delimited, aristocratic democracy in the Athenian sense—a democracy of intelligence, of strength, of superior fitness—a democracy at the top."11 Just as the popular image unduly degraded Germany, Mencken's image unduly idealized it. The truth lay somewhere between the extremes.

The American reaction to the war, including the wave of anti-German feeling, convinced Mencken that many of the trends he had been combatting and ridiculing were being accelerated. The fact that even in the early stages public opinion was predominantly on the side of England and the Allies reinforced the Anglo-Saxon elements in the native culture. As a result, the conflicts between the assumptions of the native culture and those of the German-Americans and other dissenting minority groups came increasingly into the open.

The Anglo-Saxon tradition, as Mencken interpreted it, was roughly equivalent to the genteel tradition. In his view, its dominance in American foreign policy meant that we were dedicated to Anglophilism and a "combination of shameful rapacity and pretended virtue." In theory, the policy of neutrality allowed manufacturers to sell arms to any of the belligerents, but, in fact, the British blockade prevented our ships from reaching German ports. "We thus deliberately ranged ourselves," commented Mencken, "on the side of England, though under the cover of neutrality." The Germans expected a "frank and honest dealing with the problem of war in the United States"; instead, they were confronted with "our characteristic Anglo-Saxon hypocrisy." The same Americans who denounced the Germans for "making war upon the enemies that have sworn to destroy them" countenanced the profitable trade with the Allies. Meanwhile, the State Department held the German government strictly accountable for any hostile acts by German vessels against American ships.[12]

Mencken had previously avoided identifying himself publicly with any particular group, but now he began to speak out on behalf of German-Americans. Most of them, he admitted, had expected American opinion to run against Germany.

But when the English cut the cables and the country was suddenly flooded with violently anti-German "news" and arguments, the effect was vastly greater than they had ever anticipated. What they had before them was the familiar American spectacle of the mob running amok—with the newspapers gallantly beating the tom-toms. At one stroke everything German became anathema.

Anyone who favored Germany, no matter how calmly and reasonably, was generally regarded as a criminal or a traitor. "Surely it is not surprising," Mencken remarked, "that the German-Americans, in the face of such an onslaught, were forced into a separateness which, before the war, had never marked them." "It is useless," he added, "to denounce them for imaginary offenses against their Americanism; they have already received plain notice that they stand in a separate class, and haven't the rights of other Americans."[13]

Before the war, he had justified his iconoclasm in "The Free Lance" on the ground that it fulfilled a temperamental need and that it was, besides, the main agent of progress. Now, when one reader congratulated him for not taking refuge behind a false name, he attributed his outspokenness to his German blood. "The great virtue of all Germans, and likewise their great curse," he asserted, "is their lack of tact, their unashamed egoism, their constitutional inability to dissemble."[14]

One View of the "Archangel Woodrow"

Mencken felt increasingly that the Anglo-Saxon traits he detested were typified by President Wilson and his administration. His view of Wilson can best be understood by relating it to his attitudes toward progressivism, the dominant political movement of the prewar years. He approved of certain policies and reforms the progressives, both Democratic and Republican, advocated, but he objected to certain of their basic assumptions and to the moralistic tone of their campaigns. "The question which most interests us today," he had declared in 1910, "is not whether a proposed reform is theoretically justifiable, but whether it is practically effective." Although he frequently denied having any share of the reform impulse, "The Free Lance" exhibited his tendency as a truth-seeker to try to bring about certain forms of progress. Often concealed beneath his humor, ridicule, and satire was the serious purpose of goading the public into action. One of the best examples of his reformism was his campaign against the unsanitary conditions and the high incidence of infectious diseases in Baltimore. In the hope of reducing the number of deaths caused by typhoid, for example, he ridiculed popular misgivings about vaccination and urged the setting up of a mass vaccination program. When he considered Maryland politics, he was angered because Baltimoreans were at the mercy of the rural delegates who dominated the state legislature. Why not, he speculated, eliminate the legislature and substitute a board of a few trained, reliable men? Why might not the commission plan work for states as well as for cities? He also commented approvingly on such progressive measures as the corrupt practices and public service acts that had helped curb corruption in some state legislatures.[15]

In his prewar opposition to the basic assumptions of the progressives, Mencken countered their concept of democracy with the same kind of conservative *Realpolitik* that he later

presented in the *Mercury*. "A Progressive," he wrote, "is one
who believes that the common people are both intelligent and
honest; a reactionary is one who knows better." According to
Mencken's diagnosis, what was needed was not more democracy,
but less democracy. "Universal manhood suffrage," he maintained, "is the cancer that eats at the vitals of the republic."
Progressivism was "a mild narcotic, producing a pleasant glow,
but leaving the disease itself unchecked." Although progressives
claimed that their intentions were altruistic and noble, Mencken
was convinced that "the very same incentive moves reformers
and politicians alike—that is, the thirst for spoils, in glory or
actual money." Once "the sentimental rumble-bumble" is pushed
aside, democracy emerges as "a battle between two opposing
gangs . . . , one of which wants to get what it hasn't got and
the other of which wants to hold on to what it has got." In
order to obtain a following, politicians must appeal "to the
emotions of the people primarily, and to their intelligence
only secondarily." Accordingly, the man capable of "cold-blooded
intellectual honesty" has little chance in American politics unless he is willing to demean himself by "incessant bellowing
and . . . plenty of black magic."[16]

During the presidential campaign of 1912, with incumbent
William Howard Taft running for the Republicans, Theodore
Roosevelt for the new Progressive party, and Wilson for the
Democrats, Mencken observed that none of the candidates could
be specially chosen by God, since all three favored the Ten
Commandments and the conventional pieties. In reality, the
chief motive of each was to become president. Since Congress
made the laws and the courts enforced them, Mencken remarked
satirically, the main function of the president was "entertaining
and inflaming the vulgar." For this job, he argued, neither Taft
nor Wilson was well qualified. Taft was too rational and
dignified. Wilson had "taught school too long to have any
ideas left, and certainly too long to have any seltzer in him."
Mencken advised readers who wanted a good political show
to vote for "Th. Dentatus Africanus." Knowing that the American people "have no intellectual courage, that they shrink
instinctively from the real problems of life, that they cling to

platitudes like life buoys," T.R. "ladles out the swill that they like." Besides, he has a great gift for the dramatic.[17]

After Wilson's election, Mencken adopted the attitude of a skeptic waiting to be convinced. The people, he noted, apparently regarded the new president as "a statesman of almost messianic proportions. . . . He is the expert appointed to solve all their problems. He is the candy kid. Well, let us hope that he really is." By mid-1914, Mencken was still skeptical. Ignoring the much needed reforms achieved in the Underwood tariff and the Federal Reserve Act, he speculated on the reasons for the "collapse" of the Wilson regime. In his opinion, the basic trouble was that Wilson's "inherently acute and untrammeled" mind was crippled by his inbred puritanism. Like many Americans, Wilson tended "to see everything terrestrial in a pale ethical glow, to do all thinking in terms of morals."[18]

The policies of the administration after the war began increased Mencken's dissatisfaction. In October 1914, after quoting dispatches describing the war supplies being shipped to the British and the French, Mencken exclaimed sarcastically, "Ah, the blessings of bogus neutrality." Later that month, he accused William Jennings Bryan, Wilson's Secretary of State, of "submitting politely to all demands and orders of the English." Following the November elections, he was glad to note that "the Angelic Doctor lost his own Congressional district," and that "In Ohio the Hon. Mr. Bryan's moving pleas for prohibition were disregarded."[19]

When a German submarine sank the Cunard liner *Lusitania* in May 1915, the reactions of the administration and the American people confirmed Mencken's dislike of Wilson and intensified his sense of estrangement from the native culture. The deaths of nearly twelve hundred passengers, including a hundred and twenty-eight American citizens, horrified the general public. Theodore Roosevelt and other leaders, echoed by many periodicals, clamored for American intervention. Mencken recognized that the incident brought home "the ruthless tragedy and cruelty of war," but he defended the German point of view. Taking the line of argument common in the German-American press, he contended "that the *Lusitania* was an armed vessel of the

English naval reserve, engaged in transporting munitions of war to the enemies of Germany." The passengers had knowingly assumed the risk of attack because they had been explicitly warned ahead of time that the liner would be sunk on sight. (This was an indirect reference to a series of advertisements issued by the German embassy in Washington.) As for the rules of international law, British ships had consistently violated them. If the U-boat had hailed the *Lusitania,* with a view to clearing the ship of its passengers and crew in accord with the rules, the liner would have crowded on steam and easily outdistanced the submarine. "The Germans," said Mencken, "therefore torpedoed her first and hailed her afterward."[20]

Wilson's note of May 13 holding Germany to strict accountability, Mencken believed, meant "that the only way to avoid an open rupture will be for either the one Government or the other to withdraw from its position." By that autumn, the administration had won some concessions from Germany which, for the time, prevented the outbreak of war between the United States and the Central Powers. Instead of giving Wilson credit for continuing to negotiate, Mencken reiterated his opposition. In commenting on the president's opening speech in his campaign for reelection, he explained that German-Americans acknowledged that their first duty as citizens was to the United States. They did not argue that America should enter the war on the side of Germany, but they demanded the right to argue that she should not enter on the side of England. Most American newspapers denounced this last contention as treasonable. In this situation, Wilson, instead of combatting and curbing the passions of the mob, had reflected and yielded to them. If, Mencken claimed, the president "had no more than offered a gesture of sympathy to men and women passing through a great travail of spirit, he would have brought the German-Americans to his side to a man. . . . They wanted some sign that he saw and understood the affliction oppressing them, . . . that he was in favor of common justice to them, that he was veritably the President, not of one party or faction, nor even of the majority, but of the whole people." Wilson responded with "a platitudinous sermon upon the moral superiority of the United States and its altruistic concern for humanity—and on top of it a snarling attack upon all opponents, however sincere, of the arms traffic."[21]

"The Free Lance," had it not been for the war, might have continued much longer as a regular feature of the *Evening Sun,* but the clash between Mencken's views and those the *Sun* papers maintained editorially was becoming painfully apparent. In the midst of editorials and news columns supporting Wilson and voicing the prevailing hostility against the Central Powers, Mencken's column seemed almost like an enemy outpost. Mencken appreciated his freedom from editorial constraints, but he did not hesitate to attack the *Sun* policies. Finally, late in October 1915, he abruptly abandoned his column, saying "I do not believe that mutiny on the quarterdeck should be tolerated."[22] Nevertheless, some of the editorial-page articles he contributed down to the middle of 1916 were as belligerent in their German-American stance as "The Free Lance" had been.

These articles provided the last regular channel that Mencken had for his opinions on war issues until after the Armistice. *The Smart Set* did not furnish such an outlet because he and Nathan had agreed to exclude from it all but incidental references to the war. They indulged freely, however, in allusions showing that they were inoculated against the anti-German epidemic. In January 1915, for example, they printed this typical filler: "A rathskeller for my palace, a pipe for my scepter, a waltz tune for my national anthem, a napkin for my flag, a waiter for my subject, a stein for my prime-minister, a thousand tomorrows for my harem!"

Late in 1916, a few weeks after Wilson's reelection, Mencken packed his bags for a trip to Germany as a war correspondent for the *Sun.* In January 1917 the German government announced that unrestricted submarine warfare would be resumed. In February, when the United States broke off diplomatic relations with Germany, Mencken was with General Eichhorn's troops in the Riga-Dvinsk sector of the eastern front. After returning to Berlin, he proceeded to Paris on the same train as Ambassador Gerard and his staff and a number of other correspondents. At the request of the *Sun,* joined by the *New York World,* he stopped off in Havana to report the revolution that had just occurred.

When he arrived back in Baltimore in March, he was suspected in some quarters of being in the pay of the Kaiser. It
was known that General Ludendorff himself had exempted
him from the regulation requiring correspondents to remain
in the country for six weeks after leaving the front. Some of
his fellow correspondents had intervened to obtain this privilege
for him, but the assumption that he had been speeded on his
way to undertake some subversive mission fitted in better with
the prevailing mood. Within the past few weeks, German
U-boats had sunk several American vessels, with heavy casualties
among the crews. Widespread publicity was being given to the
shocking news that Alfred Zimmerman, the German Secretary
of State, had offered to arrange a military alliance with Mexico
in the event that Germany became involved in a war with the
United States. On shipboard, Mencken had written 50,000 words
telling "the truth" about the war as he saw it, but the *Sun* editors killed most of his copy.

The general public indeed would no longer tolerate news
stressing the German point of view. Demands for intervention
were reaching fever pitch. On April 2 the president, addressing
a joint session of the new Congress, called for a declaration of
war. America, he said, had no quarrel with the German people,
but only with the aggressive, autocratic, and unscrupulous German government. In inspiring, idealistic language which was
often to be quoted cynically in the era of postwar disillusionment, he called upon Americans "to fight . . . for the ultimate
peace of the world and for the liberation of its peoples, the
German peoples included: for the rights of nations great and
small and the privilege of men everywhere to choose their way
of life and of obedience. The world must be made safe for
democracy."[23]

The Loneliness of Dissent

The war, even before America's entry into it, temporarily ham-
pered the revolt against conventional values of which Mencken
was one of the leaders. Although this revolt was concerned
primarily with literature, manners, morals, and religion, it also
involved political issues. In its political aspects, it was brought

1. The Mencken house at 1524 Hollins Street, West Baltimore, H. L. Mencken's home during most of his life and the focal point of many of his reminiscences and much of his personal folklore.

2. The Mencken children, circa 1889: Charles Edward, Henry Louis, Anna Gertrude, and August. "We were encapsulated in affection," declared Henry Louis, "and kept fat, saucy and contented."

3. H. L. Mencken's mother, Anna Margaret Abhau, some three years before her marriage.

4. H. L. Mencken's father, August Mencken, Sr. (circa 1898), cigar manufacturer, and to his son "a man of illimitable puissance and resourcefulness."

5. H. L. Mencken at eighteen, "the meditative, impressionable, speculative, iconoclastic age."

6. "A free spirit and darling of the gods": H. L. Mencken in the temporary *Baltimore Herald* office in South Charles Street, 1904.

7. Wielder of "The Free Lance": H. L. Mencken in the *Baltimore Sun* office, 1913.

8. A note dated August 1, [1913], which typifies the kind of support and encouragement Mencken frequently offered Theodore Dreiser. The opening sentence refers to a review of Dreiser's *A Traveler at Forty* by Willard Huntington Wright.

9. H. L. Mencken, 1913, young man-about-town.

H.L.MENCKEN
1524 HOLLINS ST.
BALTIMORE.

Aug 1st [1913]

Dear Dreiser:— This review (by Wright) bears out what I said
the other day: that you are gaining a definite
place, by general acceptance, as the leading American
novelist. I see you mentioned constantly, & always
with the same respect. New serious novels are
no longer compared to "Silas Lapham" or to
"McTeague", but to "Sister Carrie" & "Jennie Gerhardt."
I think you will note this plainly in the reviews

of the new book.
    Temperature here: 105.

                                    Y HLM

THE FREE LANCE

RISING to a question of personal privilege, I beg to assure those gentlemen of the Letter Column who mistake my defense of the slandered and hard-pressed Germans for a laudable (or heinous) manifestation of patriotism that I am not a German and am not bound to Germany by sentimental ties. I was born in Baltimore of Baltimore-born parents; I have no relatives, near or remote, in Germany, nor even any friends (save one Englishman!); very few of my personal associates in this town are native Germans; I read the German language very imperfectly, and do not speak it or write it at all; I never saw Germany until I was 28 years old; I have been there since but twice; I am of English and Irish blood as well as German.

WHAT is more, the most massive influences of my life have all been unmistakably English. I know Kinglake's "Crimea" and Steevens' "With Kitchener to Khartoum" a great deal better than I know any history of the American Revolution or Civil War; I make a living writing the language of Thackeray and Huxley, and devote a good deal of time to studying it; I believe thoroughly in that imperialism for which England has always stood; I read English newspapers and magazines constantly, and have done so for 15 years; I regard the net English contribution to civilization as enormously greater than the German contribution; I am on good terms with many Englishmen, always get along well with them, and don't know a single one that I dislike.

ALL this by way of necessary explanation. But the Englishman upon whom the glory and greatness of England rests is not the Englishman who slanders and blubbers over Germany in this war. The England of Drake and Nelson, of Shakespeare and Marlow, of Darwin and Huxley, of Clive and Rhodes is not the England of Churchill and Lloyd-George, of Asquith and McKenna, of mongrel allies and bawling suffragettes, of "limehousing" and "mafficking," of press-censors and platitudinarians, of puerile moralizing and silly pettifogging. The England that the world yet admires and respects was a country ruled by proud and forthright men. The England that today poses as the uplifter of Europe is a country ruled by cheap demagogues and professional pharisees. The slimy "morality" of the unleashed rabble has conquered the clean and masculine ideals of the old ruling caste. A great nation has succumbed to mobocracy, and to the intellectual dishonesty that goes with it.

WHAT is the war really about? Why are the nations fighting one another? In so far as Germany and England are concerned, the cause is as plain as a pike-staff. Germany, of late years, has suddenly become England's rival as the boss of Europe, and with Europe, of the world. German trade has begun to prevail over English trade; German influence has begun to undermine English influence; even upon the sea, the new might and consequence of Germany have begun to challenge England's old lordship. The natural result is that the English have grown angry and alarmed, and the second result is that they yearn to crush and dispose of Germany before it is too late—i.e., before the Germans actually become their superiors in power, and so beyond their reach.

SUCH a yearning needs no defense. It is natural, it is virtuous, it is laudable. National jealousies make for the security, the prosperity and the greatness of the more virile nations, and hence for the progress of civilization. But did England, filled with this yearning, openly admit it, and then proceed in a frank and courageous manner to obtain its satisfaction in a fair fight? England did not. On the contrary, she artfully dissembled, her mouth full of pieties, until Germany was beset by enemies in front and behind, and then she suddenly threw her gigantic strength into the unequal contest. And did she, even then, announce her cause, state her motive, tell the truth? She did not. She went into battle with a false cry upon her lips, seeking to make her rage against a rival appear as a frenzy for righteousness, shedding crocodile tears over Germany's sins, wearing the tin halo and flapping chemise of a militant moralist.

I DO not like militant moralists, whether they be nations or individuals. I distrust the man who is concerned about his neighbor's sins, and who calls in the police (or the Turcos, or the Sikhs, or the Russians) to put them down. I have never known such a man who was honest with himself, nor is there any record of such a one in all history. They were a nuisance in the days of Christ, and His most bitter denunciations were leveled against them. They are still a nuisance today, though they impudently call themselves Christians, and even seek to excommunicate all persons who object to their excesses. That their shallow sophistries appeal to the mob, that they are especially numerous and powerful under a mobocracy, is but one more proof that mobocracy is the foe of civilization, and not only of civilization, but also of the truth.

FOR the manly, stand-up, ruthless, truth-telling, clean-minded England of another day I have the highest respect and reverence. It was an England of sound ideals and great men. But for the smug, moralizing, disingenuous England of Churchill and Lloyd-George, of hollow pieties and saccharine protestations, of Japanese alliances and the nonconformist conscience—for this new and oleaginous England, by Gladstone out of Pecksniff, I have no respect whatever. Its victory over Germany in this war would be a victory for all the ideas and ideals that I most ardently detest, and upon which, in my remote mud-puddle, I wage a battle with all the strength that I can muster, and to which I pledge my unceasing enmity until that day when the ultimate embalmer casts his sinister eye upon my fallen beauty.

WHEN I think of this new, this saponaceous, this superbrummagem England, so smug and slick without and so full of corruption and excess within, I am beset by emotions of the utmost unpleasantness. I snort, I swear; I leak large globulous tears. It is my hope and belief that this sick and bogus England will be given a good licking by the Deutsch, to the end that truth and health may prevail upon the earth. If the Mailed Fist cracks it, I shall rejoice unashamed. The Mailed Fist is dedicated to the eternal facts of life, the thing behind the mere word, the truth that is above all petty quibbling over theoretical rights and wrongs. I am for the Mailed Fist, gents, until the last galoot's ashore.

MEANWHILE, the Hon. William Jennings Bryan continues to make sheep's eyes at the Nobel prize. Like all uplifters, a thrifty fellow!

READ the Towsontown *New Era* and escape the Sunday drought.
Adv.   H. L. MENCKEN.

10. "The Free Lance," *Baltimore Sun,* September 29, 1914: an important statement of the significance for Mencken of the cultural and political traditions of both England and Germany.

11. A cartoonist's view of the "subconscious" Mencken. This conception, drawn in 1912 by McKee Barclay, a friend and colleague, was inspired by the belligerent German-Americanism of Mencken's "The Free Lance" column in the *Baltimore Sun.*

12. Laying plans for *The American Mercury*: George Jean Nathan and H. L. Mencken at Alfred A. Knopf's summer home in Portchester, New York, 1923.

almost to a standstill until the end of the war. Mencken's major political aim during the war years was not merely to champion the German-American minority, but to defend the right of any minority or any individual to oppose the will of a tyrannous majority. As Mencken discovered in reading the letters retorting to his sallies in "The Free Lance," vituperation and abuse were the reward of anyone who openly defied the prevailing pro-Allied political ideology. References to Mencken in national perodicals between 1914 and 1917, though not necessarily abusive, were likely to be unfavorable. In 1915, for instance, a contributor to *The Bookman* felt called upon to protest against Mencken's pro-German stand.[24]

Once the United States entered the war, patriotic sentiment, now continually stirred up by government propaganda, often became frenzied. The Espionage Act and the Sedition Act expressed the dominant mood by making political heresy a criminal offence. If legal censorship and police action were not used to put down political dissent, it was almost certain to be put down by mob violence.

Mencken felt the full force of the heightened anti-German hysteria after returning from his tour of duty as a war correspondent. The *Baltimore Sun* gave him no further assignments. *The Smart Set,* largely because of his association with it, fell under suspicion despite its policy of avoiding war issues. Operatives of the National Security League, an organization of volunteers eager to detect and squash subversive activities, reported that Mencken was an intimate friend of "the German monster, Nietzsky [*sic*]."[25] At the suggestion of Eltinge F. Warner, publisher of *The Smart Set,* Mencken, tongue-in-cheek, composed a memorandum for the Department of Justice portraying himself as a genuine patriot. The charges against him amused him and convinced him of the ignorance of his accusers, but he resented being deprived of the right of free speech. Until after the Armistice, the expression of his views on the war and the conduct of the Wilson administration had to be restricted mainly to his private correspondence.

His wartime experiences brought to its height his long-standing quarrel with the dominant native culture. Since the start of his career as a journalist, he had been commenting satirically

on the shortcomings of the majority of Americans. He had attributed to them a "habit of reasoning almost wholly by emotion, abruptly, extravagantly." He had described the typical
American's "brummagem Puritanism, . . . his great dislike of
arts and artists, . . . his pious faith in quacks and panaceas, his
curious ignorance of foreigners, his bad sportsmanship, . . . his
weakness for tin pot display and strutting, his jealous distrust
of all genuine distinction, his abounding optimism, his agile
pursuit of the dollar." Although Mencken maintained that such
traits resulted from the inferior hereditary endowment of most
Americans, he nevertheless condemned them for not striving for
what he regarded as worthier standards. America, he said, provided the opportunity for making money, for launching new
religions, for rephrasing old platitudes.

But [he added] certainly not opportunity to tackle head on and
with a surgeon's courage the greater and graver problems of
being and becoming, to draw a sword upon the timeworn delusions of the race, to clear away the corruptions that make government a game for thieves and morals a petty vice for old maids
and patriotism the last refuge of scoundrels—to think, in brief,
as men whose thinking is worthwhile, cleanly, innocently, ruth-
lessly![26]

Wartime conditions made more remote than ever the chance
that a significant number of Americans would be moved by
such ideals.

   The popular American response to the war challenged not
only the values based on Mencken's German-Americanism and
his interpretation of the tradition of the Old South, but also
his standards as an iconoclast, a libertarian, and an aesthetic
rebel. What made Mencken differ fiercely from the dominant
groups of Americans was the regimentation of opinion and the
suppression of individual liberties. The "mob man" seemed to
be taking over. The trend toward the tyranny of the majority
was accelerated. Super-patriotism, intolerance, puritanism, and
philistinism came increasingly into prominence. Mencken's
strong biases made him acutely critical of the propaganda activities of the Creel Committee, the arrests and prosecutions made
under the Sedition and Espionage Acts, and the muzzling of
nonconformist newspapers and magazines. He derived many of

the examples supporting his postwar indictments of American culture from his observation of

the tyrannies that went on during the war—by the Postoffice, by the gunmen and *agents provocateurs* of the ironically named Department of Justice, by the hordes of private cads . . . , by blackmailers disguised as advocates of the Liberty Loans, by profiteers disguised as patriots, by political scoundrels aspiring to higher office, by weak, pusillanimous and dishonest judges, by hysterical juries and unconscionable newspapers.[27]

In a series of letters to Louis Untermeyer, Mencken vividly recorded his reactions to the interference with civil rights authorized by the Wilson administration. Untermeyer, whose verses occasionally appeared in *The Smart Set,* was at this time a Socialist. Mencken, despite his abhorrence of the general political aims and principles of the Socialists, strongly sympathized with their stand against American intervention and against infringement of civil rights. His letters consider the question whether the radical *Masses,* to which Untermeyer was a contributor, would be forced to suspend publication. Mencken especially admired the June 1917 issue in which Max Eastman, the editor, had challenged Wilson's statement that we were fighting a war for democracy. "We will Prussianize ourselves," declared Eastman, "and we will probably not democratize Prussia." "That you may look for trouble," Mencken told Untermeyer, "goes without saying. Wilson is fully determined to shut off all criticism; his Presbyterian blood seems to be raised to a true Puritan temperature."[28]

This prediction was fulfilled when Postmaster-General Burleson barred *The Masses* and other radical publications from the mails. Mencken knew that in wartime some curtailment of freedom of speech was inevitable, but he interpreted the general approval given the repressive policies as one more proof of the weaknesses of democracy and the emotional suggestibility of the "mob." A major problem of any democracy, he pointed out, is

that the very free speech it is based upon makes war impossible unless the desire for it is practically unanimous. When such unanimity is absent, as is usual, it has to abolish free speech by orgy. The spectacle is staggering, but not without its logic. To

argue anything in such a time seems to me to be as impossible as
to stop a stampede by playing on an E clarinet. . . .

All appeals to any intrinsic love of free speech are futile. There
is no such passion in the people. The masses are invariably
cocksure, suspicious, furious and tyrannical. This, in fact, is the
central objection to democracy: that it hinders progress by penal-
izing innovation and noncomformity.[29]

Such remarks should not be construed to mean that Mencken
was becoming completely alienated from American culture. In
1915 he had prophesized sardonically in a letter to Dreiser that
the uplifters, whose ideal was "a nation devoted to masturbation
and the praise of God," would succeed in forbidding copula-
tion, just as they would succeed in putting through prohibition.
Although he had concluded by proposing to perfect his German in order to "spend his declining years in a civilized country," in fact the notion of becoming an expatriate appealed to
him only momentarily. The excesses to which chauvinism drove
many Americans aroused his fighting spirit. In a coldly angry
mood generated by the strongly anti-German bias in newspaper
reviews of The "Genius," he wrote to Dreiser: "There can
never be any compromise in future between men of German
blood and the common run of 'good,' 'right-thinking' Americans.
We must stand against them forever, and do what damage
we can to them, and to their tin-pot democracy."[30] His ambition
was not to escape to the Continent in order to harass from
that distance those Americans who asserted the ideal of Anglo-
Saxon supremacy, but rather to fire his broadsides directly at
them.

Another characteristic which made it unlikely that he would
book passage on the first postwar boat to Europe was that he
drew his spiritual nourishment not primarily from Germany,
but from parts of the American tradition. His statement that
during the war he was "purged of the last remaining vestiges
of patriotic feeling"[31] can best be interpreted to mean that he
lost his faith in the nationalism manifested in his earlier approval
of the Spanish-American War. Except for traces of this kind of
political nationalism, his "patriotism" had always taken the
form of a provincialism with a cosmopolitan dimension. His
disgust with what was happening nationally reinforced his al-

legiance to Baltimore and "the usable past" that he found in
the German-American and the pre-Jacksonian southern traditions. Against the values of the majority as represented by the
national culture he pitted the values based on his interpretation
of the attitudes and rights of minority groups. To the ideal of
Anglo-Saxon hegemony he opposed his ideal of a national culture and a national literature which would reflect all the racial
strains in the country. At the same time, he observed with grim
satisfaction the weaknesses in the national culture which the
stresses of war brought out. By confirming his worst suspicions
about the "Anglo-Saxon" elements in the American heritage,
the wartime frenzies increased his sense of the essential rightness
of his own opinions.

Like his essays and articles in the twenties, Mencken's wartime writing shows an alternation between an intense scrutiny
of current happenings and a nostalgic evocation of the past. He
was already developing the feeling that the year 1914 marked
the end of an era better and happier than the coming age was
likely to be. The views which isolated him from the majority
of his countrymen increased the nostalgia with which, at times,
he contemplated his idealized images of bourgeois German-
American life at the turn of the century and of plantation society in the Old South.

His intellectual and social life now depended much more
fully than they had previously upon German and German-
American interests. In 1917, as if in defiance of the claims that
the Allies were championing Christian civilization, he used some
of the leisure forced upon him to translate Nietzsche's *The
Antichrist* (published 1920). For counsel and companionship,
he relied mainly on a few like-minded friends, many of them
of German descent. A common German-American background
was one of the ties that bound him to Untermeyer and Dreiser.
The Saturday Night Club, whose music making Mencken continued to share throughout the war, was dominated by German-
Americans. One of his closest friends was Theodor Hemberger,
a choral director from whom he learned a great deal about
music and with whom he liked to discuss his literary projects.
While walking in the country, he and Hemberger sometimes
sang the German marching song, *"Ich hatt' einen Kameraden."*

In Hemberger's honor, Mencken placed a few notes from this tune at the beginning of *A Little Book in C Major* (1916), a collection of humorous epigrams from *The Smart Set*. This was the nearest thing to a dedication that he ever included in any of his books.[32]

His reflections upon life as he remembered it to have been in Baltimore in the eighties and nineties were stimulated particularly by his association with Philip Goodman, an advertising man turned publisher. In 1918 Goodman's firm published Mencken's *Damn! A Book of Calumny,* a collection of short pieces from *The Smart Set,* and his *In Defense of Women.* Goodman, brought up in a German-Jewish environment in Philadelphia, loved German beer, German food, and the German way of life. He had neither the financial resources nor the skill to market books successfully, but his shortcomings as a publisher did not interfere with Mencken's enjoyment of their friendship. During the last year of the war, they began an extensive correspondence in which they exchanged memories of their early days. Typical of the at least partly apocryphal subject matter and the humorous tone of Mencken's letters is the following:

> Let Kurt Bradtmeier keep his tongue off the subject of Moselle. Does he think the clergy and laity have forgotten the time he was taken by the Customs men for smuggling five bottles of Affenthaler from the Norddeutscher Lloyd Schnellpostdampfer Dessauer, back in 1894? It cost his father-in-law, Emil Schandt, at least $700 to get him off. You may recall the scandal that followed the case. The wine disappeared during the trial: all the trace it left was some sinister hiccoughing among the jurymen. The foreman was Bruno Lilienthal, the Wurst butcher, and it is generally believed that he got $100. They acquitted Kurt on the ground that there was no evidence that he knew what was in the bottles.[33]

Mencken's preference for the Old as opposed to the New South is illustrated by his portrayal of George Washington as a man who, in modern America, would be the object of suspicion and scorn. Significantly, Mencken attributed to the first president traits which, on a smaller scale, might have characterized any enterprising German-American burgher. Washington, he declared, had a liking for all forthright and pugnacious men, and a contempt for all lawyers, platitudinarians and other such fact-dodgers. He was not pious. He drank red liquor whenever he felt chilly, and kept a jug of it handy. He knew far more profanity than Scripture, and used and enjoyed it more. He had no faith in the infallible wisdom of the common people, and did his best to save the country from it. He advocated no sure cure for all the sorrows of the world. He took no interest in the private morals of his neighbors.

If Washington were alive in 1915, Mencken argued, he

would be ineligible for any public office of honor or profit. He would be on trial in all the uplift magazines and yellow journals for belonging to the Invisible Government, the Hell Hounds of Plutocracy, the Money Power, the Interests. The . . .triumphant prohibitionists of his native Virginia would be denouncing him (he had a still at Mount Vernon) as a debaucher of youth, a recruiting officer for insane asylums. . . . The suffragettes would be on his trail threatening him with their black-list.[34]

Thus Mencken, with humorous exaggeration, suggested that the United States had declined so much from its past greatness that even the most revered of the Founding Fathers would be rejected by twentieth-century Americans.

Fighting the Anglo-Saxon Critics and Censors

If the wartime censorship had been even more rigorous, Mencken might have been forced to live more fully in the past, or at least to bide his time until the end of hostilities. But, despite such indignities as having his mail intercepted, he still enjoyed considerable freedom to write and publish. He and Nathan managed to keep *The Smart Set* going, even though a drop in circulation and a rise in printing costs put it in precarious financial straits. Late in 1917, at the suggestion of John Cullen, a former *Baltimore Sun* man who had become managing editor of the *New York Evening Mail,* he contracted to provide three articles a week for that paper. Constantly threatened by government censorship, the *Mail,* owned by Edward A. Rumely, was trying to live down its past reputation for being strongly pro-

German. The editors rejected some pieces in which Mencken referred to touchy issues, but they printed his articles on a wide range of subjects. Now that the pages of the *Baltimore Sun* were closed to him, the connection with the *Mail* stimulated some of his best writing. To it he submitted his entirely imaginary history of the bathtub, a hoax which in many quarters was taken seriously; his story of the suppression of *Sister Carrie;* and the first version of "The Sahara of the Bozart," his indictment of the New South.[35] Book publication offered still another outlet for his views.

As a result, even though the war silenced his criticism of the administration and the whole trend in American politics, he could still express in print his rebellious attitudes toward accepted standards in literature, manners, and morals. Undismayed because the wartime ideology temporarily gave the advantage to the spokesmen for the genteel tradition, he was determined to maintain his stand against gentility in either life or art.

Much as he had formerly used Mark Twain as a test case for assessing the quality of literary criticism, he now used Dreiser. "In England," he observed in 1916, ". . . Dreiser is better understood, and even in wartime and despite his German name, he is usually discussed with the greatest respect." "Arnold Bennett, H.G. Wells, W.J. Locke, Frank Harris and others of their kidney," he remarked in *The Smart Set,* "venture upon the atrocity of putting Dreiser above Howells." Most American critics, on the other hand, fell into two groups: those who ignored Dreiser and those who indignantly attacked him. Typical of the first group were "the acknowledged heavyweights of the craft—the Babbitts, Mores, Brownells and so on." Most academic critics belonged in the same category. Mencken could find no reference to Dreiser in Reuben Halleck's *A History of American Literature* (1911), Henry Pancoast's *An Introduction to American Literature* (1912), and Fred Lewis Pattee's *A History of American Literature since 1870* (1915). Even Phelps, whom Mencken had congratulated in 1910 for recognizing Twain's stature as an artist, completely neglected Dreiser in his *The Advance of the English Novel* (1917). It seemed that Dreiser was "a sort of bugaboo to the rev. pundits, to be put into Coventry with Beelzebub."[36]

While Babbitt and More maintained their Olympian aloofness from contemporary literature, Stuart Sherman, a young professor at the University of Illinois, extended the rift between Mencken and the New Humanists into a quarrel that was to continue through the twenties. While a graduate student at Harvard, Sherman had become a disciple of Babbitt and an admirer of More. He first proceeded to the attack in December 1915 in an article in *The Nation* entitled "The Naturalism of Mr. Dreiser." Staunchly upholding the Anglo-Saxon tradition, he noted sarcastically that Dreiser's novels represented "a new note in American literature, coming from that 'ethnic' element of our mixed population which, as we are assured by competent authorities, is to redeem us from Puritanism and insure our artistic salvation." The true realist, he insisted, did not confuse animal and human behavior but sought to create specifically human characters. Dreiser's failure to distinguish sharply between the human and the animal made him not a realist, but a naturalist, and hence he did not deserve to be classed with George Eliot, Thackeray, Trollope, and Meredith. "Since a theory of animal behavior can never be an adequate basis for a representation of the life of man in contemporary society," Sherman concluded belligerently, "such a representation is an artistic blunder. When half the world attempts to assert such a theory, the other half rises in battle."[37]

Mencken's most sustained reply to this "irate flubdub" was his article on "The Dreiser Bugaboo" in *The Seven Arts* for August 1917. He first questioned whether there was any distinction between realism and naturalism "that anyone save a pigeonholing pedagogue can discern." Whatever label one applied to Dreiser's philosophy, it did not result in "the empty, meticulous nastiness" of Zola's *Pot-Bouille,* but in a sense of "compassionate compassion" for characters caught up in "the universal and inexplicable tragedy." As for Dreiser's alleged emphasis on "animal behavior," Mencken declared that "the behavior of such men as Cowperwood and Eugene Witla and of such women as Carrie Meeber and Jennie Gerhardt, as Dreiser describes it, is no more merely animal than the behavior of such acknowledged and undoubted human beings as Dr. Woodrow Wilson and Dr. Jane Addams." *The Financer* and *The Titan,* for instance, dramatize the "conflict, in the ego of Cowperwood, between aspiration and ambition, between the passion for beauty and the passion for power." "Is either passion animal?" Mencken inquired. "To ask the question is to answer it." Sherman, as his praise of Arnold Bennett's "pseudo-philosophy" reveals, gives his allegiance to

a sweet commingling of virtuous conformity and complacent optimism, of sonorous platitude and easy certainty. . . . The offense of Dreiser is that he has disdained this revelation and gone back to the Greeks. Lo, he reads poetry into "the appetite for women"—he rejects the Pauline doctrine that all love is below the diaphragm! . . . He sees the life of man, not as a simple theorem in Calvinism, but as a vast adventure, an enchantment a mystery. It is no wonder that respectable schoolteachers are against him.[38]

Mencken was willing to argue with a critic who, like Sherman, tried to present a reasoned case against Dreiser, but he had only invective for critics who automatically condemned all works which defied "Anglo-Saxon" norms. The smearing of Dreiser as "German" incensed him much more than similar charges against himself. As a journalist constantly engaged in heated controversy and putting his German sympathies on public record, he had learned to welcome counterattacks. He regarded the denunciations which poured in from readers of "The Free Lance" as a sign of his success in "stirring up the animals." Dreiser, on the other hand, had abandoned journalism in order to write novels. He had not publicized his views on the war and thus had not invited the abuse heaped upon him. Mencken himself considered *The "Genius"* artistically inferior to Dreiser's earlier novels, but he felt indignant that many reviewers resorted to name-calling instead of considering the book on its merits. Elia W. Peattie of the *Chicago Tribune,* for example, was so eager to repudiate the idea that *The "Genius"* was "the American prose-epic" that she proclaimed, "I have not yet lost my patriotism, and I will never admit such a thing until I am ready to see the American flag trailing in the dust dark with the stains of my sons, and the Germans completing their world rule by placing their Governor general in the White House." Mencken had the hysterical reactions to *The "Genius"* in mind when he commented, "To the moral balderdash which poisons American criticism now add patriotic fustian."[39]

He atttributed the censorship imposed on *The "Genius"* to "the same muddled sense of Dreiser's essential hostility to all that is safe and regular—of the danger in him to that mellowed Methodism which has become the national ethic." In July 1916 the Western Society for the Prevention of Vice, with its head-quarters in Cincinnati, secured the removal of the novel from nearly every book store in the city. It also obtained a temporary cessation-of-circulation order from postal authorities and filed a complaint with the New York Society for the Suppression of Vice. John S. Sumner, the New York Society's executive secretary, notified J. Jefferson Jones of the John Lane Company that unless Lane's removed all offensive passages from *The "Genius"* or discontinued its publication and sale, the Society would file criminal charges. On July 28 Jones agreed to withdraw the book, but declared he would take legal steps to contest the Society's ruling. He, and Mencken too at first, urged Dreiser to try to pacify the censors by permitting the deletion of some passages. "After all," Mencken wrote Dreiser, "we are living in a country governed by Puritans and it is useless to attempt to beat them by a frontal attack—at least at present." However, when he saw that Dreiser was determined to make no compromises, he modi-fied his stand and agreed that a fight might force Sumner to back down.[40] He then plunged immediately into the task of helping organize support for Dreiser.

Mencken's strategy was to get as many authors as possible to come out publicly on behalf of Dreiser. Ordinarily he looked askance at the Authors' League of America, but the popular and respectable members of this organization were typical of the group he now most wanted to reach. With this in mind, he persuaded Harold Hersey, an admirer of Dreiser's and as-sistant to the secretary of the League's executive committee, to enlist in the cause. By August 25 both Mencken and John Cowper Powys had drafted protests for writers to sign, Jones had started seeking help from English authors through Lane's

in London, and a quorum of the executive committee of the
League, after meeting with Dreiser, had urged League members
to speak out against the suppression of *The "Genius."* Contending that the novel was not lewd, licentious, or obscene, the committee pointed out that the unfair test applied to it, if not
modified, would prevent the sale of many classics.[41]

Many editors, writers, and publishers, including Willard
Huntington Wright, Frank Harris, Ezra Pound, Alfred Knopf,
and Ben W. Huebsch, helped publicize the Dreiser Protest,
but Hersey and Mencken did the major share of the work.
While Hersey circulated leaflets among the hundreds of individuals who might be willing to sign of their own accord, Mencken
wrote personal appeals to the more prominent and respectable
authors. "I am sending out about twenty-five letters a day, each
carefully designed to fit the mental capacity of the recipient,"
he wrote Dreiser on November 24, "and the response is becoming
very gratifying." His letters to Ellis Parker Butler, who had at
first declined to sign, illustrate his persuasive techniques. Deferring to Butler's doubts about *The "Genius,"* he noted that his
own review of it in *The Smart Set* had been unfavorable, but
he emphasized the general significance of the "contest between
free expression and a most arbitrary and insufferable censorship." After praising Dreiser for his integrity as an artist, he
cited examples like James Lane Allen, Mrs. Atherton, and Booth
Tarkington to show that the signers of the protest included
"the majority of American authors of any distinction whatever."
In his next letter, Mencken waved to one side Butler's misgivings about the phrasing of the protest and congratulated him
on his willingness to oppose "the excesses of the Comstocks."
Knowing that Butler was a member of the executive committee
of the Authors' League and might be able to goad that organization into further action, Mencken argued that "the authors
of America must form a defensive league against those who seek
to deprive them of their common right of free speech."[42]

Concerned about the unfavorable publicity that might result
from any rash acts by Dreiser, Mencken warned him not to
alienate possible supporters by publicly denouncing common
American beliefs or by listing among his backers a number of
"tenth-rate Greenwich geniuses." Mencken was particularly dis-

turbed by Dreiser's insistence on printing, while *The "Genius"* case was still unsettled, *The Hand of the Potter,* a play with a sexually depraved youth as its chief character. The subject matter, he informed Dreiser, was "impossible on the stage," and the play itself was artistically inept, with "no more dramatic structure than a jelly-fish." Rejecting Dreiser's protests that an artist's subjects should not be dictated by popular conventions, Mencken concluded that "you stand in serious danger, through this play, of being definitely labeled as a mere shocker of boobs."[43]

By the time Mencken left for Germany, it was apparent that all the agitation had made little impression on Sumner. He was not interested in the possible literary merits of Dreiser's work, nor in the opinions of the many authors who signed the protest. His concern was with the potentially harmful effects of *The "Genius,"* especially "on female readers of immature mind," and he believed that laymen were just as competent to judge such matters as professional writers. Besides, he considered novels which dealt with the sordid aspects of life as foreign rather than American in spirit. As a result, he did not offer to make any concessions. Legally, Jones and Dreiser were in a difficult position. Since Jones had voluntarily withdrawn *The "Genius"* when Sumner first threatened to bring suit, there had been no indictment, and therefore no opportunity to obtain a judicial opinion. All attempts to have the censorship nullified in the courts or to force Lane's to distribute the book were futile, and it remained in the Lane stockrooms until Horace Liveright reissued it in 1923.[44]

Signs of Hope for Postwar Revolt

One effect the war had on Mencken was to harden his opposition to certain sets of ideas and the groups that represented them. The twenties provided new examples of what he regarded as government tyranny and assorted kinds of fraud and imbecility, but the lines of battle along which he fought did not undergo much change. Even when he became an object of suspicion after his return from Germany, he had reasons for not indulging in despair and self-pity. He continued to be as much attracted by the American scene as he was repelled by it. There was no lag in his concern with popular morals and popular culture. Although the war increased his dislike of certain features of the national ethos, it also increased his determination to subject those features to satire and ridicule. Furthermore, he foresaw that the war was bound to be followed by a general disillusionment with Wilsonian idealism and a revolt against wartime restraints. "Wilson," he told Untermeyer in 1917, "seems determined to shut off all free discussion absolutely. My own feeling is that the more he suppresses magazines and newspapers the more quickly a reaction against this intolerable Russianism will arise."[45] Such predictions show that Mencken still had some faith in the good sense of the American people.

He had some specific evidence to suggest that the rebellion he had been advocating could be brought to a successful conclusion. Despite the failure of the Dreiser Protest to attain its immediate object, the large number of signatures was one of the signs that made him hopeful for the future. The "orthodox gladiators"[46] who refused to sign included Hamlin Garland, Howells, Joyce Kilmer, Brander Matthews, and William Lyon Phelps, but they were greatly outnumbered by their colleagues who, without necessarily approving of either Dreiser or his novel, went on record against the action of the censors. Belonging to the latter group were writers of great popular reputation like Robert W. Chambers, Mary E. Wilkins Freeman, Rupert Hughes, Meredith Nicholson, Mary Roberts Rinehart, and William Allen White. As for the younger writers, the Protest contains many names which were to achieve varying degrees of prominence in the twenties. The socialist opponents of American entry into the war were represented by Max Eastman and John Reed; the idealistic, mildly socialistic literary critics by James Oppenheim, editor of *The Seven Arts,* and his associate, Van Wyck Brooks; the young progressives by Walter Lippmann, editor of *The New Republic;* and the novelists just getting established by Sherwood Anderson, Willa Cather, Floyd Dell, and Sinclair Lewis.

As Dreiser's champion, Mencken emphasized one aspect of the fin de siècle: its demand for a literature dealing forthrightly with the full range of American experience. Like Huneker, he also dramatized for his readers the aestheticism of the nineties.

In reviewing Frank Harris's privately printed biography of Oscar Wilde, for example, he made an analogy between English and American prudery. Why had all the American publishers to whom Harris had submitted the book refused to print it even after he had deleted the passages they objected to? Wilde's sexual irregularities were "disgusting enough, in all conscience," but they are not "so rare in our own land that we can afford to go through any hocus-pocus of holy horror." In either England or America, artists are likely to be persecuted. Behind Wilde's prison sentence and the cruelty and contempt with which he was treated lay the "Puritan philosophy" which sees in the artist "a prophet of that innocent gusto, that pagan joy in life, which is its chief abomination."[47]

Through such comments, Mencken undoubtedly helped stimulate the revival of interest in the rebellion of the nineties which occurred from about 1910 to 1918 in some American colleges and universities. In authors like Wilde, Pater, Swinburne, Shaw, and Compton Mackenzie, college intellectuals found confirmation for the view that artists were a small elite beleaguered by philistines. Among the undergraduates whose literary radicalism was strengthened by this cult of the artist were Edmund Wilson, John Peale Bishop, and Scott Fitzgerald at Princeton, Randolph Bourne at Columbia, and Malcolm Cowley at Harvard. They experienced a disillusionment with American culture which anticipated the much greater disillusionment many of them felt later when returning from war service.[48]

The efforts of *The Smart Set* to keep its readers abreast of recent literary developments abroad also appealed to young writers. As Wright had done before them, Mencken and Nathan got much help from Ezra Pound, who, from his vantage point in London, acted unofficially as a literary scout for *The Smart Set* as well as for *Poetry*. Because of Pound's efforts, for instance, Mencken was able to refer to several of Joyce's stories from *Dubliners* as having "already appeared in this favorite family magazine." Although Pound at times urged Mencken to move as soon as possible to Europe, he also encouraged him to persist in his attacks on American moralism, advising a more serious onslaught than that illustrated by the bantering tone of *The Smart Set*. " 'Hell' in the person of Comstock's following, [Billy]

Sunday, and all the rest," Pound warned, "will do you in, unless you get some heavy artillery."[49]

Mencken was becoming more confident that enough of the needed "artillery" could be assembled. Back in 1908 he and Huneker and Pollard, in their efforts to keep alive the American form of the moral and literary rebellion of the nineties, had been comparatively isolated figures. By 1917 many young writers, however much they might differ from Mencken in detail, had begun to share his opposition not only to literary censorship, but also to literary colonialism and to the genteel and "puritanical" aspects of the traditions of England and New England. If they were critics, they were likely to call for a literature embodying honest reactions to American experience. If they were poets, novelists, or dramatists, they often strove to approximate this ideal in their own works. Mencken did not, of course, singlehandedly create the new movement, but he was one of its pioneers. His writing did much to help create the atmosphere which made it possible.

He singled out for attention in *The Smart Set* the essays and books showing the new direction that American literary criticism was taking. One of the landmarks was Joel Spingarn's "The New Criticism," first printed in 1911. When this paper was reprinted in 1917, Mencken chose it as a starting-point for an article called "Criticism of Criticism of Criticism." He welcomed Spingarn's work as indicating that at least some academic critics realized that art should not be judged primarily by moral standards. Imagining how indignantly critics like Brownell and Phelps would respond to such heresy, he gleefully noted that Spingarn

> tackles all the varying camorras of campus-pump criticism seriatim, and knocks them out unanimously—first . . . the burblers for the sweet and pious; then the advocates of unities, metres, all rigid formulae; then the historical dust-snufflers; then the experts in bogus psychology; then the metaphysicians; finally, the spinners of aesthetic balderdash.[50]

Mencken found in Spingarn's views support for his own conception of art and criticism. Paraphrasing Spingarn, he declared, "Every sonnet, every drama, every novel is *sui generis;* . . . it must be judged by its own inherent intentions." In asserting that Spingarn's critical theory was "a doctrine of Benedetto Croce out of Johann Wolfgang Goethe," he misled his readers; in fact, it stemmed primarily from Croce.[51] Mencken summed up this theory in the question, "What is the poet [i.e., the artist] trying to do? . . . and how has he done it?" Delighted to find that Spingarn conceived of the critic as an artist, he quoted with approval the statement that "aesthetic judgment and artistic creation are instinct with the same vital life." Such an approach, he added, presupposes a critic who "is a civilized man, hospitable to new ideas." Since critics like Brownell and More lack this capacity, they cannot "understand all that is most personal and original and hence most forceful and significant in modern literature." Anything which does not fit the approved formulas alarms them. Critics like Huneker and Georg Brandes, on the other hand, "have within them the gusto of artists and so carry with them the faculty of understanding."[52]

To Spingarn's assumption that criticism should aim at the "intuitive re-creation of beauty,"[53] Mencken added several qualifications derived from his own practice. He maintained that the critic must make his "interpretation comprehensible to the vulgar, else it will leave the original mystery as dark as before." He was also dubious about Spingarn's rejection of "the race, the time, the environment of a poet's work as an element in Criticism." Beauty, Mencken commented, is not an "apparition in vacuo," but "has its social, its political, even its moral implications. The finale of Beethoven's C minor symphony is not only colossal in beauty; it is also colossal in revolt. . . . Brahms wrote his Deutsches Requiem, not only because he was a great artist, but also because he was a good German." Possibly aware that Croce's philosophical idealism sustained Spingarn's concept that expression is the essence of art, Mencken added this dictum: "The really competent critic must be an empiricist." In the best of Huneker, "a sensitive and intelligent artist recreates the work of other artists, but there also comes to the ceremony a man of the world, and the things he has to say are apposite and instructive, too." Finally, the critic as an empiricist must be ready to use violent methods. "If pills fail, he gets out his saw. If the saw won't cut, he seizes a club and knocks in the patient's head."[54]

Although Spingarn's critical theory might attract young critics, Spingarn himself made little effort to apply it to contemporary letters. But a concern for current literature and a call for works truly representative of American experience were expressed not only in Mencken's reviews, but also in such books as John Macy's *The Spirit of American Literature* (1913) and Van Wyck Brooks's *America's Coming-of-Age* (1915). Mencken's most important bid for continued leadership in the new movement was *A Book of Prefaces* (1917), in which he listed Macy and Brooks as among the few critics in America who showed real promise.[55]

After first encountering Macy's book in 1917, Mencken called it "the antidote to the pedagogues." "No book," he announced enthusiastically, "has set my own notions to bubbling more furiously." He did not specify which of Macy's ideas impressed him most, but it is easy to imagine his pleasure at finding a critic who stated "in a piquant and intriguing style" views similar to his own. Macy, too, chided the writers of handbooks for deferring to politely genteel standards and neglecting contemporary authors. "American literature," declared Macy, "is on the whole idealistic, sweet, delicate, nicely finished. . . . The notable exceptions are our most stalwart men of genius, Thoreau, Whitman, and Mark Twain." Envisioning the possibility of a great national literature, Macy claimed that "the whole country is crying out for those who will record it, satirize it, chant it. As literary material, it is virgin land, ancient as life and fresh as a wilderness." In fiction, Dreiser's *Jennie Gerhardt* and Edith Wharton's *Ethan Frome* showed how some young novelists were beginning to respond to this challenge.[56]

Perhaps because Mencken was concerned mainly with the total effect of *The Spirit of American Literature,* he did not pause to object to Macy's faith in democratic ideals and political reform.[57] He was, however, very conscious of the political idealism of Van Wyck Brooks and his associates, including James Oppenheim, Waldo Frank, and Randolph Bourne. Unlike Mencken, Brooks and his friends shared the optimism of the progressive movement, even though they were dissatisfied with the results of many of the specific reforms it had advocated. They were typical of the "artists" who supplanted the muckrakers as the standard intellectual types.[58] Except for the crisis brought on by America's entry into the war, they were more interested in morals and literature than in politics.

In *America's Coming-of-Age,* Brooks's thesis was that in American culture there was "no community, no genial middle ground" between the genteel idealism of the highbrows and the "catchpenny opportunism" of the lowbrows. The idealism originated in "the piety of the Puritans" as transformed by transcendentalism; the opportunism "in the practical shifts of Puritan life, becoming a philosophy in Franklin, passing through the American humorists, and resulting in the atmosphere of contemporary business life." The cleavage between "stark theory and . . . stark business" gave our intellectual life an air of unreality and made our practical life cynically materialistic.[59]

What Brooks hoped would appear in the middle ground between these extremes, and transform our culture, was the ideal of self-fulfillment (as opposed to self-assertion). He suggested that some form of socialistic collectivism was the logical means to that individualistic goal. In this way, he tried to reconcile the ideals of intellectuals whose interests were primarily aesthetic with those of the muckrakers. He did not give much idea of what kind of socialism he favored or how he thought it could be put into effect. His chief American cultural hero was Whitman, who, he said, had cast all the warring elements in the national character into a crucible from which "they emerged, harmonious and molten, in a fresh democratic ideal, which is based upon the whole personality." The task of our intellectuals was to draw, like Whitman, on "the rude material of right personal instinct," and then to proceed, with a sureness on the plane of ideas that Whitman lacked, to introduce "fruitful values and standards of humane economy" into "the unchecked, uncharted, unorganized vitality of American life."[60]

In *The Smart Set,* Mencken dismissed *America's Coming-of-Age* as one among a number of "hortatory and pontifical books," remarking that it "instructs the rest of us in our opportunities in the manner of the *New Republic.*"[61] These comments suggest the reservations he had about Brooks and his associates. He approved when they rallied to Dreiser's defense or attacked superpatriotism and puritanism, but he objected when they wrote in the manner of prophets and soothsayers. His own study

of wartime conditions made him cautiously optimistic about
the future, but their optimism seemed to him to rest on nothing
more substantial than ideals smacking of the uplift.

He saw a parallel between politically minded writers like
Walter Lippmann and his colleagues on *The New Republic* and
aesthetically oriented intellectuals like Brooks. In 1915 Mencken
had refused to do an article on Dreiser for *The New Republic,*
explaining to his friend that there was "no more oleaginous
and forward-looking gazette in These States." He had, nevertheless, commended Lippmann's *A Preface to Politics* for "telling the bitter truth about the whole vice of vice crusading,"
and had praised *Drift and Mastery* for showing "how little sense
there is in the New Freedom of Dr. Woodrow Wilson or in the
multitudinous sovereign balms of the Hon. William Jennings
Bryan." But, Mencken noted, Lippmann retained his faith
"in the general aims and purposes of the uplift" in spite of his
"many disquieting doubts about most of its specific perunas."
After reviewing such progressive efforts as trust-busting, the
initiative and referendum, and the recall of judges, Mencken
concluded that "the uplift has failed signally." Lippmann reminded him of the spiritualists "who admit that . . . every one
of their proofs of communication with the dead and damned
is open to serious question, but . . . argue . . . that the aggre-
gate of such dubious testimony should be sufficient to convince
any intelligent man."[62]

Mencken could tolerate the vaguely socialistic ideals of "literary radicals" like Brooks and Bourne with much better grace
than he could stomach Max Eastman's doctrinaire socialism or
Lippmann's articulate liberalism. Oppenheim and Bourne, the
chief spokesmen for *The Seven Arts* on political issues, were
not of German-American descent nor were they sympathizers
with Germany, but their pacifism and their concern for human
rights led them to adopt views similar to Mencken's. They
sensed the ironic contrast between the professed American war
aims and the actual effects of mobilization. Bourne upbraided
American intellectuals for being so duped by slogans and sentiment that they conceived of our participation in the war as a
glorious enterprise. Much like Mencken, though not out of the
same motives, Bourne objected to the "one-sidedly and partisanly

colonial" emphasis our thinkers and writers put on the Anglo-Saxon tradition. "America might have been made," he commented, "a meeting-ground for the different national attitudes. An intellectual class, cultural colonists of the different European nations, might have threshed out the issues here as they could not be threshed out in Europe." Instead there had come "the collapse of neutrality and the riveting of the war-mind on a hundred million people." People might talk about saving the world for democracy, but democratic rights could not be preserved even on the home front. "Never has a government in wartime," Bourne pointed out, "been known to refuse the use of relentless coercion against 'forces moving in another direction.' The attaching of one's conscience to any such forces is infallibly taken to be the allying of oneself with the disloyal, and the inadvertent aiding of the nation's enemies." In keeping with its commitment to preserve civil rights, *The Seven Arts* vigorously protested the suppression of the August 1917 issue of *The Masses* and the threatened indictment of the editors.[63]

Mencken realized that many young intellectuals shared his aims in moral and literary matters, despite the differences in background, point of view, and emphasis that partially divided him from them. They, in their turn, were not always willing to accept his opinions, but, as Brooks says, they came to regard him as "a literary statesman whose strategy and decisions affected us all." The literary radicals were, on the average, only a few years younger than Mencken. Like him, they were the heirs of the literary movement of the nineties. *The Seven Arts,* which sought to hasten the "coming-of-age" for which Brooks had called, reveals the extent to which their efforts paralleled Mencken's. In the first issue, the editors announced their "faith . . . that we are living in the first days of a renascent period, a time which means for America the coming of that national self-consciousness which is the beginning of greatness." "Our arts," the statement of purpose continued, "show signs of this change. It is the aim of *The Seven Arts* to become a channel for the flow of these new tendencies: an expression of our American arts which shall be fundamentally an expression of our American life." In the light of this objective, it is evident that Brooks was being highly complimentary in his review of *A Book of Burlesques* when he said that Mencken "is as completely 'aware' of the American scene as any of Mr. Dreiser's heroes in their awarest moments."[64]

The positive aim of *The Seven Arts,* as in Mencken's criticism, implied a negative aim as well: that of opposing any features of the national life which limited the freedom of American artists. The editors, like the bohemian critics to whom they were the successors, were conscious of the contrasts between European and American cultural standards. As in Mencken's case, the national culture simultaneously repelled and attracted them. The editors and other contributors, in order to carry out the destructive part of their mission, attacked the preoccupation with material values and the emotional sterility they believed were dominant in American life. They exposed the bigotry and prudery behind much literary censorship. They refused to listen to critics like Babbit and More, whose narrowly defined traditionalism made them incapable of understanding contemporary needs. They rejected pragmatism, with its rationally conceived goals of adjustment and social efficiency, and sought instead ideals embodying personal feeling and imaginative insight.[65]

Brooks and his colleagues, again like Mencken, were fascinated by the American character and wanted it explored more fully and dramatized more vividly in literature. They also resembled him in being literary journalists. Although they did not ignore matters of form, their primary concern was with the content of the work of art and the degree of force and originality with which it was presented. Their aims were broadly social and cultural rather than narrowly literary. Although they stressed the new poetry more than Mencken did, many of their literary preferences were similar to his. In October 1916, for example, Mencken praised Sherwood Anderson's *Windy McPherson's Son,* compared it to Dreiser's *The Titan,* and found "the gusto of a true artist in it." In *The Seven Arts* for November, Waldo Frank declared that reading Anderson's novel had made him realize "that Theodore Dreiser was a classic," for he "has caught the crass life of the American, armoring himself with luxury and wealth that he misunderstands, with power whose heritage of uses he ignores." Dreiser's typical hero is "too unknowing to know that he is ignorant," but Anderson's hero seeks self-knowledge. Thus Anderson gives us "a presentation of life shot through with the searching color of truth, which is a signal for a native culture."[66]

As coeditor of *The Smart Set,* Mencken could often print the work of young authors as well as praise it critically. In December 1915, almost a year before the founding of *The Seven Arts, The Smart Set* published a short story by Oppenheim and a novelette by Waldo Frank. In some instances, the efforts of *The Seven Arts* to encourage promising authors reinforced those that Mencken and Nathan had made earlier. Dreiser had frequently contributed to *The Smart Set;* he contributed his essay "Life, Art and America" to *The Seven Arts.* As early as January 1916, Mencken and Nathan had printed a story by Sherwood Anderson, three of whose stories were featured by Oppenheim and Frank. Others whose work appeared in both magazines were Louis Untermeyer and Carl Van Vechten. The rapprochement that existed between Mencken and the new review is also illustrated by his willingness to have "The Dreiser Bugaboo" published in it.

One of the books reviewed in *The Seven Arts* was *The Young Idea,* edited by Lloyd Morris and published in 1917. No statement by Mencken appears in the book, nor do any of the thirty contributors, most of whom were concerned mainly with the new poetry, mention him by name. Yet the moral and literary rebelliousness which permeates the collection strongly suggests the mood of critical self-consciousness he and the literary radicals were helping to create. Only four contributors were classified among "The Pessimists." The rest were sure that a revolution was occurring, especially in poetry. "The War," declared John Gould Fletcher, "has had the effect of making Americans realize that they are . . . essentially different . . . from the English; and in spite of the accident of migration, from the European stocks. America is now engaged in the process of discovering itself." Oppenheim demanded "a more general revolt against . . . the English, or the New England, tradition," with the goal of making us "really self-conscious as Americans" and making our poetry "a renascence of common experience." Young poets, according to Arthur Davison Ficke, were discarding "Victorian pruderies and reticences" and rediscovering "the virile freedom of the Elizabethans." As for novelists, Dreiser, Stephen Crane,

David Graham Phillips, and Frank Norris were mentioned as having dared to break away from the accepted kinds of "amiably superficial and romantically idealistic" fiction. In a summary statement, Morris found the basis of the movement in "a determination to express a reaction to experience in terms of the thoughts and feelings of our own time and country."[67]

A Book of Prefaces (1917): A Summons to Rebellion

Mencken's *A Book of Prefaces* did not at first reach a wide audience, but it helped to establish his reputation among young writers and intellectuals. Although the volume included much material from magazine and newspaper articles, Mencken used some of his newly acquired leisure for careful rewriting and editing. Because of the danger of censorship, he did not touch directly upon current political issues, but the animus against democracy which was intensified by his wartime experiences pervades the book. Within the first twenty-five pages he attacked the "essentially moral [,] . . . believing, certain, indignant" Anglo-Saxon mind, with its faith in "the master delusion that all human problems . . . are readily soluble, and that all that is required for their solution is to take counsel freely, to listen to wizards, to count votes, to agree upon legislation." Out of "this notion that there is some mysterious infallibility in the sense of the majority" two erroneous assumptions have developed. One is "that no concept in politics or conduct is valid (or more accurately respectable), which rises above the comprehension of the great masses of men, or which violates any of their inherent prejudices or superstitions." The second is "that the articulate individual in the mob takes on some of the authority and inspiration of the mob itself, and that he is thus free to set himself up as a soothsayer." In these circumstances, men of genuine ideas are hedged in by taboos, but quacks find a ready audience. The result of these tendencies is the *"Sklavenmoral* that besets all of us of English speech—the huggermugger morality of timorous, whining, unintelligent and unimaginative men—envy turned into law, cowardice sanctified, stupidity made noble, Puritanism."[68] Although Mencken does not specifically mention wartime restrictions on individual rights, the phrasing of his invective makes it clear that he had them in mind.

"Puritanism as a Literary Force," the key essay in *A Book of Prefaces,* develops at greater length the view of the dominant native culture Mencken had frequently voiced in the *Baltimore Sun* and *The Smart Set.* At the beginning of this essay, he discredits Puritan theology and morality by quoting Leon Kellner, a German student of American literature. By using this strategy, he was able to protest indirectly against the prevailing anti-German hysteria.

A strong anti-New England bias colors his treatment of Puritanism. He does not consistently distinguish between Puritanism as a religious movement and a theology existing in a particular historical period and puritanism as a kind of narrow moralism which has existed in a number of cultures. In the theology of the New England Puritans, the conception that God as well as man was bound by a series of covenants into which they had mutually entered mitigated the sense of God's limitless and wrathful power. The hope of grace stirred the Puritans quite as much as the fear of hell. Mencken grossly misrepresents this theology when he calls it "no more than a luxuriant demonology," in which "even God himself was transformed into a superior sort of devil, ever wary and wholly merciless." "That primitive demonology," he maintains, "still survives in the barbaric doctrines of the Methodists and Baptists, particularly in the South; but it has been ameliorated, even there, by a growing sense of the divine grace." But, he asserts, the Puritan preoccupation with ethical concerns, as opposed to its theology, still dominates American culture, except in cities like New York, San Francisco, and New Orleans "where Continental influences have measurably corrupted the Puritan idea." Thus, "the prevailing American view of the world and its mysteries is still a moral one, and no other human concern gets half the attention that is endlessly lavished upon the problem of conduct, particularly of the other fellow."[69]

Mencken's main purpose, however, is not to establish a historical link between Puritan theology and contemporary moral attitudes, but to expose and combat bigotry. For the most part, he uses "Puritanism" to designate a narrow moralism, a usage

which is at least as old as Shakespeare's *Twelfth Night*.[70] Closely
related to this concept of puritanism, which "holds beauty to be
distracting and corrupting," is philistinism, which "holds beauty
to be a mean and stupid thing." He distinguishes between "the
elder Puritanism," as manifested, for example, in the earlier
phases of the nineteenth-century antislavery campaign, and the
"new Puritanism" illustrated in the rise of comstockery and the
recent prohibition movement. The proponents of the elder Puritanism appealed to the individual conscience and sensed their
own responsibility for the evils they attacked; the converts to
the new Puritanism, instead of accusing themselves, forcibly
collar sinners and bring them to the bar of judgment. The
prosperity following the Civil War, with "the national sense
of energy and fitness" which accompanied it, gave the American
puritan " a lusty will to power." Wealthy supporters financed
organizations like the Y.M.C.A., the Society of Christian En-
deavor, and the Anti-Saloon League. Laymen, not clergymen,
dominated these groups, and they brought to the task of moral
crusading all the techniques of modern business, "from skilful
sales management to seductive advertising, and from rigorous
accounting to the diligent shutting off of competition." Beginning with the Comstock Postal Act of 1873, the legislation which
the new puritans forced through, in addition to many local and
state regulations, swept upward to the Mann Act of 1910 and
the Webb Act of 1913. The first of these "ratifies the Seventh
Commandment with a salvo of artillery, and the second . . .
put the overwhelming power of the Federal Government behind
the enforcement of the prohibition laws in the so-called 'dry'
States."[71]

According to Mencken's analysis, American artists suffer from
two great handicaps. The first is a "Puritan impulse from
within" which tends to curb any impulse to revolt and to encourage "conformity to the national prejudices," in accordance
"with set standards of niceness and propriety." The second handi-
cap, represented by the Comstock Postal Act and the proliferation of groups favoring censorship, is "the heavy hand of a
Puritan authority from without." Not only do American writers
constantly face the threat of censorship, but they also realize
that they have little chance of successfully opposing it. As Drei-

ser's experience showed, the support they get from publishers is likely to be half-hearted. Summing up his case against comstockery, Mencken concludes that "It constitutes a sinister and ever-present menace to all men of ideas; it affrights the publisher and paralyzes the author."[72]

As Randolph Bourne protested, Mencken greatly exaggerated the extent to which strictly literary censorship threatened American letters. "I cannot see," Bourne remarked, "that the younger writers—particularly the verse-writers—are conscious of living under any such cultural terrorism as he describes." In "Puritanism as a Literary Force," Mencken does not refer to the developments which gave him hope for the future, such as the large number of signatures on the Dreiser Protest and the increasing number of publishers and magazines eager to print candid and forceful writing. In this essay, he even contends that the assaults on the national prejudices by rebels like Dreiser have proved ineffectual. At the same time, he omits much evidence which would have justified his gloomy tone. If he had added a vivid account of the political censorship and the persecution of minorities that were going on in mid-1917, he might have quieted the doubts of readers like Bourne. He deliberately refrained from dealing with these issues because of the danger that his own book would be suppressed, but his indignation at the legalized effort to force dissenters into conformity helps to answer Bourne's question, "How is it that so robust a hater of uplift and puritanism becomes so fanatical a crusader himself?"[73]

"The new generation, urged to curiosity and rebellion by its mounting sap," Mencken observed at the end of "Puritanism as a Literary Force," "is rigorously restrained, regimented, policed." Despite his somber analysis of how effectively the puritan impulse from within and the puritan authority from without controlled American artists, he had no intention of counseling young authors to submit to these restraints. "We have yet no delivery," he noted, "but we have at least the beginnings of a revolt or, at all events, of a protest."[74]

In part, Mencken's efforts to encourage this revolt involved trying to create what Van Wyck Brooks later called "a usable past." Looking back to the nineteenth century, Mencken called attention to such exemplars of literary unorthodoxy as Poe,

Whitman, and, to a lesser extent, Mark Twain. Poe's criticism, Mencken claimed, shows that he "sensed the Philistine pull of a Puritan civilization as none had before him, and combatted it with his whole artillery of rhetoric." "His scathing attacks . . . keep a liveliness and appositeness," Mencken declared, "that the years have not staled."[75] Although Whitman's vision of an ideal democracy did not appeal to Mencken as it did to Brooks and Oppenheim, he nevertheless praised Whitman for challenging "the intolerable prudishness and dirty-mindedness of Puritanism" and for seeking "the themes and even the modes of expression in his poetry in the arduous, contentious and highly melodramatic life that lay all about him." As for Mark Twain, Mencken featured the rebellious aspects of his career less than one might expect. As presented in *A Book of Prefaces,* Twain emerged as at best only a partial rebel. He had "instinctive gifts that lifted him, in 'Huckleberry Finn,' to kinship with Cervantes and Aristophanes," but he never completely escaped the influence of the "Puritan village of the American hinterland" in which he was born. His decision not to allow *What Is Man?* to be published until after his death revealed his "incapacity for defying the taboos which surrounded him."[76]

In contrast to Brooks, who had picked Whitman as the cultural hero to whom America should turn, Mencken chose as his heroes three living authors—Conrad, Dreiser, and Huneker. His essays on these men suggest more definitely than his discussion of nineteenth-century figures the form the needed revolt might take. These "prefaces" reiterate his opposition to the genteel tradition and to literary commercialism; they renew his championship of a literature honestly and fearlessly bodying forth American life. Conrad is a supreme example of the European in whom artistry and aristocracy are united; Dreiser, with "his gigantic steadfastness," is the kind of "great, instinctive artist" who will emancipate American fiction from its timorousness; Huneker is the herald of zest for life and appreciation of beauty. That a true cosmopolitan like Huneker was allowed to exist and exert a civilizing influence within American culture led Mencken to confess "to a somewhat battered optimism." If men like Dreiser and Huneker were making headway, he implied, the younger generation of writers should rally to their support.[77]

"The reviews of the prefaces, in the main," Mencken wrote to Ernest Boyd, "are very unfavorable, and some of them are furious." Stuart Sherman's attack in *The Nation* illustrated a kind of controlled ferocity. His manhandling of Mencken's book contrasted strongly with the ideals he professed a few months later in a propaganda pamphlet written for the Creel Press Bureau. After asserting "that the ideals of the Allies have been the ideals of just men in all ages," he observed, "We need not fear lest we become venomous haters, for our very object is the inculcation of the sense of human brotherhood and human compassion." Still smarting from Mencken's onslaught in "The Dreiser Bugaboo," most of which was reproduced in *A Book of Prefaces,* Sherman proved himself a good hater. He made no attempt to explain his opponent's thesis or to counter his arguments. Instead, he ironically praised Mencken as "a lover of the beautiful," grouped him with writers like Huneker, Otto Heller, Untermeyer, and G.S. Viereck, and concluded that "his quarrel with American criticism is not so much in behalf of beauty as in behalf of a *Kultur* which has been too inhospitably received by such of his fellow citizens as look to another *Stammvater* than his." In his pamphlet, Sherman, protesting "I do not see how the American scholar's sympathies can be strongly enlisted in a feud in behalf of Anglo-Saxon blood," warned against the assumption that the English-speaking peoples had a monopoly on Allied ideals, but in his review he swung to the defense of the Anglo-Saxon tradition. Mencken's "continuous laudation of a Teutonic-Oriental pessimism and nihilism in philosophy, of antidemocratic politics, of the subjection and contempt of women, of the *Herrenmoral,* and of anything but Anglo-Saxon civilization," Sherman declared, "is not precisely and strictly *aesthetic* criticism; an unsympathetic person might call it infatuated propagandism." "But, of course," he added sarcastically, "all these things are properly to be regarded as but the obiter dicta of a quiet drummer for beauty."[78]

At the opposite extreme from Sherman's tirade were the reviews indicating that *A Book of Prefaces* was likely to increase

Mencken's audience among the younger writers. Through *The Smart Set* he had already attracted a following in the Middle West as well as in the East. Although New York was still un-rivaled among American cities as a center for publishing and for the arts in general, Chicago, nearly two decades after its "renaissance" of the nineties, was once more asserting its claim to cultural importance. There, in 1917, Harriet Monroe's *Poetry* and Margaret Anderson's *The Little Review* were being pub-lished. Among those who often met with the editors of these stimulating journals to discuss new works, new techniques, or their own projects were Sherwood Anderson, Carl Sandburg, Vachel Lindsay, Floyd Dell, Edgar Lee Masters, Ben Hecht, and Burton Rascoe. Hecht, then a young newspaper reporter, was one of Mencken's most ardent disciples and imitators. After Mencken and Nathan accepted Hecht's short story, "The Un-lovely Sin," printed in *The Smart Set* for August 1917, he be-came a frequent contributor. In a review of *A Book of Prefaces* in the *Chicago Sunday Tribune,* Rascoe, a young literary journal-ist from Oklahoma, set out to get his readers to join Mencken's "all too meagre audience." He was particularly struck by Mencken's serious concern with "the whole process of daily life in this republic." "His vivid combinations, his apt coinages of words," said Rascoe, "are traceable to a close observation and appraisal of daily affairs. Add a nimble and often grotesque imagination and you have the formula of his style—the most vigorous, the most individual, and the most frequently imitated in this country." *A Book of Prefaces,* in Rascoe's opinion, repre-sented an advance beyond Mencken's magazine criticism because it displayed less intolerance and fewer snap judgments. In giving "an equitable estimate and a keen analysis of the artistic aims" of Conrad, Dreiser, and Huneker, Mencken had achieved the true aim of the critic—to arouse "a desire to find pleasure in their writings."[79]

Mencken's friendly interest in the Chicago writers helped make his reputation there even more favorable than it might otherwise have been. In an article in the *Chicago Tribune,* he claimed that Chicago was not only "the most civilized" but also "the most thoroughly American" of our big cities. "A culture," he explained, "is bogus unless it be honest, which means unless it be truly national—the naif and untinctured expression of a national mind and soul." Reacting against the dominance of "Puritanism" and the doctrine of Anglo-Saxon supremacy in the East, Mencken characterized Philadelphia as "a Sunday school with a family entrance up the alley," and called Boston the home of "the fourth rate colonial snob" who "at his best . . . is still ashamed of his nationality." "The trouble with New York," he complained, "is that it has no nationality at all. It is simply a sort of free port—a place where the raw materials of civilization are received, sorted out, and sent further on." New York "puts much higher values upon conformity, acceptance, intellectual respectability, than it puts upon actual ideas," but "In Chicago originality still appears to be put above conformity." He recalled that "It was Chicago, and not New York, that launched the 'Chap Book' saturnalia of the nineties—the first of her endless efforts to break down formalism in the national letters and let in the national spirit." As examples of original and enterprising authors who had spent at least some time in Chicago, he cited, among novelists, H.B. Fuller, Norris, and Dreiser; among humorists and short-story writers, Dunne, Ade, and Lardner; among poets and critics of poetry, Sandburg, Lindsay, Masters, and Harriet Monroe. He concluded his article with this eulogy: "I give you Chicago. It is not London-and-Harvard. It is not Paris-and-buttermilk. It is American in every chitling and sparerib, and it is alive from snout to tail."[80]

7

POSTWAR TRIUMPH

Mentor of a Disillusioned Generation

During America's participation in the war, political heresy was put down by force, but moral and literary rebellion, though checked, was not completely curbed. As we have seen, it had a healthy development in the work of young critics, poets, and novelists whose careers were not interrupted by military service. Mencken, as a critic, helped to imbue a significant number of these authors with the spirit of the literary movement of the nineties. As coeditor of *The Smart Set,* he was also in a position to offer them practical advice and, at times, to publish their writings. The end of the war, as he had foreseen, created an atmosphere which allowed the revolt to move quickly to its climax. He was soon accepted as a mentor not only by an increasingly large number of the young intellectuals who had remained at home, but also by many of those who had returned from service in the armed forces or in ambulance brigades.

Looking back on this period in 1923, he reflected that

it was the war, in the end, that really broke down the old tradition. The bald fact that the majority of the adherents of that old tradition were violent Anglomaniacs, and extravagant in their support of the English cause from the first days of 1914, was sufficient in itself to make most of the younger writers incline the other way. The struggle thus became a battle royal between fidelity to the English cultural heritage of the country and advocacy of a new national culture that should mirror, not only the influence of England, but also that of every country that had contributed elements to the American strain. . . .

. . . So long as the war-time laws against free speech were in force, the professors seemed to have everything their own way, but the moment those laws were suspended there was a reaction so violent that they were completely unhorsed and undone. The more intelligent young soldiers, returning from . . . [the] war . . . , proceeded at once to a realistic and often extremely destructive discussion of its motives and conduct. On the purely political side, the effect of this grim autopsy was made visible in the astounding collapse of Wilson, and his ignominious retirement to private life. On the literary side, it had the effect of liberating all the new authors.

Even though Mencken realized that writers like Henry van Dyke, William Allen White, and Owen Wister may have succumbed honestly, though naively, to the emotional contagion of the time, he believed that they had betrayed their calling as artists by becoming superpatriots and propagandists. "The whole history of the war period," he held, "is a history of the subsidence of the van Dykes and the rise of the Cabells, Dreisers, Masterses, Andersons, and Sinclair Lewises—in brief, of the men who continued to question the national culture, despite the colossal effort to endow it with a mystical sort of perfection."[1]

Once Mencken was again free to express the whole range of his ideas, he was in a particularly strategic position to gain a wider audience among the young intellectuals, whether they were nonveterans, veterans, or college students. More quickly and acutely than the majority of Americans, they experienced a feeling of disillusionment with the war leaders and the war aims, of disgust with the standards of an industrial civilization, of skepticism about accepted religious and moral axioms, of uncertainty about the future. In the words of F. Scott Fitzgerald, the younger generation had "grown up to find all Gods dead, all wars fought, all faiths in man shaken." They did not want to run with the herd or even to form coteries among themselves; they wanted to seek out their own values and work out their own careers as individuals. Mencken's views and personality as projected in his style strongly appealed to them in the three or four years immediately after the war when they were still

engaged in the adventure of self-discovery. They could sympathize with his expressions of a seeking and questioning mood,
as when he wrote,

The only thing I respect is intellectual honesty, of which, of
course, intellectual courage is a necessary part. A Socialist who
goes to jail for his opinions seems to me a much finer man than
the judge who sends him there. . . . But though he is fine, the
Socialist is nevertheless foolish, for he suffers for what is untrue.
If I knew what *was* true, I'd probably be willing to sweat and
strive for it, and maybe even die for it to the tune of bugle-
blasts. But so far I have not found it.[2]

More typically, Mencken spoke out with a refreshing posi-
tiveness that had a tonic and bracing effect. He had already
undergone his time of testing. His personal anguish, the controversies in which he had engaged, and his constant quarrel
with the national culture had put him on his mettle. His feeling
during the war that the tyranny of the majority was rapidly
becoming a reality convinced him more than ever of the essential
rightness of his opinions. Since he shared few, if any, of the
illusions the younger generation was just discarding, he stood
clear of the prevailing confusion. On a wide variety of topics—
from the Ku Klux Klan to the new psychology, from Fitzgerald
to Billy Sunday—he expressed with verve and humor, satire and
invective, the kinds of attitudes toward which young people were
reaching. At one and the same time, he could guide, console,
and entertain.

Although the revolt he advocated was primarily religious,
moral, and literary, it also had its economic and political facets.
Speaking for the intellectuals among the veterans, John Peale
Bishop and Edmund Wilson protested against "the commercialism and industrialism which had caught up the very professors
from the great universities," against the "dreary stultification" to
which mass production condemned young men and women,
and against the use of violence to put down strikes.[3] Mencken
did not hide his basic economic conservatism, but he regarded
most American capitalists as "disgusting cravens, eternally afraid
of something, always demanding that their enemies be ham-
strung."[4] He ridiculed "the office-holding and commercial bour-

geoisie" of the New South who were responsible for its "present 'industrial prosperity' . . . , *i.e.,* its conversion from a region of large landed estates and urbane life into a region of stinking factories, filthy mining and oil towns, child-killing cotton mills, vociferous chambers of commerce and other such swineries." He condemned the gullibility of the public and the spectacle of the American manufacturer who "simply packs his surplus in gaudy packages, sends for an advertising agent, joins an Honest-Advertising club, fills the newspapers and magazines with lying advertisements, and sits down in peace while his countrymen fight their way to his counters." In commenting on the steel strike of 1919, he stated plainly that he did not sympathize with the strikers' cause, but he was contemptuous of the industrial leaders who denied the workers their right to free assemblage and free speech, employed thugs to attack and even murder them, and then got police and soldiers called out to terrorize them further. The "raucous clamor against the so-called Reds," many of whom were deported without being granted a fair hearing, was another sign of "the true weakness of modern capitalism . . . : it is the creation, not of genuinely strong men, but of timorous bounders hiding behind policemen."[5] Such views made sense to those who were beginning to question the values of a business civilization.

Unlike the progressive and socialist intellectuals of the period 1908 to 1918, the majority of the young intellectuals of the post-war decade were not primarily interested in politics. Little of the old zeal for political crusading survived the collapse of war-time ideals. Confronted by the triumph of Prohibition and the ineptness and corruption of the Harding administration, the young writers tended to agree with Mencken that organized political reform was a lost cause. Mencken's own political views were too individualistic, too distrustful of organized action, to enable him either to accept the program of any existing party or to devise a coherent program of his own. But his determined affirmation of the right to dissent gave his revolt a political dimension. His prejudices, hardened by his wartime reactions, prepared him to recognize more quickly than most commentators many of the key problems of the new era. He was ready at once to conduct a boisterously destructive campaign against the political influence wielded by religious sects through the Anti-Saloon League, against the fear and intolerance embodied in the hounding of aliens during the Red Scare, against all kinds of repressive legislation and political graft. From one point of view, "the Mencken approach," as Eric Goldman has suggested, "was really a kind of latter-day muckraking, exposing and assailing The Shame of Prohibition, The Shame of Comstockery, The Shame of the Babbitts." The positive value sustaining Mencken's campaign was his intense libertarianism. His call "to heed the inner voice and to be one's own man" was one to which the young artists readily responded.[6]

Mencken undoubtedly helped stimulate young men and women in the early 1920s to question the codes they had been taught in childhood, to oppose puritanism and hypocrisy, and to search for a more realistic ethic.[7] When told by a college professor that he had many readers in the universities, Mencken replied, "If you are right, then I'll certainly write the book I have had in mind for a long while, to wit, 'Advice to Young Men,' a frank, realistic, unsentimental treatise on such things as politics, education, business, sex, etc., revolving around the doctrine that the most precious possession of man is *honor.*"[8] Although Mencken did not carry out his plan for such a book, he used the title for one section of his *Prejudices: Third Series.*

As his concern for his own personal code shows, his religious and moral iconoclasm was not directed at religion and morality as such, but at hypocrisy and fraud wherever they appeared. For him the key distinction was between the gentleman or man of honor, typified by George Washington, and the man of morals, "the self-bamboozled Presbyterian," typified by Woodrow Wilson. It was not the doctrines or the ritual of the evangelical churches to which he objected, but the moral fervor which compelled the clergy and the lay members of these denominations to try to impose puritanical norms on the public at large. Because his German-American and semisouthern standards clashed with those common in the native culture, he was better prepared than most critics to expose the conflict between the actions of many Americans and the traditional religious or moral beliefs they professed. "This disparity between what is publicly approved and what is privately done," he claimed, "is at the heart of the Anglo-Saxon, and especially of the American character."

It is the cause of the astounding hypocrisy that foreigners always see in us. . . .

. . . We bawl about the malefactions of Big Business—and every man in Little Business is trying to gouge and rob his way into Big Business as fast as he can. . . . We deafen the world with our whoops for liberty—and submit to laws that invade and destroy our most sacred rights. . . . We play policeman and Sunday-school superintendent to half of Christendom—and lynch a darkey every two days in our own back-yard. Thus the curious dualism of the land. . .

"The thing needed," he explained, "is obviously a thorough overhauling of the outworn national code—perhaps its forthright abandonment and the formulation of an entirely new one, closer to the unescapable facts."[9]

In *The Smart Set* and in Mencken's books, readers could find both a satirical and a serious treatment of sexual morality. If they wanted a deftly amusing survey of such topics as "The Feminine Mind," "The War between the Sexes," "Marriage," and "Woman Suffrage," they could turn to his *In Defense of Women.* In the indexes of the first two series of *Prejudices,* they found the names of Freud and Havelock Ellis duly listed. In these volumes, they discovered much sense as well as satire in "The Blushful Mystery" and "Appendix on a Tender Theme." In "The National Letters" in *Prejudices: Second Series,* they noted the serious demand that the power of sex should be recognized more frankly in American life and literature. "Even the shy and somewhat stagy carnality that characterizes the Village . . . ," Mencken contended,

proves that, despite repressions unmatched in civilization in modern times, there is still a sturdy animality in American youth, and hence good health. The poet hugging his Sonia in a Washington square beanery, and so giving notice to all his world that he is a devil of a fellow, is at least a better man than the emasculated stripling in a Y.M.C.A. gospel-mill, pumped dry of all his natural appetites and the vacuum filled with double-entry book-keeping, business economics and auto-erotism. In so foul a nest of imprisoned and fermenting sex as the United States, plain fornication becomes a mark of relative decency.[10]

For the reader won over to Mencken's point of view, there was much truth in this charge. It also provided an excellent rationalization for youthful defiance of the accepted sexual taboos.

As an agent of literary revolt, Mencken functioned much as he had before the war, but with many more recruits rallying to his cause. As a literary critic, he never surpassed the achievement of *A Book of Prefaces*, but his newly acquired prestige greatly increased the audience for that seminal book. Neither his aims nor his tastes changed, but many more young writers now looked to him for advice and help. He rejoined the staff of the *Baltimore Sun*, and his critiques appeared there and in other newspapers as well as in *The Smart Set* and other magazines. He remained practically anaesthetic to the best of the new poetry, but through reviews, editorial notes, and personal meetings he cheered on dozens of critics and novelists.

In fiction, he continued to encourage the development of two main phases of the literary movement of the nineties: its experiments in realism and naturalism and its cultivation of an urbane and mannered romanticism.

His effort to sponsor realism and naturalism is well illustrated in a list of eighteen books he recommended late in 1919, commenting that "the American novel begins to take on an unmistakable dignity." As one would expect, he included titles by his prewar favorites: Mark Twain, Norris, Phillips, Wharton (*Ethan Frome*), and Dreiser. Among more recent works, he stressed novels and story collections like Ring Lardner's *You Know Me, Al*, Abraham Cahan's *The Rise of David Levinsky*, Willa Cather's *My Antonia*, and Sherwood Anderson's *Winesburg, Ohio*. In 1920 Mencken sanctioned revolt from the village as a theme in fiction by praising Zona Gale's *Miss Lulu Bett* and Sinclair Lewis's *Main Street*. Mencken's suggestion that some enterprising novelist should portray life in a medium-sized American city encouraged Lewis to persevere in his plan to use such a setting for his next novel, *Babbitt*.[11]

Mencken was also in a good position to explain to the would-be sophisticates of the twenties the tradition illustrated by the romances of Hergesheimer, Cabell, and Van Vechten. These and other authors of the cosmopolitan school benefited from the increasing vogue of aestheticism. In 1918 the young editors of the new Modern Library chose Wilde's *The Picture of Dorian Gray* as their first selection. In the same year Mencken himself contributed an introduction to a new edition of Wilde's *A House of Pomegranates*. In 1919, when Carl Van Vechten excitedly announced his "discovery" of Saltus, Mencken was able to speak with the authority of one long familiar with the life and writings of this leading American spokesman for decadence. He reminded his readers that Saltus was "still very much alive, and even engaged with the pen." After commenting on the New York socialite's "pagan contumacies and polychromatic parts of speech," he recalled how Saltus' novel, *The Truth about Tristram Varick,* had startled and delighted him back in the early nineties.[12]

As for Cabell, Hergesheimer, and Van Vechten—in some respects the heirs of Wilde and Saltus—Mencken knew and corresponded with all of them. For a number of years he had been helping to establish their reputations, and in 1919 he included titles by them in his list of recommended novels. They were typical of a group of writers who reacted against what they considered provincial and petty in American life and strove to create a literature that would be aristocratic, urbane, witty, and ironic. In one sense, their jeweled prose and their stress on other times and countries represented an effort to escape the present and renounce responsibility for it. At the same time, despite their differences in approach and method, they and the realists had a common objective: to protest against the conditions that made it hard for a sensitive artist to survive. This shared aim explains why members of the two groups were usually on friendly terms and often publicly admired and supported each other's efforts.[13]

The most famous example of satire disguised as romantic fantasy was Cabell's *Jurgen*. It dealt ostensibly with the medieval, mythical land of Poictesme, but Mencken called it "the most bitter attack on current American Kultur that I have ever read." Although he suspected that much of its irony and bawdy symbolism were too subtle for the general public, he felt sure that some of the more direct thrusts struck home. As an appropriate commentary on the United States in 1919—"the year of the 100% American's apotheosis"—he liked to quote Jurgen's discovery that "The religion of Hell is patriotism, and the government is an enlightened democracy."[14] Early in 1920, when the New York Society for the Suppression of Vice proceeded against *Jurgen,* he offered his help in protesting this action as quickly as he had in *The "Genius"* case five years before.

One of the less familiar aspects of Mencken's influence in the early twenties is the stimulus he gave to the southern literary renaissance. To begin with, he applied a form of shock treatment to the New South. The thesis of "The Sahara of the Bozart," reprinted in revised form in *Prejudices: Second Series,* is that the modern South,

> that stupendous region of fat farms, shoddy cities and paralyzed cerebrums . . . , is almost as sterile, artistically, intellectually, culturally, as the Sahara Desert. If the whole of the late Confederacy were to be engulfed by a tidal wave tomorrow, the effect upon the civilized minority of men in the world would be but little greater than that of a flood on the Yang-tse-kiang. It would be impossible in all history to match so complete a drying-up of a civilization.[15]

Such pungently phrased overstatements caught the public eye, aroused controversy, and gave this particular essay a fame not shared by Mencken's earlier and later pieces on the South.

Many southern reviewers and editors resorted to the expedient of dismissing "The Sahara" as an outburst of Prussian malice, but a scattering of articulate southerners took a different view. They noticed that the strategy of the essay was to contrast the New South, not with European cultures, past or present, nor even with other regions of the United States, but with the "civilization of manifold excellences" that, according to Mencken, prevailed in the Old South. As Donald Davidson was to remark later, they sensed that Mencken was perhaps "a disguised Confederate raider" whose surprise attack might be his way of trying to arouse the New South to a greater awareness of its cultural problems and to greater efforts to solve them.[16] Among the minority who recognized this possibility were Emily

Clark, Mary D. Street, Hunter Stagg, and Margaret Freeman, all of Richmond, Virginia. They were laying plans for *The Reviewer,* one of several experimental magazines which sprang up about the same time and helped revive southern letters. *The Reviewer's* first number, dated February 15, 1921, which carried a review of the new *Prejudices,* accepted "The Sahara" as a suitable challenge to southern authors.

Emily Clark, the first editor of the magazine, describes how Mencken encouraged the new venture in both the *Baltimore Sun* and *The Smart Set* and also befriended her and other staff members. In one of his letters to Miss Clark, he told her, "In general, your chief aim should be to develop new Southern authors. The South is beginning to emerge from its old slumber. You have a capital chance to lead the way." He accompanied such suggestions with the names of young southern writers then unknown to Miss Clark, including Frances Newman, Julia Peterkin, and Gerald W. Johnson, all of whom later contributed to the journal. In *The Smart Set* for August 1921, Mencken cited *The Reviewer,* the *Double-dealer* of New Orleans, and *All's Well* "out in trackless, unexplored Arkansas" as evidences of artistic ferment. "What is going on down there," he declared, "is almost precisely what went on in the Middle West in the 1890's, to wit, a gathering revolt of the more alert and competent youngsters against the constraints of an ancient, formalized and no longer vital tradition." He particularly admired Cabell for his upholding of the aristocratic tradition of the Old South, despite his being as isolated as "a solitary civilized European in Iowa." Noting that *The Reviewer* lacked "bellicosity, . . . the will to hammer upon skulls," Mencken hoped that its editors could persuade Cabell to turn critic and make an onslaught on southern "tripe-sellers and cheese-mongers." He advised young southerners, depicting the life of their region, to "question it sharply and a bit raucously, and try to visualize something superior to it." Writing a few months later in *The Reviewer,* he again pointed out that a new interest in the arts was developing in the South, and urged the "intellectual aristocracy" to speak out against the prevailing philistinism.[17]

Despite the thinness of their editorial purse, Mencken and Nathan made *The Smart Set* an important vehicle for the new talent. They had the distinction of being the first editors to buy a story by Scott Fitzgerald, whose "Babes in the Woods" appeared in September 1919. In 1919 and 1920 they featured, in addition to more Fitzgerald, such stories as Dreiser's "Sanctuary," Sherwood Anderson's "I Want to Know Why," and Willa Cather's "Coming, Eden Bower!" They also published work by such typical successors of the bohemian poets and critics as George Sterling, Vincent O'Sullivan, Benjamin de Casseres, Hecht, and Van Vechten.

One of the controversies about Mencken which arose among the advocates of literary revolt was whether his preoccupation with the manners and morals of the "mob" was a strength or a weakness. Randolph Bourne, in 1917, had felt that "Mencken too often . . . wastes away into a desert of invective, yet he has all the raw material of a good critic—moral freedom, a passion for ideas and for literary beauty, vigor and pungency of phrase, considerable reference and knowledge." "Has he not," Bourne inquired, "let himself be the victim of that paralyzing Demos against which he so justly rages?" Just as the artist writes to an ideal audience, Bourne argued, the critic should judge for the ideal audience and leave Demos to "its commercial magazines and its mawkish novels." This was substantially the view of the literary expatriates, who added the proviso that it was better to put the Atlantic Ocean between oneself and the United States. Pound predicted that once Mencken made his escape, he would begin his real work. "Certainly you will lose a great part of your public," Pound asserted, "when you stop trying to civilize the waste places; and you will gain about fifteen readers."[18]

Some critics, however, realized that Mencken's attitudes toward Demos and the places it inhabited involved not merely rage and scorn, but an exasperated affection. O'Sullivan expressed this idea by saying that Mencken's treatment of America "is in the manner of Him who chasteneth because He loveth." In Rascoe's opinion, Mencken was not primarily a literary critic, but a critic of ideas whose efforts were sustained by the "hope that . . . stupidity, narrowness, hypocrisy, and mean living will be in some trifling way decreased, so that intelligent and honest artists may live their lives in These States without interference by the police." Edmund Wilson noted a contrast between Menck-

en's "comic mask" and the critic, evangelist, and artist behind
it. The fact that Mencken was "a genuine artist and man of
first-rate education and intelligence who is thoroughly familiar
with, even thoroughly saturated with, the common life" accounted for the power of his satire. Wilson would have agreed
with Mencken's claim that young American artists needed a
"view of the world . . . grounded upon observation of the world
. . . as it actually is today." In Wilson's judgment, Mencken
was "the civilized consciousness of modern America, its learning,
its intelligence and taste, realizing the grossness of its manners
and mind and crying out in horror and chagrin."[19]

If Mencken's revulsion from the moral attitudes and habits
of mind of the common people produced a satirical commentary
alternating between horror and the horse-laugh, his feeling of
kinship with them provided much of the motive force behind
The American Language (1919), a work of major literary as
well as linguistic importance. His explicit assertion of this kinship is all the more remarkable because he completed the
manuscript in 1918 when his sense of isolation from the majority
of Americans was most extreme. In that colloquial idiom he had
admired in the work of writers like Mark Twain, George Ade,
and Ring Lardner, and which formed an integral part of his
own style, he found that the spirit of liberty still survived. The
feature of American speech which most impressed him was "its
impatient disdain of rule and precedent, and hence its large
capacity (distinctly greater than that of the English of England)
for taking in new words and phrases and for manufacturing
locutions out of its own materials." There can be no mistaking
his sympathy for the traits revealed in the common language:

Such a term as *rubber-neck* is almost a complete treatise on
American psychology; it reveals the national habit of mind
more clearly than any labored inquiry could ever reveal it. It
has in it precisely the boldness and disdain of ordered forms
that are so characteristically American, and it has too the grotesque humor of the country, and the delight in devastating
opprobriums, and the acute feeling for the succinct and the
savory.[20]

The American Language reinforced Mencken's efforts to create an American as opposed to an Anglo-Saxon tradition. He

took note of the assumption that it is "an anti-social act to examine and exhibit the constantly growing differences between English and American, as certain American pedants argue sharply," but dismissed it as "a somewhat childish effort to gain the approval of Englishmen—a belated efflorescence of the colonial spirit, often commingled with fashionable aspiration." Freely admitting his amateur status as a philologist, he said his aim was to "pave the way for a better work by a more competent man."[21]

One effect of the book was to give a new dimension to the reputation he had acquired in academic circles. The academic critics who had once deemed him a mere journalist could not help but be impressed by the capacity he now showed for scholarship and for orderly and vivid exposition. They could not, of course, foresee that his "Preliminary Inquiry" marked the beginning of a new movement in American linguistic studies —a movement to which Mencken, with the help of innumerable professors and interested laymen, was to contribute significantly by turning out three revised editions and two supplements. Nor could they foresee how accurate would be Mencken's prophecy at the end of the first edition that the idiom of everyday speech would form an increasingly important part of the American literary tradition. "Given the poet," he predicted,

there may suddenly come a day when our *theirns* and *would'a hads* will take on the barbaric stateliness of the peasant locutions of old Maurya in "Riders to the Sea." They seem grotesque and absurd today because the folks who use them seem grotesque and absurd. But that is a too facile logic and under it is a false assumption. In all human beings, if only understanding be brought to the business, dignity will be found, and that dignity cannot fail to reveal itself, soon or late, in the words and phrases with which they make known their high hopes and aspirations and cry out against the intolerable meaninglessness of life.[22]

Authors who, at least at times, were to justify this prophecy included Anderson and Lewis, Hemingway and Dos Passos, Cummings and Frost, Faulkner and Salinger.

The Search for a Wider Audience:
Laying Plans for the *Mercury*

By 1922 many young writers began to question whether they should any longer look to Mencken for leadership. They acknowledged that he had helped them in many intangible as well as in many practical ways, but it was natural that, as they themselves matured, they should become more conscious of his limitations. Most of them did not share his interest in popular culture and politics. Many of them felt that his religious and moral revolt had been salutary, but that it had now served its purpose. In 1921 Scott Fitzgerald, after commenting on Mencken's success in stirring up anti-Puritanism, asked, "how of the next twenty years? Will he find new gods to dethrone?" Others observed that Mencken was contributing to magazines like *The Nation* and *The New Republic,* was being widely quoted in the press, and was even letting some of his statements be used as advertising copy.[23] Was he not becoming too respectable?

As for literary issues, many young authors believed that their interests and tastes had developed beyond Mencken's range. In some cases, as among the Greenwich Villagers, this feeling was partly a defensive reaction against his frequent jibes at their literary efforts, in which he found "not a touch of the prodigious gusto and gaudiness of American life," but only "technique, piffle, artificiality . . . —the hollow agonies of studio, tea-shop and magazine ante-room." Anyone who wished to could easily collect examples of Mencken's shortcomings as a literary critic—his lack of a consistent aesthetic, his ineptitude as a judge of poetry, his oversimplifications, his inability to appreciate the subtleties of artists like Henry James, T.S. Eliot, or the later Joyce. Mencken's literary sensibility consisted of strong fibers knotted in a coarse net; nuances tended to escape it. His impatience with any kind of intricate symbolism or stream-of-consciousness technique can also be accounted for by the fact that he belonged to the avant-garde of the nineties, not to that of the new generation coming up in the twenties. Edmund Wilson, viewing the twenties in retrospect, made clear this difference between the two generations. Wilson had consciously allied himself with the tradition of literary journalism represented by Shaw and Mencken, but he had felt in the early twenties that the battle being fought by Mencken and his supporters had mostly been won. "There remained for the young journalist, however," he writes, "two roads that had still to be broken; the road to the understanding of the most recent literary events in the larger international world—Joyce, Eliot, Proust, etc.—which were already out of the range of readers the limits of whose taste had been fixed by *Egoists* and *The Quintessence of Ibsenism;* and to bring home to the 'bourgeois' intellectual world the most recent developments of Marxism in connection with the Russian Revolution."[24] Neither Mencken nor most of the young intellectuals in 1922 wanted to help clear the second road, but nearly all the young writers wanted to explore the first. Mencken had no desire to lead them.

Even before Mencken's reputation among the young authors had reached its climax, his interest in social and political issues had begun to overshadow his literary concerns. This change was accompanied by the hope of discovering or founding a magazine much broader in scope than *The Smart Set,* one which would reach "the Forgotten Men" he later described as the ideal audience for which the *Mercury* was intended. Soon after the Armistice, he told Louis Untermeyer, "You will escape from literary criticism, too, as I am trying to do. The wider field of ideas in general is too alluring. . . . We live, not in a literary age, but in a fiercely political age." "Soon or late," he predicted, "some one will start a weekly that we can write for." In a sketch of his career written in 1922, he explained that after publishing his first book of criticism (*Shaw*), "I moved steadily from practical journalism, with its dabblings in politics, economics and so on, toward purely aesthetic concerns, chiefly·literature and music, but of late I have felt a strong pull in the other direction, and what interests me chiefly today is what may be called public psychology, *i.e.,* the nature of the ideas that the larger masses of men hold, and the process whereby they reach them."[25]

A few years before, in describing the kind of nonliterary, middle-class audience to whom E.W. Howe's writings appealed, he anticipated his later accounts of the group to whom he directed the *Mercury*. Howe, Mencken thought, was "thoroughly anti-democratic at bottom, though he probably does not realize it." Unlike "other national sages," Howe "practices resolutely a relentless honesty, sacrificing every appearance, however charming, to what he conceives to be the truth." He "stands for the thought of the higher stratum of men who, starting from the mass, have lifted themselves to a certain measure of security, and with it of self-respect and dignity. . . . They are men who have risen to a capacity for disillusion which is the first step toward a capacity for free speculation." Such men, suspicious of "the shibboleths that have served the mob so long," discontented "with the mountebanks who monopolize the political arena," have begun a "slow, uncertain, still somewhat timid movement toward a saner and more candid ethic." They constitute "an audience that likes to hear things discussed frankly, and to find its secret notions put into plain words."[26]

Mencken, like Howe, had the "old journalist's incurable itch to have his say," but he did not discover any adequate vehicle for his social and political commentary until the founding of the *Mercury*. As a practical journalist, he made use of whatever outlets were available, including *The Nation* and *The New Republic*, but he felt uncomfortable about having his name identified with these politically liberal journals. At the same time, he did not want to be identified with the "Tories." The political dilemma as he saw it in 1920 was the same that he described when laying plans for the *Mercury* in 1923. Because "the party system . . . herds men into undifferentiated masses," it seriously handicaps "the man of independent spirit, wide information and self-respect." "Either he must be a so-called Liberal," Mencken complained, "or he must swallow the whole nauseous dose of plutocratic poppycock—either he must follow John Reed, Amos Pinchot and *The New Republic*, or he must bring down his intelligence to the level of General [Leonard] Wood, the Union League Club and the *New York Times*."[27] The *Mercury*, in large measure, represented Mencken's effort to establish an organ to speak for the third force between those extremes—for the Forgotten Men, the saving remnant of the middle class.

Mencken, as his feeling of kinship with Howe suggests, had a real affinity with the audience to which he appealed with such great success in the *Mercury*. It was a minority within the middle class, but it was much larger and more diverse than the group of young intellectuals, most of whom were also of middle-class origin. For Mencken, there was "a lot of fun" to be got out of addressing the larger audience of the *Mercury*. Now at the height of his powers, he proved "that iconoclasm, whatever its perils, is at least one of the most gallant and stimulating of sports." As behooved a journalist speaking to "the higher stratum of men who . . . have lifted themselves to a certain measure of security," he also demonstrated that he could make his new venture financially profitable. By putting the "secret notions" of his new audience into "plain words," by twitting it for its lingering Puritanism and Philistinism, by appealing to its aspirations to be "in the know" about artistic matters, by sketching a *Realpolitik* which swore at liberalism at one extreme and toryism at the other, and by satirizing the less enlightened elements of the population, he ideally fulfilled Shaw's definition of the Critic as confessor to "the sovereign people." "Criticism," Shaw remarked,

is not only medicinally salutary: it has positive popular gratification given to envy by its attacks on the great, and to enthusiasm by its praises. It may say things which many would like to say, but dare not, and indeed for want of skill could not even if they durst. Its iconoclasms, seditions, and blasphemies, if well turned, tickle those whom they shock; so that the critic adds the privileges of the court jester to those of the confessor.[28]

Thus Mencken, as editor of and contributor to the *Mercury*, simultaneously shocked and tickled his readers.

8

CONCLUSION

Despite the changes which transformed America during Mencken's lifetime, his basic attitudes remained much the same in his maturity as they had been in his youth. His wide-ranging interests, the soundness of his information on many issues, and the common sense with which he treated them were offset, to a considerable extent, by his failure to see any need for modifying his premises. He was no more capable of renouncing the dogmas of "scientism" and social Darwinism, even though they were outmoded by the twenties, than the more sincere of the Fundamentalists he derided were able to renounce theirs. In an age when scientists were developing the theory of relativity and psychologists were exploring the power in human affairs of the instincts and the unconscious mind, his faith in the mechanistic science and the rationalism of the late nineteenth century was itself naive. His opinions on such topics as mysticism and psychical research, though expressed pungently and amusingly, reflect a corresponding naiveté.

Although he delighted in commenting on literature, music, economic and political issues, the social sciences, and the natural sciences, he was not an original or a systematic thinker in any of these fields. His prejudices were the themes of his art, not the building blocks of a coherent system of thought. When viewed as the materials of his art, his ideas take on a unity of mood and emotion generated by the vigor of his style and by the intensity of his commitment to certain values, especially those he associated with the truth-seeker and the gentleman. Scrutinized as the materials of a philosophy, his ideas are baffling in their ambiguity. Just as we think we have grasped the quintessential Mencken, another and contradictory phase of his thought emerges. His theoretical determinism is at odds with his faith in individual initiative, his libertarianism, and his belief that the small group of truth-seekers can bring about at least a limited kind of progress. His social and political views range from conservatism in the manner of William Graham Sumner, at one extreme, to Jeffersonian liberalism and distrust of all government, at the other. On the purportedly scientific ground that Negroes are far behind the whites in the process of evolution, he stereotypes them unfavorably, but he is quick to praise individual Negroes who have vitality and talent. Similarly, he condemns farmers as "Puritans" who want to impose Prohibition and other restraints on city people, but he sees that the struggles and problems of farmers can make moving subject matter for fiction. Politically, despite many shrewd hits and insights, he proved himself as utopian as any of the liberals or radicals to whom he applied that label. He called upon the United States to "invent" a genuine aristocracy, but failed to explain how she could do so.

He professed to be a skeptic even about his own beliefs, but he did not subject them to a truly skeptical analysis. Nevertheless, he had certain qualities which tended to counterbalance his rigid adherence to his prejudices and the contrarieties inherent in them. To begin with, he had a temperamental distrust of all systems and system-makers, and he made no pretence of being consistent except in the matter of expressing forthrightly the opinions which seemed to him most relevant to a particular topic at a particular time. He also had the ability to laugh at himself as well as at others. As an expert in controversy, he welcomed attacks on himself, partly because they showed that his thrusts had gone home, partly because he defended everyone's right to have his say, and partly because he felt that destructive criticism, even of his own work, was much more stimulating than acclaim. "I have learned more from attacks than from praise," he once told Dreiser.

In even the most vicious of them there is a touch or two of plausibility. There is always something embarrassing about unqualified praise. A man knows, down in his heart, that he doesn't deserve it. When he sees all his petty bluffs and affectations accepted seriously, the sole result is to make him lose respect for the victim.[1]

As this statement suggests, Mencken was embarrassed whenever he converted an opponent to his way of thinking. Dogmatic as he was about his own opinions, he admitted the right of others to maintain conflicting views. He admired spunk and spark wherever he discerned them, even though they were present in people whose ideas he detested. In the case of individuals whose integrity as artists he respected, he acknowledged that, if his advice was at variance with their own best insights, they should reject it. After telling Dreiser that his *Hey Rub-a-Dub-Dub,* a collection of essays, "appeals . . . to the defectively educated," he commented, "I could have written the book much better myself, whereas I couldn't have done a single chapter of *Twelve Men* or *Sister Carrie.*" Then, in a characteristic vein, he added, "You are writing your books, and I am writing mine. . . . When you offend my pruderies I shall howl, but I'd consider you an ass if you let it influence you."[2]

If it were not for Mencken's provincial origins, the dissonant traditions to which he was exposed, and the tensions and ambivalences in his thought, his career might have taken an entirely different direction. Without the stimulus from these sources, he would probably not have entered into that half affectionate, half exasperated, quarrel with America which furnished his major theme and helped create his national reputation. A remark he made about Theodore Roosevelt applied with equal force to himself: "Life fascinated him, and he knew how to make his own doings fascinating to others." His youthful writings reveal two impulses that coalesced and shaped his mature work as artist and critic. The first was the impulse to lash out at the institutions, individuals, and values which he saw as forcing into conformity potential truth-seekers and artists (or members of any other dissident minority). The second was the impulse toward self-expression—"to give outward and objective form to ideas that bubble inwardly and have a fascinating lure."[3]

In championing the rights and freedoms of an intellectual or artistic minority against the cramping effects of the culture of the majority, Mencken was, of course, by no means unique. In this respect, he belonged in a major tradition in American letters, represented in the nineteenth century by such diverse figures as John Randolph of Roanoke, James Fenimore Cooper, Emerson, Thoreau, Melville, Emily Dickinson, Mark Twain, and Ambrose Bierce, and in the twentieth by many of the authors for whom Mencken had a kindred feeling, including John Macy, Van Wyck Brooks, Dreiser, Ring Lardner, and Sinclair Lewis.

When compared with his contemporaries, Mencken is remarkable, first, for the extent to which his concern with all aspects of the national culture dominated his consciousness and, second, for the great flow of energy he poured into his iconoclasm. The tensions implicit in his ambivalent attitudes toward the American scene provided much of this motive power. On the one hand, he sensed in the "gorgeous and prodigal" manifestations of American culture a vitality matching his own. On the other, he was moved to indignation by the discrepancy between the realities he observed about him and his vision of the kind of art, ethics, and personal behavior a society composed exclusively of truth-seekers and artists would produce. Caught up in this process of mutual attraction and repulsion, he developed an omnivorous appetite for all phases of the national life and letters. His iconoclasm, despite his disclaimers, had some reformist overtones, but it took the form mainly of such negative emotions as scorn and humorous disdain for whatever conflicted with his conception of what should be.

A minor paradox here is that, like most iconoclasts and satirists, he would have been extremely unhappy in his own version of Utopia. If Swift's compatriots, for example, had fully lived up to their responsibilities as animals capable of reason, the resulting uniformity of their behavior, however admirable, would have shorn the ideal of rationality of much of its luster. Swift might have experienced more peace of mind, but he would have been deprived of the delight he took in perfecting his satirical art. Similarly, Mencken—with nothing in American economics, politics, society, criticism, or art to react against—

would have lost his chief joy and main motive as an artist-journalist. His orientation developed out of "an aesthetic of aggression"—an awareness "that stimulation comes only by opposition." He described his mission in life as "the tracking down of quacks of all sorts, and the appreciative exhibition of their multifarious tricks to catch coneys." Of his own writing, he said, "It always seeks to expose a false pretence, to blow up a wobbly axiom, to uncover a sham virtue."[4] If puritanism, philistinism, chicanery, and logic-chopping had all been replaced by their opposites, the American scene would no longer have been gaudy and glorious. To retain his sanity and happiness, Mencken would have had to create an imaginary world in which they existed.

Literary journalism was the main workshop in which the writers of Mencken's generation studied their craft. In wanting to develop an individual style capable of dramatizing his impressions, Mencken was like many of his colleagues with literary interests. With that aim in mind, he carefully pondered the essays of Thomas Huxley, whose ability to deal lucidly with difficult subjects he never ceased to admire. At various times, he took as his models the works of Thackeray, Kipling, Shaw, O. Henry, Mark Twain, Ambrose Bierce, and George Ade. His style inevitably reflected both the strengths and weaknesses of the kind of training he received in the hurly-burly of daily journalism. The *New York Sun,* as we have previously noted, helped him to learn to see the life about him and to interpret it vividly, much as novelists like Crane, Norris, and Dreiser had learned to do during their newspaper experience. The *New York Sun* editorials also encouraged him to attack those he regarded as frauds and mountebanks, but to bring good sense and good humor to the process. The same paper had its bad effects "because," as he commented many years afterward, "it showed a considerable artificiality of style, and made me overestimate the value of smart phrases."[5] He never completely succeeded in suppressing the impulse to use the smart phrase rather than one more apt or just. Another part of his apprenticeship was learning to write quickly and copiously in order to meet deadlines—a virtue in a newspaper writer but not necessarily in a literary or social critic.

His newspaper experience left an indelible mark on his personal attitudes. Throughout his working life, he cherished his concept of newspapermen, especially those he had known in his youth, as a privileged group who observed the human comedy from the front row and could say pretty much what they pleased about it, providing they had a style which would attract as well as startle readers. He looked upon himself as a newspaperman before all else, with magazine editing and literary criticism in second place.

As illustrated by his reviewing for *The Smart Set,* literary journalism had still another significance: it was the major channel through which the spirit of the moral and literary revolt of the nineties was transmitted to the twenties. With his efforts sometimes paralleling and sometimes differing from those of bohemian critics like Huneker and Pollard, he exerted a major influence in bringing about the transition between the two periods. The fixity with which he held to his basic premises accentuates the fact that the eighties and nineties, not the twenties, shaped his attitudes. Through denunciation and ridicule similar to those in the more extreme of the little magazines of the nineties, he publicized the dangers of literary commercialism and defied the genteel tradition, with its insistence that American letters should be predominantly "Anglo-Saxon," optimistic, and morally uplifting. By discussing and urging his audience to read authors like Ibsen and Shaw, Pinero and Wilde, Sudermann and Hauptmann, Zola and Wells, Mark Twain and Norris, Crane and Dreiser, he helped popularize the idea that art and artists are important and that one function of art may legitimately be to question accepted axioms and standards. In these ways he assisted in creating a climate of opinion which once again made a moderate degree of revolt possible. By attacking hypocrisy, puritanism, philistinism, and censorship, and pointing out the need for a new national ethic, he suggested the form the moral rebellion might take and what it might seek to accomplish. By stressing the tradition of Norris, Crane, and Dreiser and calling on American writers to challenge the shibboleths of the native culture and deal realistically or satirically with the life they knew, he indicated the goals he hoped the literary uprising would attain.

His reactions to World War I help explain his determination to exploit the opportunities for insurrection he felt sure would occur after the lifting of wartime restrictions. As he saw the refurbishing of the Anglo-Saxon tradition, the solidifying of public opinion behind the tyranny of the majority, and the squashing of the rights of German-Americans and other dissenting minorities, he was more certain than ever of the soundness of the standards by which he had previously condemned various aspects of the native culture. Though more than ever repelled by what was happening nationally, he was also more fully resolved to see that the group with which he identified himself, whether he conceived of it as the German-Americans or as an intellectual and aesthetic elite, should not only regain their rights as American citizens, but should also puncture the pretensions of their "Anglo-Saxon" enemies. At the same time, he was still fascinated by the American people, championed their speech as a language distinct from British English, and predicted that they would have enough sense to rise up against Wilsonian policies.

He would, however, have found the trials of wartime much less bearable if a considerable number of young intellectuals and writers, beginning about 1912, had not sympathized with the kind of revolt he advocated. Their disillusionment with American culture, preceding the greater disillusionment many of them felt later when they returned from war service, was partly inspired by the revival of interest in the literary movement of the nineties Mencken had helped stimulate through such pieces as his review of Frank Harris's biography of Wilde. Although Mencken's background and motives differed considerably from those of the young intellectuals, his conviction that the United States needed a moral and literary reawakening, together with the assurance and literary bravura with which he stated it, strongly impressed them. They began to look to him for guidance, and he was able to profit from the alliance he formed with them.

It would be superfluous, at this point, to repeat the conclusions reached in chapters 6 and 7 regarding his strengths and weaknesses as a mentor to the younger generation in the first few postwar years, the significance of the continued swing of his interests away from literary to social and political issues, and the reasons for his success in reaching a much larger audience through the *Mercury* than he had ever reached through *The Smart Set*. By 1922, when many young writers believed they had absorbed his message and taken his measure, he was already reaching a larger and more diverse public through his newspaper articles and his series of *Prejudices*. At first, he knew of no magazine through which he could regularly reach this wider range of readers, to many of whom his ideas were novel, exhilarating, and even shocking. The *Mercury*, backed by a reputable and financially solvent publisher, provided exactly the vehicle he needed. It reflects the shrewdness of his judgments about the interests and needs of middle-class Americans who were seeking to be sophisticated and enlightened. With the exception of a small minority of political radicals and those young writers who felt they had outgrown him, even his more venturesome readers were likely to think that his unorthodoxy took them as far as they cared to go. His more cautious and conservative customers, on the other hand, might grumble at his ridicule of the politics of "normalcy," his insistence that even radicals were entitled to speak, publish, and organize freely, or his slams at professors or fraternal organizations; but the more perceptive of them, at least, realized his kinship with them. They knew that he was "safe" on essentials—that he stood opposed to labor agitation, socialism, or anything else that threatened the free-enterprise system. They realized that, like themselves, he assumed that capitalism, sparked by economic individualism, was a stable and permanent system, governed by economic laws as inevitable in their operation as natural laws.

His middle-class traits helped him, then, to size up the audience of the *Mercury*, especially in the years between 1924 and the crash of 1929, but they also restricted his ability to recognize and grasp the significance of certain major problems of his time. The norms embodied in his own way of life were themselves the product of a transitional period in the history of Baltimore, but he tended to assume that they had a universal validity. His basic conservatism was accompanied by a corresponding distrust of sudden innovations and radical proposals to make over society and the existing political system. He had no desire to be identified with artistic and political movements at either the extreme right or the extreme left. Conscious of belonging to an elite, he was not much concerned about the economic problems of farmers and workingmen, whom he usually classified as members of the mob. Though critical of the plutocracy, he was not much concerned, either, about the economic and social problems caused by the concentration of great wealth in a few hands.

Ironically, it was his persistent economic conservatism which, with the onset of the depression of the thirties, alienated many readers whom it had previously attracted. The crisis in finance and banking, the slump in business and industry, and the inability of local and state governments to cope with social unrest and mass unemployment shocked millions of Americans into questioning the old economic verities. Mencken did not react in the same way. Following the principles he had learned from his father and from Sumner, he argued that in time the economic system would right itself. Previously, he had goaded and guided his readers, but now many of them were beginning to move beyond his range. As the circulation of the *Mercury* dropped, the only advice he had to offer in a time of national catastrophe was to leave well enough alone. In 1932, partly out of sympathy with the Democratic aim of repealing Prohibition, he supported Franklin Roosevelt, but by early 1933 he was worrying about the assertion of federal power under the New Deal and the "visionaries whooping up gaudy schemes to succor the depressed and lay on new taxes."[6] Late that year, realizing that he was breasting currents too strong for him, he wisely retired from the *Mercury*. In the *Baltimore Sun* and in occasional magazine articles, he continued to snipe at "Roosevelt Minor" and the Brain Trust, but he also devoted himself to such works as *Treatise on Right and Wrong* (1934) and the early chapters of his memoirs.

During this period, several major changes occurred in his personal life. He had created a public image of himself as a resolute bachelor who valued independence above all else, but privately he was as loyal to home and family as his father had been. "Next to agreeable work as a means of attaining happiness," he declared, "I put what Huxley called the domestic affections—the day to day intercourse with family and friends."

In 1925, explaining why he had never married, he wrote, "I have always had a home in Baltimore, with my mother and sister, that is more comfortable than any I could set up myself." His mother's death in December of that year broke this pattern. "I begin to realize," he confided to Dreiser, "how inextricably my life was interwoven with my mother's. A hundred times a day I find myself planning to tell her something or ask her for this or that. . . . The house seems strange, as if the people in it were deaf and dumb." This feeling of emptiness in his life helps account for his long courtship of Sara Haardt, culminating in their marriage in 1930. Although he was made the butt of much joshing comment among his friends and in the national press, he could have cited chapter and verse from *In Defense of Women* to justify his action. One reason for "the relatively late marriages of superior men," he had noted, "is . . . that, as a man grows older, the disabilities he suffers by marriage tend to diminish and the advantages to increase."[7]

When he first met Sara in 1923, she had just turned twenty-five and was teaching English at Goucher College. A native of Montgomery, Alabama, she was a witty and charming southern belle. She had the additional merit of being partly of German descent and having considerable talent as a writer of fiction. Only her perilously frail health, constantly threatened by tuberculosis, prevented them from marrying sooner. They established themselves in a large apartment at 704 Cathedral Street decorated with the Victorian bric-a-brac she loved to collect. Even with his constant care and skillful nursing, she lived only five years after their marriage. After her death, he called their life together "a beautiful adventure," adding, "Now I feel completely dashed and dismayed. . . . What a cruel and idiotic world we live in!"[8] Soon afterward, he rejoined his brother August at the old family home in Hollins Street.

No matter how much understanding is brought to bear upon a study of Mencken, he will always remain a controversial figure. Because of the wide range of his interests, the tensions and contradictions in his thought, his intermingling of humor with contentiousness and dogmatism, and the multiplicity of roles he assumed as journalist, literary critic, social and political commentator, and scholar, he inevitably invites a wide range of responses. Those who dismiss him as a "mere" journalist or a third-rate disciple of Shaw and Nietzsche greatly underestimate his importance, while those who rank him with Swift and Voltaire probably unduly exaggerate it. Since this study has tried to steer a middle course between these extremes, it is fair to ask one final question: what were his most enduring contributions to American culture?

On balance, the two aspects of his work which seem most durable are his libertarianism—his affirmation of the right to dissent—and the gusto and artistry with which he expresses it. The evils he attacked on behalf of "common decency" take different forms today than they did in the twenties, but they still exist, as they have in every age. While recognizing that many of his principles were basically conservative and that those he brought to his iconoclastic mission were not fully thought out, one may yet hope that America will continue to produce rebels as determined and able as he. Although he often indulged in stereotyping and namecalling, he usually did so with a characteristic humor which warned the reader not to be completely taken in. By and large, his weapons were those he urged the young southerners to wield in their fight against the old tradition—the "weapons of sound information, of common sense, of good taste, of lively wit, of ready humor." His style conveys his delight in combat, his sense of exhilaration at "dancing with arms and legs" in defiance of the multitude. "The unimaginative and ignoble man," he maintained, "likes the grayness, as a worm likes the dark; he wants to be made secure in his wallow; he craves certainties to protect him—a simple and gross religion, safety for his precious money, no wild ideas to craze his wife, Prohibition, the rope for agitators, no bawdy twanging of lyres. It is the business of the artist to blast his contentment with the sounds of joy."[9] At his best, Mencken performed this function supremely well. The "bawdy twanging" of his own lyre is his legacy to America.

Notes

Since the notes give due acknowledgment to the sources which proved most valuable for the purposes of this study, they are the equivalent of a selective bibliography. A comprehensive and authoritative record of works by and about Mencken is readily available in *H.L.M.: The Mencken Bibliography,* compiled by Betty Adler with the assistance of Jane Wilhelm (Baltimore: Johns Hopkins Press, 1961). This volume is supplemented and brought up to date by the check lists in *Menckeniana,* a quarterly published by the Enoch Pratt Free Library, Baltimore.

Among the noteworthy studies which reached me only after my own manuscript was in its final form are Guy J. Forgue's *H. L. Mencken: L'Homme, L'Oeuvre, L'Influence* (1967), Carl Bode's *Mencken* (1969), and Ellen Moers's *Two Dreisers* (1969).

In the notes that follow, full information is given about an item the first time it is presented. If subsequent references are made to the same source, a short title is used. If a letter is available in both manuscript (holograph, typescript, or copy) and in printed collections, the published version is consistently cited.

The abbreviations used are as follows:

AM	*The American Mercury*
EPBP	Ellis Parker Butler Papers, Manuscript Division, New York Public Library
EPL	Mencken Collection, Enoch Pratt Free Library, Baltimore
HLM	H.L. Mencken
HoL	Houghton Library, Harvard University

IGP   Isaac Goldberg Papers, Manuscript Division, New York Public Library

PaL   Dreiser-Mencken Collection, Rare Book Room, University of Pennsylvania Library

PL   Letters to and from HLM, microfilm collection, Princeton University Library

SS   *The Smart Set*

1. MENCKEN AND *THE AMERICAN MERCURY,* 1924–1926

1. How it came about that the new magazine was given this title is discussed in M.K. Singleton, *H.L. Mencken and the American Mercury Adventure* (Durham, N.C.: Duke University Press, 1962), pp. 33–34.

2. "Editorial," *AM,* I (January 1924), 30. This unsigned editorial announcing the scope and aims of the magazine ostensibly speaks as much for George Jean Nathan, the coeditor, as for HLM, but its substance, style, and tone show that it was written by the latter without much deference to Nathan's views. This judgment is confirmed by a letter to Gamaliel Bradford, January 2, [1924], in which HLM, referring to the editorial, uses such phrases as "I admit" and "I offer." See Guy J. Forgue, ed., *Letters of H.L. Mencken* (New York: Knopf, 1961), pp. 263–64.

3. The time of the first meeting between HLM and Nathan is incorrectly given as May 1908 in *The Intimate Notebooks of George Jean Nathan* (New York: Knopf, 1932), p. 94, and William Manchester, *Disturber of the Peace: The Life of H.L. Mencken* (New York: Harper, 1951), p. 38. This earlier date is obviously in error since it precedes HLM's own association with *The Smart Set.*

4. Owen Hatteras [joint pseudonym of HLM and Nathan], "Conversation VII–On Editing a Magazine," *SS,* LXV (June 1921), 105.

5. *A Personal Word* ([New York]: *The Smart Set,* 1921), p. 7.

6. "Foreword," *The World in Falseface* (New York: Knopf, 1923), pp. x–xi.

7. I have followed the account of the founding of the *Mercury* in Carl R. Dolmetsch, *The Smart Set: A History and Anthology* (New York: Dial Press, 1966), pp. 84–88; it differs in some respects from that given in Singleton, *H.L. Mencken,* pp. 28–54.

8. In the preface to *Americana 1925* (New York: Knopf, 1925), HLM explained that the purpose of the "Americana" department was "to make the enlightened minority of Americans familiar, by documentary evidence, with what is going on in the minds of the masses—the great herd of undifferentiated good-humored, goose-stepping, superstitious, sentimental, credulous, striving, romantic American people." The quotations selected from a wide variety of

sources dripped "with the juices of Kiwanis, the American Legion, the Ku Klux, Rotary, the Mystic Shrine, the Elks, the Sons of the Revolution and the Y.M.C.A." The items were preceded by brief and often artfully ironic introductions. The contribution of "Americana" to folklore, humor, and satire is analyzed in Singleton, *H.L. Mencken,* pp. 43–45, 96–110, and passim.

Manchester, in *Disturber,* p. 150, errs in saying that Nathan alone was responsible for "Clinical Notes." Mencken and Nathan wrote the section jointly from January 1924 through July 1925. It first appeared under Nathan's name alone in August 1925 and was continued by him until February 1930, when the department was dropped.

9. HLM to Howard Mumford Jones, July 31, [1923], HoL.
10. [Announcement of the relinquishing of the editorship . . . and founding *The American Mercury*] (New York: [*The Smart Set*], October 10, 1923) .
11. Singleton, *H.L. Mencken,* pp. 55–59.
12. HLM to Louis Untermeyer, July 20, 1916, PL.
13. Figures from N.W. Ayer & Son's *American Newspaper Annual and Directory,* vols. for 1915 through 1924. The figures for the earlier years, based on publisher's estimates, may represent the total copies printed and sent out to subscribers and newsstands more accurately than they do the net paid circulation. The figure for 1923, the certified estimate submitted to the Audit Bureau of Circulations, is probably substantially accurate.
14. HLM, "Postscript," *Three Years, 1924–1927* (New York: *American Mercury,* 1927) , p. 35; figures from *Three Years,* pp. 7–8, and N.W. Ayer & Son's *American Newspaper Annual and Directory,* vols. for 1926 through 1930.
15. "Postscript," *Three Years,* p. 35. A more detailed survey of the *Mercury* readership appears in Singleton, *H.L. Mencken,* pp. 156–63.
16. George Jean Nathan and HLM, "Clinical Notes," *AM,* III (September 1924) , 63; reprinted in HLM, *Prejudices: Fifth Series* (New York: Knopf, 1926), p. 304; "Clinical Notes," *AM,* I (March 1924) , 323–24; "Editorial," *AM,* III (September 1924) , 34.

As illustrated in the preceding entry, a piece in "Clinical Notes" is attributed to HLM only when he reprinted it as his own or when the content and phrasing clearly indicate that it is by him rather than by Nathan.

17. *Prejudices: Third Series* (New York: Knopf, 1922), pp. 12–14.
18. "Editorial," *AM,* VI (November 1925) , 286.
19. "Editorial," *AM,* I (March 1924) , 296, 295; revised and reprinted as "The Husbandman," *Prejudices: Fourth Series* (New York: Knopf, 1924) , pp. 43–60.
20. Lippmann, "H.L. Mencken," *Men of Destiny* (New York: Macmillan, 1927) , p. 70.

21. "A Hero of the Open Spaces," *AM*, VIII (May 1926), 126–27. Like other reviews in HLM's book section, "The Library," this one has its own title. All notes referring to these reviews will, as in this case, cite the title of the specific review.

22. "Three Volumes of Fiction," *AM*, I (February 1924), 252.

23. "Other Biographies," *AM*, V (August 1925), 510; "Clinical Notes," *AM*, II (May 1924), 56; *AM*, VII (March 1926), xx, xxii.

24. "Mark Twain," *SS*, LX (October 1919), 143.

25. "The Literary Olio," *SS*, XXVII (February 1909), 156; HLM to Will Durant, n.d., quoted in Durant, *On the Meaning of Life* (New York: Ray Long & Richard H. Smith, Inc., 1932), p. 31.

26. Davis, "Prolegomena to a Future Christology," *Show Window* (New York: John Day Co., 1927), p. 143.

27. "Stevenson Again," *AM*, IV (January 1925), 125: "Religion," p. 2, IGP. All items citing "IGP" as the source refer to the autobiographical notes HLM dictated early in 1925 for the use of Isaac Goldberg, who was then writing *The Man Mencken: A Biographical and Critical Survey* (New York: Simon and Schuster, 1925).

28. The State of the Country," *AM*, III (September 1924), 123–24.

29. *The Education of Henry Adams*, Modern Library ed. (New York: Random House, 1931), pp. 224, 231; "Preface" [by HLM alone] in Nathan and HLM, *The American Credo* (New York: Knopf, 1920); Davis, *Show Window*, p. 132.

30. "Counter-Offensive," *AM*, VIII (May 1926), 124.

31. The articles HLM dispatched from Dayton, Tennessee, the scene of the Scopes trial, ran in the *Baltimore Evening Sun* from July 9 through July 18, 1925; several of them are reprinted in "The Baltimore Nonpareil," *Star Reporters and 34 of Their Stories*, ed. Ward Greene (New York: Random House, 1948), pp. 226–255. In the "Editorial" in the *Mercury* for October 1925, HLM commented on the career of William Jennings Bryan, who died a few days after acting as chief prosecuting attorney in the trial. In the expanded form in which this editorial is reprinted in *Prejudices: Fifth Series*, it is one of the most brilliantly sustained of HLM's satirical portraits of popular American leaders. HLM reminisces about his experiences in Dayton in "Inquisition," *The Days of H.L. Mencken*, 3 vols. in 1 (New York: Knopf, 1947), III, 214–38.

    Ray Ginger, *Six Days or Forever?* (Boston: Beacon Press, 1958) is a thorough study of the Scopes trial and its religious, social, and political implications.

32. *AM*, VIII (May 1926), 123–24.

33. "Editorial," *AM*, III (December 1924), 422.

34. "The Origin of Variations," *AM*, VIII (July 1926), 379. Morley Roberts was the author of the volume reviewed.

35. "Genesis vs. Sense," *AM*, VI (November 1925), 382; "Osler," *AM*, V (August 1925), 507.

36. "Sabbath Meditation" in Nathan and HLM, "Clinical Notes," *AM,* II (May 1924), 60, reprinted in part, under the same title, in *A Mencken Chrestomathy,* ed. H.L. Mencken (New York: Knopf, 1949), pp. 84–85; "Fides ante Intellectum," *AM,* VII (February 1926), 251–52; William James, *The Varieties of Religious Experience,* Modern Library ed. (New York: Random House, 1902), p. 414; author's italics.

37. Sumner was Spencer's main American disciple. In a letter to Albert G. Keller, dated January 5, 1932, HLM said, "The books of your old chief, Dr. Sumner, made a powerful impression on me when I was young, and their influence has survived. I only wish that such things as 'The Forgotten Man' could be printed as circulars in editions of millions" *(Letters of H.L. Mencken,* p. 337).

38. *AM,* I (January 1924), 28; Sumner, "The Forgotten Man" (lecture delivered before the Brooklyn Historical Society on January 30, 1883), in *Sumner Today,* ed. Maurice R. Davie (New Haven: Yale University Press, 1940), pp. 15, 11.

39. "Preface," *The Days,* I, viii.

40. *Sumner Today,* p. 14; "Editorial," *AM,* II (May 1924), 26.

41. "Birth Control" in Nathan and HLM, "Clinical Notes," *AM,* IV (April 1925), 452; HLM, "The Afraamerican: New Style," *AM,* VII (February 1926), 255.

42. *Sumner Today,* p. 15; HLM, "Babbitt as Philosopher," *AM,* IX (September 1926), 125–26.

43. *Sumner Today,* pp. 6, 25; *AM,* I (January 1924), 27.

44. Quotations in the preceding two paragraphs are from *AM,* I (January 1924), 28–29.

45. *AM,* II (May 1924), 26; *Sumner Today,* p. 25; Richard Hofstadter, *Social Darwinism in American Thought, 1860–1915* (Philadelphia: University of Pennsylvania Press, 1945), p. 176.

46. "Editorial," *AM,* VIII (July 1926), 287–89.

47. "The Heroic Age," *AM,* VII (March 1926), 382–83. Illustrating how "a sinister minority" could force through restrictive legislation, HLM added, "Law Enforcement becomes the new state religion. A law is something that A wants and can hornswoggle B, C, D, E and F into giving him—by bribery, by lying, by bluff and bluster, by making faces. G and H are thereupon bound to yield it respect—nay, to worship it."
This argument was one of his favorites and was drawn from Sumner. See *Sumner Today,* pp. 4, 17, and Sumner, *What Social Classes Owe to Each Other* (New York: Harper & Bros., 1883), pp. 123, 132. On the latter page, Sumner uses the argument to show how prohibition laws worked a hardship against the Forgotten Man.

48. *AM,* VIII (July 1926), 289, and VII (March 1926), 382.

49. "Editorial," *AM,* VIII (May 1926), 34.

50. "Editorial," *AM*, VIII (August 1926), 416.
51. "The Immortal Democrat," *AM*, IX September 1926), 124; "Editorial Notes," *AM*, IX (September 1926), xxxvi; "Editorial," *AM*, IV (February 1925); HLM's italics.
52. "Books about Books," *SS*, LXV (June 1921), 143. Speaking in this article of More's "pertinacity," HLM remarked, "The vacillating type of man, believing one thing this year and the contrary next year, and always ready to be converted back and forth—this fellow I dislike intensely."
53. "The National Letters," *Prejudices: Second Series* (New York: Knopf, 1920), p. 65; *Notes on Democracy* (New York: Knopf, 1926), pp. 205–6.
54. "Towards a Realistic Aesthetic," *Prejudices: Fourth Series*, pp. 237–40, and "Veritas" in Nathan and HLM, "Clinical Notes," *AM*, V (June 1925), 215–16; *AM*, I (January 1924), 27.
55. "Editorial," *AM*, II (June 1924), 158; "Critical Note" in Nathan and HLM, "Clinical Notes," *AM*, I (January 1924), 74, reprinted in "From a Critic's Notebook," *Prejudices: Fourth Series*, pp. 139–40; HLM's italics.

2. CHILD OF BALTIMORE

1. "Editorial," *AM*, I (April 1924), 408–9; "Katzenjammer," *AM*, VII (January 1926), 125.
2. "On Being an American," *Prejudices: Third Series*, p. 14.
3. Hulbert Footner, *Maryland Main and the Eastern Shore* (New York: Appleton-Century Co., 1942), p. 8; "Back to Normal," in *Rededicating America: Life and Recent Speeches of Warren G. Harding*, ed. Frederick Schortemeier (Indianapolis: Bobbs-Merrill, 1920), p. 223; Harding's encomium on the American village is quoted in Roger Butterfield, *The American Past* (New York: Simon and Schuster, 1957), p. 381.
4. "The Last Round," *Baltimore Evening Sun*, October 4, 1920, reprinted in *A Carnival of Buncombe*, ed. Malcolm Moos (Baltimore: Johns Hopkins Press, 1956), p. 23; "A Short View of Gamalielese," *The Nation*, CXII (April 27, 1921), 621.
5. *The Nation*, CXIV (May 3, 1922), 517–19.
6. *AM*, VII (March, 1926), 382.
7. *Minority Report: H.L.M.'s Notebooks* (New York: Knopf, 1956), p. 118.
8. Charles Hirschfeld, *Baltimore, 1870–1900: Studies in Social History*, Johns Hopkins University Studies in Historical and Political Science, series LIX, no. 2 (Baltimore: Johns Hopkins Press, 1941), p. 32.
9. *The Nation*, CXIV (May 3, 1922), 517; Woodward, *Origins of the New South, 1877–1913* ([Baton Rouge]: Louisiana State University Press, 1951), p. 162.

10. The details about the financial and industrial development of Baltimore are from Hirschfeld, *Baltimore,* pp. 32–44.

11. For the facts of HLM's life and his mature impressions of the significance of his early experiences, this chapter relies to a considerable extent on the autobiographical notes written for Isaac Goldberg in 1925 and on *The Days,* especially the first volume. Since HLM responded to an artistic compulsion to embroider some incidents while writing his memoirs, a question might be raised as to the accuracy of his details. "A Girl from Red Lion, P.A." in vol. 1 and the account of the visit to the Vatican in vol. 3, for example, are in the tradition of the tall tale. But even these stories had their basis in fact, and throughout *The Days* statements about specific names, dates, and events are usually correct. With a reporter's concern for accuracy, HLM did not rely on memory alone, but referred to his own extensive files, including the notes for Goldberg, and consulted relatives and friends. Once the easily detected elaborations are discounted, *The Days* remains, therefore, the most reliable record we have of the author's boyhood and youth.

12. *The Days,* I, 92–93, vii.

13. Ibid., I, 212–15. HLM also reminisced about the *Ellicott City Times in* "The Grandstand Flirts with the Bleachers," *SS,* XLV (April 1915), 434.

14. *The Days,* I, 84–85, 255–62.

15. "My Father," pp. 4–5, IGP.

16. *The Days,* I, 92; "My Grandfather," pp. 1, 5, IGP.

17. "My Father," p. 7, IGP; *The Days,* I, 251–52.

18. "My Father," p. 7, IGP.

19. "Heretics," *AM,* III (October 1924), 250–51.

20. This general account of German-Americanism is based chiefly on John A. Hawgood, *The Tragedy of German-America* (New York and London: G.P. Putnam's Sons, 1940), pp. xi-xviii, 21–53, 267–86, and Carl Wittke, *The German-Language Press in America* (Lexington: University of Kentucky Press, 1957), pp. 162–68.

21. A small group who dissented from this typical view were the German Methodists, organized in the 1830s by Wilhelm Nast, who was converted to Methodism after his arrival in the United States. Like many American leaders of his church, Nast favored prohibition and strict observance of the Sabbath. See Wittke, *The German-Language Press,* pp. 182–84.

22. *The Days,* I, 100–101.

23. HLM to Albert G. Keller, December 15, 1939, *Letters of H.L. Mencken,* p. 441. HLM depicted his father as satirically cross-examining him and Charlie on their return from Sunday school with such questions as " 'Have you got to Jonah yet? Have you heard about him swallowing the whale?' " (*The Days,* I, 177–78.)

24. HLM to Will Durant, n.d., quoted in Durant, *On the Meaning of Life,* p. 34.
25. "My Reading," p. 4, IGP.
26. A detailed account of the European Menckens based on information supplied by HLM is given in Goldberg, *The Man Mencken,* chap. II; it is supplemented in HLM, "Preface by the Editor" in Johann Burkhard Mencken, *The Charlatanry of the Learned,* trans. Francis E. Litz (New York: Knopf, 1937), pp. 3–45. HLM arranged for the publication of the latter volume as a means of paying tribute to his favorite ancestor, whose satire on pedantry and pretence was written in Latin and first printed in 1715. HLM was forty before he read the translation. In his preface, he said that "it . . . no little delighted me, to find that a man of my name, nearly two hundred years in his grave, had devoted himself so heartily to an enterprise that had engaged me day in and day out in a far country—the tracking down of quacks of all sorts, and the appreciative exhibition of their multifarious tricks to catch coneys."
27. Goldberg, *The Man Mencken,* p. 53; *The Days,* I, 99.
28. Goldberg, *The Man Mencken,* p. 48; "My Father," pp. 6–7, IGP. In 1919 HLM, responding to a request from Alfred A. Knopf, chose the family coat of arms as the design to be stamped on the front cover of each of his books.
29. The quotations in the preceding two paragraphs are from "Miscellaneous Notes," V, 3, and XI, 5–6, IGP.
30. *The Days,* I, 25–26.
31. See HLM's definition of "home" in "On Living in Baltimore," *Prejudices: Fifth Series,* p. 240; "Miscellaneous Notes," XI, 6, IGP.
32. *The Days,* I, 60–61, 236.
33. Review of I.A.R. Wylie, *The Germans,* in "The Prophet of the Superman," SS, XXXVI (March 1912), 157.
34. *The Days,* I, 252; *Wisconsin Banner,* October 16, 1855, quoted in Hawgood, *The Tragedy of German-America,* p. 47.
35. Bradford to HLM, December 31, 1923, in *The Letters of Gamaliel Bradford, 1918–1931,* ed. Van Wyck Brooks (Boston and New York: Houghton Mifflin, 1934), p. 165; HLM to Bradford, January 2, [1924], *Letters of H.L. Mencken,* p. 263.
36. "Editorial Notes," *AM,* VII (January 1926), xx.
37. Wilson, "Mencken Through the Wrong End of the Telescope," *The New Yorker,* XXVI (May 6, 1950), 113.
38. The information and quotations about HLM's reading are from *The Days,* I, 157–75.
39. "The Greatest of American Writers," SS, XXXI (June 1910), 153; "A Nietzschean, a Swedenborgian and Other Queer Fowl," SS, XL (June 1913), 146; "My Reading," pp. 2–3, IGP.

40. *The Days*, III, 40; "My Reading," p. 3, IGP; *The Days*, I, 173; "A Glance at the Spring Fiction," *SS*, XXX (April 1910), 153.

In justifying his preference for H.G. Wells's novels as opposed to those of Dickens, HLM wrote, "I know very well that the author of 'David Copperfield' was a greater artist than the author of 'Mr. Polly,' just as I know that the Archbishop of Canterbury is a more virtuous man than my good friend, Fred the Bartender; but all the same, I prefer Wells and Fred to Dickens and the Archbishop. In such matters one must allow a lot to individual taste and prejudices" (*SS*, XXXI [June 1910], 154–55).

41. Thackeray, *The History of Henry Esmond, Esq., The Memoirs of Barry Lyndon, Esq., Denis Duval*, 3 vols. in 1 (Boston: Samuel E. Cassino, 1887), II, 309, and footnote, 246.

42. "Oyez! Oyez! All Ye Who Read Books," *SS*, XXVI (December 1908), 156.

43. Quoted in Jay B. Hubbell, *The South in American Literature, 1607–1900* ([Durham, N.C.]: Duke University Press, 1954), p. 718.

44. The passages from *The Manufacturers' Record* are quoted in Woodward, *Origins of the New South*, pp. 140, 148.

45. "My Father," p. 4, IGP.

46. "Good Old Baltimore," *SS*, XL (May 1913), 107.

47. "A Preposterous Pretence," November 22, 1907, in "Editorials and Dramatic Reviews Contributed to the *Baltimore Sun*, 1906–1910," p. 55, one of several scrapbooks kept by HLM and deposited in EPL. Dates of the clippings cited in this and succeeding notes are indicated as shown in the scrapbooks.

In this editorial, HLM uses the spelling, *Pittsburg*, accepted at the time. The final "h" was not officially added until a few years later.

48. "Explaining the Returns," 1910, in "Editorials and Other Articles, The Baltimore *Evening Sun*, 1910–1912," 2 vols., I, 178 (EPL); also "A Preposterous Pretence."

49. EPL has two copies of this scarce "monograph."

50. *The Nation*, CXIV (May 3, 1922), 518. Valuable accounts of how southern writers after the Civil War made use of the myth of the plantation appear in Hubbell, *The South in American Literature*, pp. 738–43, 789–804, and passim; Gregory Paine, "Introduction," *Southern Prose Writers: Representative Selections* (New York: American Book Co., 1947), pp. lxxxvii-xciii, cv-cviii; Francis P. Gaines, *The Southern Plantation: A Study in the Development and Accuracy of a Tradition* (New York: Columbia University Press, 1925), pp. 62–94.

51. *SS*, XL (May 1913), 112.

3. YOUNG REBEL

1. The phrase, "the genteel tradition," was probably originated by
   George Santayana, who featured it in his address, "The Genteel
   Tradition in American Philosophy" (1911) and again in *The
   Genteel Tradition at Bay* (New York: Scribner's, 1931). The first
   of these appears in *Winds of Doctrine* (New York: Scribner's,
   1913) and has frequently been reprinted.
   Among the more valuable commentaries on the concept of the
   genteel and its advocates are Henry F. May, *The End of American
   Innocence: A Study of the First Years of Our Own Time, 1912–
   1917* (Chicago: Quadrangle Books, 1964), pp. 3–79; Willard
   Thorp, "Defenders of Ideality," in *Literary History of the United
   States*, 3 vols., ed. Robert E. Spiller, et al. (New York: Macmillan,
   1948), II, 809–26; and Danforth R. Ross, "The Genteel Tradition:
   Its Characteristics and Its Origins" (Ph.D. dissertation, University
   of Minnesota, 1954).

2. R.B. Hovey, "George Edward Woodberry: Genteel Exile," *The
   New England Quarterly*, XXIII (December 1950), 505.

3. Malcolm Cowley, "Naturalism in American Literature," in *Evolutionary Thought in America*, ed. Stow Persons (New Haven:
   Yale University Press, 1950), p. 301.

4. *The Writings of Thomas Bailey Aldrich*, Ponkapog edition, 9 vols.
   (Boston and New York: Houghton Mifflin, 1907–11), II, 71–72;
   Edmund Clarence Stedman, ed., *An American Anthology, 1787–
   1899* (Boston and New York: Houghton Mifflin, 1900), p. 478.

5. For a discussion of the policies of the major publishers and maga-
   zines from the 1890s through the early 1900s, see William Charvat,
   "Literature as Business," *Literary History of the United States*,
   II, 953–68.

6. Stedman, "What is Criticism?," in *Genius and Other Essays* (New
   York: Moffat, Yard and Co., 1911), p. 39, author's italics; Howells,
   A Hazard of New Fortunes, 2 vols. in 1 (New York: Harper,
   1891), I, 186–87.

7. Gilder to an unnamed superintendent of public schools, enclosed
   in a letter to Mark Twain, January 8, 1886, in *Letters of Richard
   Watson Gilder*, ed. Rosamond Gilder (Boston and New York:
   Houghton Mifflin, 1916), pp. 398–99.

8. HLM, "My Reading," p. 4, IGP.

9. HLM, "Dichtung und Wahrheit," in *Damn! A Book of Calumny*
   (New York: Philip Goodman Co., 1918), p. 70.

10. HLM, "In Gowns of White," May 22, 1899, in "Early News
    Stories, *Baltimore Morning Herald*, 1899–1901," pp. 32–33 (EPL).

11. The discussion of American literary taste is based on Grant C.
    Knight, *The Critical Period in American Literature* (Chapel Hill:
    University of North Carolina Press, 1951), pp. 4–27; the quotation

is from the poem, "At the Funeral of a Minor Poet," in Aldrich, *Writings*, II, 94.

12. Knight, *The Critical Period*, pp. 11–12; Frank Luther Mott, *Golden Multitudes: The Story of Best Sellers in the United States* (New York: Macmillan, 1947), pp. 310–11.

13. Stedman, "Kipling's Ballads of 'The Seven Seas,' " in *Genius and Other Essays*, p. 270.

14. The preceding two paragraphs, including the quotation from Burgess, are derived from Sidney Kramer, *A History of Stone & Kimball and Herbert S. Stone & Co.* (Chicago: H. W. Forgue, 1940), pp. 30, 38–39.

    As Kramer points out (p. 31), the first issue of *The Chap-Book* was being made up at the time the first issue of *The Yellow Book* reached America. Because of this correspondence in time of issue and the differences in content and emphasis, it is inaccurate to say that *The Chap-Book* was merely an echo of the aestheticism of *The Yellow Book*.

15. HLM in *SS*, LXV (June 1921), 139, and "The American Novel," *Prejudices: Fourth Series*, p. 286.

16. HLM, *The Days*, II, 61; Huneker, *Steeplejack*, 2 vols. in 1 (New York: Scribner's, 1922), II, 190. Arnold T. Schwab gives a full account of *M'lle New York* in his *James Gibbons Huneker: Critic of the Seven Arts* (Stanford, Calif.: Stanford University Press, 1963), pp. 94–101.

17. The quotations are from the following articles in *M'lle New York:* "Polite Letters," I, no. 2 (August 23, 1895); "Foreword," I, no. 1 (August 1895); "Leader," I, no. 3 (September 1895); "The Doomed Republic," I, no. 1 (August 1895) and "Leader," II, no. 2 (November 1898); "Leader," I, no. 6 (October 1895).

    As the first two entries above illustrate, the issues were not always consistently dated. The pages were not numbered.

18. Gelett Burgess's reminiscences about *The Lark* are included in his *Bayside Bohemia: Fin de Siècle San Francisco and Its Little Magazines* (San Francisco: Book Club of California, 1954); James D. Hart's introduction to the same volume is also useful. *The Lark* is discussed chattily in Albert Parry, *Garrets and Pretenders: A History of Bohemianism in America* (New York: Covici, Friede, 1933), pp. 228–33 and passim.

19. HLM, "The Boudoir Balzac," in *Prejudices: First Series* (New York: Knopf, 1923), p. 129.

    The Criterion originated in St. Louis, but started up as a literary weekly in New York in 1897. Its contributors included conservatives as well as bohemians, but it continued to be irregularly bohemian until 1900, when it was converted into a relatively commonplace monthly. Darrell I. Drucker surveys its history and its wavering editorial policy in his "The Genteel

Rebellion: A Study of American Journalistic Impressionism in Terms of Its Audience, 1890 to 1920" (Ph.D. dissertation, University of Minnesota, 1954), pp. 451–81. See also Percival Pollard, *Their Day in Court* [reprint of the original edition published in 1909], Series in American Studies, ed. Joseph J. Kwiat (New York and London: Johnson Reprint Corporation, 1969), pp. 308–11.

20. HLM, *Prejudices: First Series,* p. 129, and "James Huneker" in *A Book of Prefaces* (Garden City, N.Y.: Garden City Publishing Co., 1927), pp. 190–91.

21. HLM, "Theodore Dreiser," *A Book of Prefaces,* p. 74.

22. HLM, *George Bernard Shaw: His Plays* (Boston and London: John W. Luce & Co., 1905), p. 91.

23. HLM, *The Philosophy of Friedrich Nietzsche* (Boston: Luce and Co., 1908), note 1, p. 148; note 3, p. 140; p. 89.

4. APPRENTICE YEARS, 1899–1908

1. HLM to Will Durant, n.d., quoted in Durant, *On the Meaning of Life,* pp. 30–32.

2. *The Days,* II. Supplementary details may be found in Goldberg, *The Man Mencken,* pp. 95–122; Edgar Kemler, *The Irreverent Mr. Mencken* (Boston: Little, Brown, 1950), pp. 21–37; and Manchester, *Disturber of the Peace,* pp. 18–37.

3. The teachers' comments are quoted in HLM, "My Earliest Writings," p. 2, IGP; see Goldberg, *The Man Mencken,* pp. 93–94.

4. All quotations in this paragraph are from HLM, *The Days,* II, ix-xi.

5. "Two Journalists," *AM,* III (December 1924), 505.

6. "Constructive Suggestion" in George Jean Nathan and HLM, "Clinical Notes," *AM,* III (November 1924), 310.

7. *AM,* III (December 1924), 505–6.

8. All the newspaper pieces cited in this section are from two scrapbooks in the Mencken Collection, EPL, entitled "Early News Stories, *Baltimore Morning Herald,* 1899–1901," and "Prose and Verse Contributed to the *Baltimore Morning Herald,* 1900–1902." In the notes that follow, dates of the clippings are indicated as shown in the scrapbooks. The symbol "ENS" is used to designate the first scrapbook, and "PV" to designate the second.

   For further information about HLM's contributions to the *Herald,* see Adler and Wilhelm, *H.L.M.: The Mencken Bibliography,* pp. 39–44.

9. *Baltimore Morning Herald,* April 28, 1899, "ENS," p. 21.

10. Ibid., 1899, "ENS," pp. 38–39; in *The Days,* II, 15, HLM ascribes this story to his "first week on the staff," i.e., the week following July 2.

11. *Baltimore Morning Herald,* 1899, "ENS," pp. 68–69.

12. Ibid., 1899, "ENS," p. 43.
13. Ibid., 1900, "ENS," pp. 171–72.
14. Ibid., 1900, "ENS," pp. 118–19.
15. "George Ade," in *Prejudices: First Series,* p. 121.
16. Quoted in *Baltimore Morning Herald,* June 6, 1899, "ENS," p. 29.
17. *The Days,* II, 158–61.
18. *Baltimore Morning Herald,* April 30, 1899, "ENS," p. 22.
19. *The Days,* II, 41–48.
20. *Baltimore Morning Herald,* May 26, 1901, "PV," p. 48.
21. "Knocks and Jollies," ibid., November 18, 1900, "PV," p. 15.
22. *Baltimore Morning Herald,* February 3, 1901, "PV," p. 36.
23. Ibid., 1900, "ENS," p. 118.
24. "Rhyme and Reason," ibid., November 11, 1900, "PV," p. 14. The quotation from *The Dunciad* appears in book III, 1. 43.
25. *Baltimore Morning Herald,* November 4, 1900, "PV," p. 13.
26. "The Burden of Humor," SS, XXXIX (February 1913), 151.
27. William Fink [pseudonym of HLM], "Thoughts on Mortality," *SS,* XLIV (November 1914), 21.
28. *SS,* XXXIX (February 1913), 153.
29. Six "Untold Tales," undated and with the explicit morals omitted, are reprinted in Goldberg, *The Man Mencken,* pp. 343–70.
30. *Baltimore Morning Herald,* December 31, 1900, "PV," p. 27.
31. *The Days,* II, 60; the verses accepted by the *Baltimore American* were probably printed some time in 1894.
32. HLM, "On Breaking into Type" in *Breaking into Print,* ed. Elmer Adler (New York: Simon and Schuster, 1937), p. 144.

      Ventures into Verse, printed in an edition of about 100 copies, is now available chiefly in special Mencken collections such as those in EPL and the Dartmouth College Library. Goldberg, *The Man Mencken,* pp. 131–49, prints and comments upon a number of HLM's verses, including some not in *Ventures into Verse,* and reproduces others on pp. 305–10.

      In "H.L. Mencken's Poetry," *Texas Studies in Literature and Language,* VI (Autumn 1964), 346–53, Edward A. Martin analyzes the "Whitmanesque sensibility" that accounts for "the startling imagery, the emphatic cadences, and the sharply defined dramatic voice" in HLM's mature prose.
33. HLM, "An Overdose of Novels," *SS,* XXXV (December 1911), 152.
34. All quotations in the two preceding paragraphs are from *Short Stories,* XLVI (May 1902), 149–56.
35. "Seven chapters of an unnamed and uncompleted novel, c. 1901," p. 5a, in "Typescripts of Early Fiction . . . ," EPL.
36. *Short Stories,* XLI (February 1901), 236–37, 240–41.
37. Ibid., 243.
38. Goldberg, *The Man Mencken,* 316.
39. *Minority Report* (New York: Knopf, 1956), p. 292.

40. "Books for the Hammock and Deck Chair," *SS*, XXVIII (June 1909), 159.
41. "My Relations to Magazines," p. 2, IGP.
42. Theodore Dreiser, *A Book about Myself* (New York: Boni and Liveright, 1922), pp. 411–12; HLM, "Introduction" to Stephen Crane, *Major Conflicts*, in *The Work of Stephen Crane*, 12 vols., ed. Wilson Follett (New York: Knopf, 1925–26), X, x-xi; HLM, "Zola," *SS*, XXXVII (August 1912), 154; HLM, "My Reading," p. 5, IGP.
43. *The Days*, II, 91–92, 122–23.
44. *George Bernard Shaw*, pp. 87–88.
45. HLM, "My Books," p. 3, IGP.
46. *George Bernard Shaw*, p. xx.
47. Ibid., ix-x. HLM discusses Ibsen's debt to Spencer and Nietzsche in a review of Huneker's *Iconoclasts, Baltimore Evening Herald*, May 6, 1905, "Editorials, Dramatic Reviews and Other Contributions to the *Baltimore Morning Herald* and the *Baltimore Evening Herald*, 1904–1906," pp. 68–69 (EPL). HLM notes that Huneker had overlooked "the probably immense influence" of Spencer on Ibsen between 1868 and 1874, when Spencer's philosophy was "the raging epidemic in the German university towns." Huneker had, however, fully acknowledged "Ibsen's debt to Nietzsche, who, like Spencer, was the son of that Intellectual Reign of Terror begun by Darwin."
48. *George Bernard Shaw*, x-xi.
49. *The Philosophy of Friedrich Nietzsche*, pp. 197–200; *Men versus the Man*, written in collaboration with Robert Rives La Monte (New York: Henry Holt and Co., 1910), p. 115. Wherever *Nietzsche* is cited in this chapter, the reference is to the first (1908) edition.
50. In "My Books," p. 3, IGP, HLM observes that he sent Shaw a copy, but received no acknowledgment or reply. The letter HLM mailed to Shaw simultaneously with the presentation copy is printed in Stanley Weintraub, "Mencken to Shaw: 'A Young Man in the Writing Trade' Writes to His Hero," *Menckeniana*, no. 26 (Summer 1968), 9-10.
51. Shaw, "The Quintessence of Ibsenism," in *Selected Prose*, ed. Diarmuid Russell (New York: Dodd, Mead & Co., 1952), pp. 585, 550–51; HLM, "Preface," *George Bernard Shaw*, [viii]; Shaw, *Selected Prose*, pp. 545–57.
52. Prefaces to "Arms and the Man" and "Mrs. Warren's Profession," *Selected Plays*, 3 vols. (New York: Dodd, Mead & Co., 1948), III, 115, 17–18.
53. "Notes in the Margin," *Baltimore Evening Herald*, December 4, 1904, "Editorials, Dramatic Reviews . . . , 1904–1906," pp. 42–43 (EPL); Shaw, *Selected Prose*, p. 575.

54. HLM, *George Bernard Shaw,* p. 88; Shaw, *Selected Prose,* p. 576; HLM, "Preface," *George Bernard Shaw,* p. vii.
55. All details and quotations in this paragraph are from *George Bernard Shaw,* pp. [1]–8.
56. *George Bernard Shaw,* pp. 14, 25, 37, 71, 77.
57. *George Bernard Shaw,* pp. 70–71; "My Books," p. 3, IGP.
58. *The Days,* II, 277; a full account of this experience is given on pp. 276–300.
59. *The Days,* II, 313.
60. HLM gives his own account of the Saturday Night Club in "The Tone Art," *The Days,* III, 77–95. Louis Cheslock, ed., comments affectionately and authoritatively on HLM's musical tastes and activities, including the Club, in *H.L. Mencken on Music* (New York: Knopf, 1961).
61. The quotations in the two preceding paragraphs are from HLM to Fanny Butcher, February 20, [1921], *Letters of H.L. Mencken,* pp. 219–20. See also *The Days,* I, 189–201.
62. HLM to Fanny Butcher, February 20, [1921], *Letters of H.L. Mencken,* p. 220, with *encounters* in the last sentence of the quotation corrected to read *encountered* as in the microfilmed copy in PL; "Brahms," *Prejudices: Sixth Series* (New York: Knopf, 1927), p. 168; *SS,* XXXVII (May 1912), 158.
63. "Beethoven," *SS,* XLV (March 1915), 240. This unsigned article is identified as HLM's in Adler and Wilhelm, *H.L.M.: The Mencken Bibliography,* p. 133. HLM expresses a similar mood in "Beethoven," *Prejudices: Fifth Series,* pp. 88–89, concluding, "But the feelings that Beethoven put into his music were the feelings of a god. There was something olympian in his snarls and rages, and there was a touch of hell-fire in his mirth."
64. "Conrad," *Prejudices: Fifth Series,* p. 38.
65. Schaff to Isaac Goldberg, August 1925, quoted in Goldberg, *The Man Mencken,* pp. 372–73.
66. HLM to Edward Stone, March 1, 1937, *Letters of H.L. Mencken,* p. 414; Kemler, *The Irreverent Mr. Mencken* (Boston: Little, Brown and Co., 1950), p. 26; the comment on Nietzsche as Spencer's successor is quoted in Schaff to Goldberg, August 1925, in Goldberg, *The Man Mencken,* p. 373; HLM, *Nietzsche,* pp. 35–36; note 3, pp. 141–42.
67. *Nietzsche,* p. xi.
68. Ibid., pp. viii-x.
69. "In the vast extent and variety of Nietzsche's writings," said Ernest Boyd in 1925, "there are texts to suit many purposes. Nothing could be more natural than that this particular commentator, at that particular time, should emphasize that element in Nietzsche's work which best fitted both his purpose and his own temperament. H.L. Mencken created Nietzsche in his own image,

hence the affecting superstition that he is a Nietzschean" *(H.L. Mencken* [New York: Robert M. McBride & Co., 1925], p. 29).

Most of the critics and biographers who followed Boyd over-looked this shrewd judgment, but Frederick J. Hoffman cites it in *The Twenties: American Writing in the Postwar Decade* (New York: Viking Press, 1955), note 1, p. 305.

70. *Nietzsche*, p. 138. A notable passage offsetting HLM's assertion occurs in *Human, All-Too-Human*, where Nietzsche argues that "rarely is degeneration, a crippling, even a vice or any physical or moral damage, unaccompanied by some gain on the other side. The sicker man in a warlike and restless tribe, for example, may have more occasion to be by himself and may thus become calmer and wiser; the one-eyed will have one stronger eye; the blind will see more deeply within, and in any case have a keener sense of hearing. So the famous *struggle for existence* does not seem to me to be the only point of view to explain the progress or the strengthening of a human being or a race. Rather, two things must come together: first, the increase of stable power through close spiritual ties such as faith and communal feeling; then, the possibility of reaching higher goals through the appearance of degenerate types and, as a consequence, a partial weakening and wounding of the stable power: it is precisely the weaker natures who, being more delicate and freer, make progress possible" *(The Portable Nietzsche,* ed. and trans. Walter Kaufmann [New York: Viking Press, 1954], pp. 55–56; Nietzsche's italics).

71. HLM, *Nietzsche*, pp. 306–7, 108.

72. Ibid., pp. 103, 72–73, 197–99, 164; on the latter page, the description of the military-judicial caste is quoted from Nietzsche, *The Antichrist*.

73. HLM, *Nietzsche*, pp. 126–45, 77.

74. Ibid., pp. 58, 186–87.

75. Ibid., pp. 193–94, 310–11, 194–95.

76. Ibid., pp. 202, 192, 320–21.

77. Ibid., pp. 124–25, 102–3, 198, 159.

78. Ibid., pp. 167–68, 102.

79. Ibid., pp. 98, xii.

5. *SMART SET* CRITIC, 1908–1914

1. Dreiser to HLM, August 23, 1907, PaL; Dreiser to HLM, October 19, 1907, *Letters of Theodore Dreiser*, 3 vols., ed. Robert H. Elias (Philadelphia: University of Pennsylvania Press, 1959), I, 85–86.

In a letter to Isaac Goldberg dated August 24, 1925 (in Goldberg, *The Man Mencken*, pp. 378–81), Dreiser reminisces about how his friendship with HLM began. A comparison of that account with his letters written in 1907 and 1908 shows that in some respects his memory played him false. For example, he says in his letter to Goldberg that he first heard about Mencken when Dr. Hirshberg called at the *Delineator* office in 1908, but his letter to HLM of August 23, 1907 (PaL), states that George Bronson Howard had brought Mencken to his attention earlier that year.

2. The account of the first meeting between Dreiser and HLM is based on the letter from Dreiser to Goldberg cited in note 1 above.

3. HLM speaks of his acquaintance with Pollock in *The Days,* II, 113.

In *Disturber of the Peace,* pp. 36–37, William Manchester implies that Dreiser had some influence in bringing about HLM's appointment, but in "A Critical Study of the Work of H.L. Mencken as Literary Critic for the Smart Set Magazine, 1908–1914" (M.A. thesis, University of Missouri, 1947), p. 11, he contended that Boyer, not Dreiser, was primarily responsible for recommending HLM. The correspondence on which this opinion was based is printed in "Manchester's Mencken," *Menckeniana,* no. 26 (Summer 1968), 1–8. Dolmetsch, *The Smart Set,* p. 24, reaches the same conclusion.

As authority for the view that Dreiser was mainly responsible, on the other hand, we have HLM's statement made in 1925: "I assumed at that time that either Pollock or Boyer had got me my job. It was not until a year or two ago that I learned that the man responsible was actually Dreiser" ("My Relations to Magazines," p. 3, IGP). This is confirmed by Dreiser's account in his letter to Goldberg, previously cited.

It is possible that both Dreiser and Boyer recommended HLM about the same time. In any event, since Dreiser, Boyer, and Pollock were apparently agreed that he was a promising choice, the question of who first suggested him for the position is relatively unimportant.

4. HLM, "Fifteen Years," *SS,* LXXII (December 1923), 139.

5. Nathan's first contribution, "The Drama Comes into Season," did not appear in *The Smart Set* until November 1909.

6. Dolmetsch, *The Smart Set,* pp. 3–12; Charles Hanson Towne, *Adventures in Editing* (New York and London: Appleton & Co., 1926), pp. 51–52.

7. Advertisements in unnumbered pages at front of issue, *SS,* XXVI (November 1908), and at back of the following issues: XXVII (April 1909); XXVIII (May 1909); XXVIII (June 1909).

8. The issues of April and May 1909, for example, include stories with their scenes laid in southern California, England, France, Italy, Switzerland, Germany, and Spain.

9. Bangs, "First Aid to the Literary," *SS,* XXVIII (May 1909), 83; Van Vechten, "How the Twelve Best Sellers Ended," *SS,* XXIV (March 1908), 160; Baury, "As They Would Have Told It," *SS,* XXVIII (June 1909), 128–30.

10. HLM in *SS,* LXXII (December 1923), 139. In this same article, HLM maintained that he was no longer reviewing plays for the

Sun in 1908, but the clippings in his scrapbooks, now in EPL, show that he was reviewing at least some plays as late as 1912.

11. HLM in *SS*, LXXII (December 1923), 139.

12. Ibid., 139–40.

13. Ibid., 140; "In Praise of a Poet," *SS*, XXXI (May 1910), 157.

14. Poe is discussed as the first American bohemian in Albert Parry, *Garrets and Pretenders*, pp. 3–13; the passages quoted from HLM occur in *SS*, XXVIII (June 1909), 155; "The Prophet of the Superman," *SS*, XXXVI (March 1912), 156; "Sunrise on the Prairie," *SS*, LVIII (February 1919), 139–40; "Footnote on Criticism," *Prejudices: Third Series*, p. 99.

15. Paul Fatout, *Ambrose Bierce* (Norman: University of Oklahoma Press, 1951), pp. 326–27; Richard O'Connor, *Ambrose Bierce* (Boston: Little, Brown, 1967), p. 291; HLM, "Ambrose Bierce," *Prejudices: Sixth Series*, pp. 259–60.

16. Four of HLM's letters are printed in "H.L. Mencken to Ambrose Bierce," comp. M.E. Grenander, *Quarterly Newsletter of the Book Club of California*, XXII (Winter 1956), 5–10; Bierce's answers, comp. Joseph Vincent Ridgely, appear ibid., XXVI (Fall 1961), 27–33.

   HLM quotes Bierce's epigrams in *Prejudices: Sixth Series*, pp. 264–65; his own epigrams are from "The Jazz Webster," *A Book of Burlesques* (New York: Knopf, 1920), pp. 205–6.

   HLM's comments occur in *SS*, LXV (June 1921), 140, and in his review of Carey McWilliams, *Ambrose Bierce, AM*, XIX (February 1930), 252.

17. Lewis E. Gates makes a perceptive analysis of critical impressionism in his *Studies and Appreciations* (New York: Macmillan, 1900), pp. 205–34.

18. HLM in *SS*, XXVIII (June 1909), 153.

19. Thomas Wright, *The Life of Walter Pater*, 2 vols. (London: Everett and Co., 1907), II, 69–75, 222; Pollard, *Their Day in Court*, pp. 284–85; Harte, *Meditations in Motley* (Boston: Arena Publishing Co., 1894), p. 181.

20. Schwab, *Huneker;* John P. Pritchard and John M. Raines, "James Gibbons Huneker, Critic of the Seven Arts," *American Quarterly*, II (Spring 1950), 53–61; Huneker, *Steeplejack*, I, 6–7, 209.

21. *Their Day in Court*, p. 448.

22. HLM, *The Days*, II, 111–12, and "Newspaper Morals," *The Atlantic Monthly*, CXIII (March 1914), 89. In this article, Carter is referred to as "an ancient" with whom HLM took counsel when aspiring "to the black robes of a dramatic critic."

23. Harte, *Meditations in Motley*, pp. 25–26; Huneker, *Steeplejack*, I, title page and p. 5; Huneker, *Iconoclasts: A Book of Dramatists* (New York: Scribner's, 1914; first published 1905), p. 13, quoted by HLM in *Baltimore Evening Herald*, May 6, 1905 (cited above,

chap. 4, note 47) ; "Books to Read and Books to Avoid," *SS,* XXX (February 1910), 157.

24. *Meditations in Motley,* p. 126; figures from Manchester, "A Critical Study of the Work of H.L. Mencken . . . ," pp. 23–25.

25. "In Praise of a Poet," *SS,* XXXI (May 1910), 156; "A Visit to a Short Story Factory," *SS,* XXXVIII (December 1912), 152.

26. "Introduction," *Essays of James Gibbons Huneker,* ed. H.L. Mencken (New York: Scribner's, 1932), p. xi; review of Huneker's *Egoists: A Book of Supermen* in *SS,* XXVIII (June 1909), 153.

27. "Translator's Note," Henrik Ibsen, *Little Eyolf,* ed. H.L. Mencken (Boston: John W. Luce & Co., 1909), pp. xxiii-xxiv.

    HLM and Koppel completed a version of "Hedda Gabler," but the series was dropped because of inadequate sales. John W. Luce & Co. could not afford to do much advertising, and it charged the relatively high price of $1.00 a volume. For only fifty cents more, readers could get three of the widely known Archer translations in an edition published by Scribner's.

    The volume by Brieux was *Blanchette and The Escape,* trans. Frederick Eisemann (Boston: John W. Luce & Co., 1913).

28. "A Counterblast to Buncombe," *SS,* XL (August 1913), 159.

29. For example, in "Brieux and Others," *SS,* XXXVI (March 1912), 153, and "Synge and Others," *SS,* XXXVIII (October 1912), 148.

30. Huneker, *Steeplejack,* II, 123; Pollard, *Masks and Minstrels of New Germany* (Boston: John W. Luce & Co., 1911), p. 58; HLM, *SS,* XXXVI (March 1912), 154, and "What about Nietzsche?" *SS,* XXIX (November 1909), 157.

31. "Notes in the Margin," *Baltimore Evening Herald,* October 16, 1904, "Editorials, Dramatic Reviews and Other Contributions . . . , 1904–1906," pp. 31–32 (EPL) ; ibid., May 6, 1905.

32. "The Burbling of the Bards," *SS,* XXXIX (April 1913), 147.

33. Louis Untermeyer, ed., *Modern American Poetry; Modern British Poetry,* 2 vols. in 1 (New York: Harcourt, Brace, 1936), I, 114: HLM in *SS,* XXXI (May 1910), 154.

34. Max Putzel discusses Reedy and the poets in *The Man in the Mirror: William Marion Reedy and His Magazine* (Cambridge, Mass.: Harvard University Press, 1963), part 3.

    HLM's comments are from "The Bards in Battle Royal," *SS,* XXXVII (May 1912), 153; *SS,* XXXI (May 1910), 153; "The New Poetry Movement," *Prejudices: First Series,* p. 95.

35. *SS,* XXXV (October 1911), 152; "George Bernard Shaw as Hero," *SS,* XXX (January 1910), 154; "Thirty-five Printed Plays," *SS,* XLIV (September 1914), 160; "The Free Lance," *Baltimore Evening Sun,* June 10, 1911, in "The Free Lance, *Baltimore Evening Sun,* 1911–1915," 4 vols. (EPL). All subsequent notes to "The Free Lance" refer to this set of scrapbooks, in which the clippings are arranged chronologically. Hereafter, the column will

be abbreviated "FL," and the citation of the *Evening Sun* and the scrapbook title will be omitted.

On Shaw, see also "The Ulster Polonius," *Prejudices: First Series,* pp. 181–90. The comments on Strindberg occur in *SS,* XL (August 1913) , 159.

36. "By the Way," *Baltimore Evening Herald,* October 22, 1905, "Editorials, Dramatic Reviews and Other Contributions . . . , 1904–1906," pp. 112–13 (EPL) ; *SS,* XXXV (October 1911), 152.

37. *SS,* XLIV (September 1914), 153–54; "FL," February 14 and February 8, 1912.

38. "FL," May 11, 1911; *SS,* XXVII (February 1909), 157.

39. *SS,* XLIV (September 1914), 153–54.

40. Sculley Bradley, "The Emergence of the Modern Drama," *Literary History of the United States,* II, 1007–13; HLM, "On American Stage Plays," *Baltimore Evening Sun,* 1910–12, "Editorials and Other Articles, . . . 1910–1912," II, 227 (EPL) .

41. "William V. Moody," *Baltimore Evening Sun,* October 22, 1910, "Editorials and Other Articles, . . . 1910–1912," I, 222 (EPL) .

The O'Neill plays published in *SS* were *The Long Voyage Home* (October 1917) , *Ile* (May 1918) , and *The Moon of the Caribbees* (August 1918) ; see Arthur and Barbara Geld, *O'Neill* (New York: Harper, 1962) , pp. 338–40 and passim.

42. "Introduction," *Essays of James Gibbons Huneker,* p. xviii; Pollard, *Their Day in Court,* p. 27.

43. *SS,* XXX (February 1910) , 157–58; cf. Pollard, *Their Day in Court,* pp. 29–52.

44. "A 1911 Model Dream Book," *SS,* XXXV (September 1911), 153; *SS,* XXVII (February 1909), 153–54; "A Hot Weather Novelist," *SS,* XXXI (August 1910) , 158.

45. *SS,* XXVII (February 1909) , 159; *SS,* XL (June 1913) , 152; "Roosevelt, Bulwer-Lytton and Anthony Comstock," *SS,* XLII (April 1914) , 154, 156–57.

46. *SS,* XXX (February 1910) , 158.

47. *SS,* XXXI (June 1910) , 153. HLM was apparently unaware that Phelps's essay on Mark Twain had first appeared in *The North American Review,* CLXXXV (July 5, 1907) , 540–48.

48. "Rounding up the Novels," *SS,* XXXVI (February 1912) , 156; *SS,* XXXI (May 1910) , 156; "The Literary Heavyweight Champion," *SS,* XXX (March 1910) , 154.

49. "The Mackaye Mystery," *SS,* XXXV (September 1911) , 156; "Mush for the Multitude," *SS,* XLIV (December 1914) , 304; "A Dip into the Novels," *SS,* XXXVII (July 1912) , 154; "Prose Fiction Ad Infinitum," *SS,* XXXVIII (September 1912) , 153; *SS,* XXVI (December 1908) , 159.

50. *SS,* XLIV (December 1914) , 304; "The Last of the Victorians," *SS,* XXIX (October 1909) , 154, 153.

51. *SS*, XXXVII (July 1912), 154; "The Good, the Bad and the Best Sellers," *SS*, XXVI (November 1908), 159; *SS*, XXXI (June 1910), 160; "The Novels That Bloom in the Spring, Tra-la!" *SS*, XXVII (April 1909), 156.

52. *SS*, XXIX (September 1909), 157; *SS*, XXX (February 1910), 157; " 'A Doll's House'—with a Fourth Act," *SS*, XXIX (December 1909), 154: *SS*, XXXVII (August 1912), 154.

53. *SS*, XXXVIII (October 1912), 150; "FL," August 24, 1912.

54. *SS*, XXVI (December 1908), 154; HLM to Howard Mumford Jones, n.d. [1921], HoL.

55. Zola, "The Experimental Novel," trans. Belle M. Sherman, in Gay Wilson Allen and Harry Hayden Clark, eds., *Literary Criticism: Pope to Croce* (New York: American Book Co., 1941), p. 593; HLM, "A Road Map of the New Books," *SS*, XXVII (January 1909), 153.

56. *A Book of Prefaces*, pp. 146, 63–64.

57. Ibid., pp. 89, 91, 137–38; "A Novel of the the First Rank," *SS*, XXXV (November 1911), 155.

58. *A Book of Prefaces*, pp. 136–37. Flaunting a borrowed erudition, HLM quotes the passage from Sophocles in the original Greek, supplying the translation in a footnote.

59. HLM to Louis Untermeyer, n.d. [1914?], PL; *SS*, XLIV (November 1914), 21: "An Overdose of Novels," *SS*, XXXV (December 1911), 151.

60. "The Leading American Novelist," *SS*, XXXIII (January 1911), 165.

61. *SS*, XXVI (November 1908), 159; *A Book of Prefaces*, pp. 68–69, 113.

62. *SS*, XXVI (November 1908), 156; *SS*, XXXI (June 1910), 154; "A Review of Reviewers," *SS*, XLIV (October 1914), 160; *SS*, XXIX (December 1909), 154; *SS*, XXVII (April 1909), 158; "David Graham Phillips," *Baltimore Evening Sun*, 1911, in "Editorials and Other Articles, . . . 1910–1912," II, 124 (EPL); *SS*, XXIX (December 1909), 153–154.

63. "The Novel Today," *Baltimore Evening Sun*, March 22, 1911, in "Editorials and Other Articles, . . . 1910–1912," II, 70 (EPL).

64. HLM to Dreiser, April 23, [1911], *Letters of H.L. Mencken*, p. 12; "A Novel of the First Rank," *SS*, XXXV (November 1911), 153.

65. Most of the comments are from *A Book of Prefaces*, pp. 79–85, 75, 93, 107–8; the passage on Dreiser and H.G. Wells is from "Again the Busy Fictioneers," *SS*, XXXIX (January 1913), 153.

66. *A Book of Prefaces*, p. 94; HLM to Dreiser, August 1, [1913], and [November 16?, 1913], *Letters of H.L. Mencken*, pp. 32, 35–36.

67. Huneker, *Steeplejack*, I, 269–70; Huneker to HLM, April 11, 1916, *Letters of James Gibbons Huneker*, ed. Josephine Huneker (New

York: Scribner's, 1922), p. 210; Pollard, *Their Day in Court,* pp. 90–94; HLM in *SS,* XXX (February 1910), 157.

I have discussed Pollard's career and criticism at greater length in my introduction to the reprint of his *Their Day in Court* issued by the Johnson Reprint Corporation.

68. *SS,* XXVII (January 1909), 157–58; "Meredith's Swan Song," *SS,* XXXII (October 1910), 166; "Conrad, Bennett, James Et Al [.]," *SS,* XXXVI (January 1912), 158; "Various Bad Novels," *SS,* XL (July 1913), 160.

69. *SS,* XXXVIII (December 1912), 156; *SS,* XL (June 1913), 146–47; *SS,* XXXV (December 1911), 151.

70. *SS,* XXX (February 1910), 153.

71. Wright, "Something Personal," *SS,* XXXIX (March 1913), 159–60. Dolmetsch, *The Smart Set,* gives a detailed account of the editorship of Wright as well as that of HLM and Nathan. William H. Nolte, *H.L. Mencken: Literary Critic* (Middletown, Conn.: Wesleyan University Press, 1966), is partisan in its championship of its subject's assumptions and views. Professor Nolte has also edited the anthology, *H.L. Mencken's Smart Set Criticism* (Ithaca, N.Y.: Cornell University Press, 1968).

6. WARTIME TRIALS AND HOPES

1. "The American," *SS,* XL (June 1913), 89; "The American: His Morals," *SS,* XL (July 1913), 86.

2. Carl Wittke, *German-Americans and the World War,* Ohio Historical Collections, V (Columbus: Ohio State Archaeological and Historical Society, 1936), p. 3.

3. "FL," January 24, 1912, and December 30, 1911.

4. "FL," July 13, 1911, and December 1, 1914.

5. *SS,* XXXVI (March 1912), 157–58; "Munich" in HLM, George Jean Nathan, and Willard Huntington Wright, *Europe after 8:15* (New York: Lane, 1914), p. 96. In addition to the chapter on Munich, HLM identified as his own in the latter work the "Preface in the Socratic Manner" and the first three and the last two paragraphs of the chapter on London *(SS,* XLIV [October 1914], 155).

6. Bourne, "The War and the Intellectuals," in *Untimely Papers,* ed. James Oppenheim (New York: B.W. Huebsch, 1919), p. 25; Wittke, *German-Americans and the World War,* pp. 4–7.

7. HLM to Dreiser, November 8, 1914, PaL, excerpted in *Letters of Theodore Dreiser,* I, 181; "FL," September 29, 1914, and September 8, 1914.

8. "FL," September 29, 1914, and October 9, 1914.

9. All the quoted and summarized comments are from *The Atlantic Monthly,* CXIV (November 1914), 598, 600–601, 605–7; the final quotation is one of several that HLM cites from *Thus Spake Zarathustra.*

10. *The Atlantic Monthly,* CXIV (November 1914), 607.
11. Ibid., 602–3.
12. "FL," February 20, 1915.
13. "FL," February 16, 1915.
14. "FL," July 26, 1912, and July 26, 1915.
15. "Exit the Maxims," *Baltimore Evening Sun,* August 11, 1910, "Editorials and Other Articles, . . . 1910–1912," I, 195 (EPL); "FL," June 8, 12, and 17, 1911; "FL," May 22, 1911, and March 19, 1912.
16. "FL," July 23, February 27, January 25, and June 11, 1912.
17. "FL," October 6, and October 31, 1912.
18. "FL," November 6, 1912, and July 8, 1914.
19. "FL," October 1, October 21, and November 4, 1914.
20. "FL," May 8, 1915; Wittke, *German-Americans and the World War,* p. 73.
21. "FL," May 14, and October 12, 1915; "Hyphenophobia," *Baltimore Evening Sun,* December 9, 1916, "Editorial Page Articles in the Baltimore Evening Sun, 1915–1916," p. 6 (EPL).
22. Quoted in Kemler, *The Irreverent Mr. Mencken,* p. 92.
23. Address delivered at joint session of the two houses of Congress, April 2, 1917, in *Documents of American History,* ed. Henry S. Commager, 3d ed., 2 vols. (New York: F.S. Crofts & Co., 1944), II, 311.
24. William Trowbridge Larned, "The Mantle of Eugene Field," *The Bookman,* XLI (March 1915), 56.
25. HLM, "Introduction," F. W. Nietzsche, *The Antichrist,* trans. and ed. H.L. Mencken (New York: Knopf, 1927), p. 15.
26. *SS,* XL (June 1913), 89–94.
27. "The Land of the Free," *SS,* LXV (May 1921), 138–39.
28. Eastman, "Advertising Democracy," *The Masses,* IX (June 1917), 5; HLM to Louis Untermeyer, [late June? 1917], PL.
29. HLM to Untermeyer, [late July 1917], *Letters of H.L. Mencken,* p. 109.
30. HLM to Dreiser, [January? 1915], *Letters of H.L. Mencken,* p. 58; HLM to Dreiser, November 2, [1915], PaL.
31. "Miscellaneous Notes, continued," XVII, 2, IGP.
32. HLM, [prefatory statement], "Carbon Copy of Original Typescript of *A Little Book in C Major* . . . ," dated 1937 (EPL). On p. 36 of the introduction to his edition of Nietzsche's *The Antichrist,* HLM acknowledges his indebtedness to Hemberger for criticism of the MS.
33. HLM to Goodman, May 1918, PL. The background information is provided in HLM's untitled introduction to the typed copies of his "Letters to Philip Goodman" (two quarto vols., EPL). The PL microfilms reproduce this introduction as well as the copies of the letters.

The continuity between HLM's earlier and later reminiscences

is revealed in his statement in the introduction just cited that his
first sketches for *Happy Days* (1940) grew out of his correspondence with Goodman. Goodman's reminiscences, also an extension
of the correspondence, passed into his daughter's hands after his
death in 1940 and were, at HLM's behest, published by Knopf
under the title *Franklin Street*.

34. HLM first commented on Washington in this vein in "FL,"
August 10, 1914. The quotations used here are from a revised
version of the latter piece in William Drayham [pseudonym of
HLM], "A Few Pages of Notes," *SS*, XLV (January 1915), 435.
A slightly different version appears in *Damn! A Book of Calumny*,
pp. 7–8.

Late in 1920 HLM brought his sketch up-to-date by remarking
that Washington "abominated professional war veterans" and
"regarded pension-grabbers as public nuisances." He was also certain that Washington would have ignored the national Prohibition
laws. "Where," HLM asked rhetorically, "would he go on idle
nights—to a patriotic meeting of the American Legion or to a
surreptitious *Bierabend* of the Arion Gesangverein?" ("Historical
Note" in HLM and Nathan, "Répétition Générale," *SS*, LXIII
[November 1920], 34.)

35. HLM's relationship with the *Evening Mail* was, however, short-
lived. Despite the editors' precautions, Rumely was jailed and the
newspaper silenced by federal censorship. When it resumed publication, the new management made a financial settlement with
HLM but did not renew his contract.

36. "Flights of Fancy," *Baltimore Evening Sun*, February 29, 1916,
"Editorial Page Articles, . . . 1915–1916," pp. 15–16 (EPL); "The
Plague of Books," *SS*, LII (June 1917), 140; "The Dreiser Bug-
aboo," *The Seven Arts* (August 1917), 507–9, reprinted in Alfred
Kazin and Charles Shapiro, eds., *The Stature of Theodore Dreiser*
(Bloomington: Indiana University Press, 1955), pp. 84–91.

37. *The Nation*, CI (December 2, 1915), 648–50, reprinted in Kazin
and Shapiro, pp. 71–80.

38. *The Seven Arts* (August 1917), 509–12.

39. *Chicago Tribune*, December 4, 1915, quoted in *Letters of Theodore
Dreiser*, I, 204–5; HLM, "Rattling the Hyphen," *Baltimore Evening Sun*, February 12, 1916, "Editorial Page Articles, . . . 1915–
1916," p. 13 (EPL).

40. *The Seven Arts* (August 1917), 512; HLM to Dreiser, July 28,
[1916], and August 4, 1916, *Letters of H.L. Mencken*, pp. 86–89.
For a fuller account of the proceedings against *The "Genius"*, see
Robert H. Elias, *Theodore Dreiser: Apostle of Nature* (New York:
Knopf, 1949), pp. 193–96.

41. Typed copy, "Excerpt from the Minutes of the Executive Committee of the Authors' League of America, Inc., sitting at the City
Club, New York, August 25, 1916" (EPL).

42. HLM to Dreiser, November 24, 1916, PaL; HLM to Butler, December 11 and December 15, 1916, EPBP. HLM reviewed *The "Genius"* in "A Literary Behemoth," *SS*, XLVII (December 1915), 150–54.

43. HLM to Dreiser, September 22, 1916, PaL; HLM to Dreiser, [October 6, 1916], *Letters of H.L. Mencken*, p. 90; HLM to Dreiser, December 16 and December 23, 1916, PaL, the first of which is excerpted in W.A. Swanberg, *Dreiser* (New York: Scribner's, 1965), p. 213.

44. John S. Sumner to Felix Shay, November 24, 1916, and to Alexander Harvey, September 19, 1916, quoted in Elias, *Dreiser*, pp. 195, 201–2.

45. HLM to Louis Untermeyer, June 12, 1917, PL.

46. HLM to Dreiser, November 24, 1916, PaL.

47. HLM, "Portrait of a Tragic Comedian," *SS*, L (September 1916), 280–84. See also his "Introduction" to Wilde's *A House of Pomegranates* (New York: Moffat, 1918), pp. v-xii.

48. Henry Dan Piper, "Fitzgerald's Cult of Disillusion," *American Quarterly*, III (Spring 1951), 69–80; Malcolm Cowley, *Exile's Return: A Literary Odyssey of the 1920's*, rev. ed. (New York: Viking Press, 1951), pp. 32–36.

49. HLM, "Criticism of Criticism of Criticism," *SS*, LII (August 1917), 143; Pound to HLM, September 27, 1916, in *The Letters of Ezra Pound, 1907–1941*, ed. D.D. Paige (New York: Harcourt, Brace, 1950), p. 98. Pound urged HLM to move to Europe in letters dated January, 1919, and March 22, 1922, ibid., pp. 145–46, 174.

50. *SS*, LII (August 1917), 138.

51. Ibid., p. 139. In a revision of the same essay in *Prejudices: First Series*, p. 13, HLM compounded his offense by speaking of the "Spingarn-Croce-Carlyle-Goethe theory." In "The Growth of a Literary Myth" (1923), Spingarn explained that Goethe and Carlyle had made no effort to elaborate statements anticipating certain of Croce's insights. Croce alone, therefore, deserved credit for incorporating those insights into a critical system. *(Creative Criticism and Other Essays* [New York: Harcourt, Brace, 1931], pp. 171–73).

52. *SS*, LII (August 1917), 138–39.

53. HLM's brief summary considerably oversimplified Spingarn's views. Arguing that both learning and taste were "vital for Criticism," Spingarn declared that "impressionistic Criticism erred only less grievously than the 'judicial' Criticism which opposed it" *(Creative Criticism and Other Essays*, p. 8).

   In 1923, Spingarn noted that what HLM had dubbed the Croce-Spingarn-Goethe-Carlyle theory had "become the rallying cry of quite a number of our younger critics," and he gave HLM much of the credit for popularizing it (ibid., pp. 166, 174). In "Scholarship and Criticism" (1922), Spingarn commented that, when his

Creative Criticism was published in 1917, "the pedants and the professors were in the ascendant, and it seemed necessary to emphasize the side of criticism which was then in danger, the side that is closest to the art of the creator. But the professors have been temporarily routed by the dilettanti, the amateurs, and the journalists, who treat a work of the imagination as if they were describing fireworks or a bull-fight . . . ; and so it is necessary now to insist on the discipline and illumination of scholarship" *(Civilization in the United States,* ed. Harold E. Stearns [New York: Harcourt, Brace, 1922], p. 99).

54. *SS,* LII (August 1917), 139–40; Spingarn, "The New Criticism," *Creative Criticism and Other Essays,* p. 34.

55. *A Book of Prefaces,* p. 157.

56. *SS,* LII (June 1917), 140; Macy, *The Spirit of American Literature,* Modern Library ed. (New York: Boni and Liveright, Inc., n.d.), pp. v–viii, 11, 15, 17.

57. Macy, for example, hoped that the democratic ideas of Shelley, Mazzini, Lincoln, and Whitman would supplant the "bourgeois ideals" of the American people so that in time "the coming world of free men" will sweep away our "capitalistic oligarchy" (ibid., pp. 210–17).

58. F.W. Dupee, "The Americanism of Van Wyck Brooks" in *Critiques and Essays in Criticism, 1920–1928,* ed. Robert W. Stallman (New York: Ronald Press Co., 1949), p. 464.

59. *America's Coming-of-Age* (New York: B.W. Huebsch, 1915), pp. 6–10, 27. In several respects, Brooks's thesis resembles that of George Santayana in "The Genteel Tradition in American Philosophy" (1911).

60. *America's Coming-of-Age,* pp. 34, 118, 121–29, 164–65.

61. "A Massacre in a Mausoleum," *SS,* XLVIII (February 1916), 157.

62. HLM to Dreiser, April 6, [1915], *Letters of H.L. Mencken,* pp. 63–64; "The Grandstand Flirts with the Bleachers," *SS,* XLV [April 1915), 434–35.

63. Bourne, "The War and Our Intellectuals," *The Seven Arts* (June 1917), 133–36; Bourne, "Conscience and Intelligence in War," *The History of a Literary Radical and Other Papers,* ed. Van Wyck Brooks (New York: S. A. Russell, 1956), p. 200; " 'The Masses' and American Rights," *The Seven Arts* (August 1917), 532.

Although *The Seven Arts* was not officially suppressed, it ceased publication in October 1917 because Mrs. A. K. Rankine, its sponsor, became convinced that the magazine was pro-German and withdrew her subsidy. See Frederick J. Hoffman, Charles Allen, and Carolyn F. Ulrich, *The Little Magazine* (Princeton, N.J.: Princeton University Press, 1947), p. 92.

64. Brooks, *Days of the Phoenix: The Nineteen-Twenties I Remember* (New York: Dutton, 1957), p. 107; *The Seven Arts* (November

1916), 52; Brooks, "Sinclair Lewis and Others," *The Seven Arts* (May 1917), 121. Brooks unintentionally anticipated an association that would be common in the twenties when he grouped his review of Lewis's *The Job* with his Mencken review.

65. Brooks, "Toward a National Culture," *The Seven Arts* (March 1917), 535–47; Dreiser, "Life, Art and America," ibid. (February 1917), 363–89; Brooks, "Our Critics," ibid. (May 1917), 103–16, and "Our Awakeners," ibid. (June 1917), 235–48. Brooks's essays from *The Seven Arts* were reprinted with only slight changes in *Letters and Leadership* (New York: B.W. Huebsch, 1918).

66. HLM, "The Creed of a Novelist," *SS*, L (October 1916), 144; Waldo Frank, "Emerging Greatness," *The Seven Arts* (November 1916), 77–78, 74.

67. *The Young Idea: An Anthology of Opinion Concerning the Spirit and Aims of Contemporary American Literature* (New York: Duffield & Co., 1917), pp. 102–3, 68–71, 40–41, 7, 149, 155–58, 212.

68. *A Book of Prefaces*, pp. 20–22.

69. Ibid., pp. 197–98.

70. Randall Stewart discusses this historically justified second meaning of "Puritanism" in his *American Literature and Christian Doctrine* (Baton Rouge: Louisiana State University Press, 1958), pp. 4–5. In *The Twenties*, Frederick J. Hoffman surveys the use of "Philistine" and "Puritan," but fails to recognize the legitimacy of this second meaning of the latter term.

71. *A Book of Prefaces*, pp. 203, 231–41.

72. Ibid., pp. 225, 270–71, 276.

73. Bourne, "H. L. Mencken," *The New Republic*, XIII (November 24, 1917), 102.

74. *A Book of Prefaces*, p. 282.

75. Brooks, "On Creating a Usable Past," *The Dial*, LXIV (April 11, 1918), 337–41; *A Book of Prefaces*, p. 221. So HLM wrote in "Puritanism as a Literary Force," but in the essay on Huneker, perhaps partly out of a desire to build up Huneker at Poe's expense, he complained that Poe "was enormously ignorant of good books" and "could never quite throw off a congenital vulgarity of taste, so painfully visible in the strutting of his style" (ibid., pp. 154–55).

76. Ibid., pp. 215–16, 204, 223.

77. Ibid., 68, 94, 192–94.

78. HLM to Ernest Boyd, December 15, [1917], PL; Sherman, *American and Allied Ideals*, War Information Series no. 12 (Washington, D.C.: Committee on Public Information, 1918), pp. 17, 23, 12, and "Beautifying American Literature," *The Nation*, CV (November 29, 1917), 593–94.

In *The Rediscovery of American Literature: Premises of Critical Taste, 1900–1940* (Cambridge, Mass.: Harvard University Press,

1967), Richard Ruland analyzes in detail the controversy between HLM and the New Humanists, with special emphasis on Sherman.

79. Hecht describes his hero worship of HLM in his *A Child of the Century* (New York: Simon and Schuster, 1954), pp. 160, 165–71. Rascoe's review of *A Book of Prefaces* was first printed in November 1917. It was reprinted in Burton Rascoe, Vincent O'Sullivan, and F.C. Henderson [pseudonym of HLM], *H.L. Mencken: Fanfare* (New York: Knopf, 1920), pp. 3–7.

80. HLM's views are quoted and summarized from "Civilized Chicago," *Chicago Tribune,* October 28, 1917, "Miscellaneous Newspaper Articles, 1904–1936," pp. 195–97 (EPL). In a revised and expanded form, this article appeared in *The Nation* [London, England] for April 17, 1920, and was reprinted in the *Chicago Daily News,* May 12, 1920, and in *On American Books,* ed. Francis Hackett (New York: Huebsch, 1920), pp. 31–38.

7. POSTWAR TRIUMPH

1. "Introduction," "Modern American Short Stories," printed from the typescript in EPL in *Menckeniana,* no. 20 (Winter 1966), 3–4; "The South Begins to Mutter," *SS,* LXV (August 1921), 143–44.

   The first of these references is to an anthology HLM edited at the request of a German publisher, but the project fell through shortly after its inception in 1923 because of the unfavorable economic conditions in Germany. The Table of Contents provides a valuable insight into HLM's literary tastes. Among the eighteen stories he had planned to include were Edmund Wilson's "The Death of a Soldier," Ruth Suckow's "Just Him and Her," John T. Frederick's "Mirage," Cabell's "Porcelain Cups," Ring Lardner's "Champion," Willa Cather's "Paul's Case," and Sherwood Anderson's "I Am a Fool" *(Menckeniana,* no. 21 [Spring 1967], 1).

2. *This Side of Paradise* (New York: Scribner's, 1920), p. 304; "Introduction," *In Defense of Women* (New York: Knopf, 1926; first published by Philip Goodman Co., 1918), pp. xvii–xviii.

3. "Preface," *The Undertaker's Garland* (New York: Knopf, 1922), pp. 18–20.

4. "The New Chivalry" in George Jean Nathan and HLM, "Répétition Générale," *SS,* LXI (April 1920), 48.

5. "Preface," *The American Credo,* pp. 90, 25–26; "Gropings in Literary Darkness," *SS,* LXIII (October 1920), 144; "On Journalism," *SS,* LXI (April 1920), 48.

6. Goldman, *Rendezvous with Destiny* (New York: Knopf, 1953), p. 316; "Preface," *The American Credo,* p. 42.

   According to Malcolm Cowley, two main points in the creed of Greenwich Village intellectuals about 1920 were "the idea of self-expression" and "the idea of liberty" *(Exile's Return,* p. 60).

7. Discussing the ideal of liberty among the Greenwich Villagers, Cowley wrote, "Puritanism is the great enemy. The crusade against Puritanism is the only crusade with which free individuals are justified in allying themselves" *(Exile's Return,* p. 60).

8. HLM to Percy Marks, December 2, (1922?], *Letters of H.L. Mencken,* p. 239; HLM's italics.

9. "Roosevelt: An Autopsy," *Prejudices: Second Series,* p. 102; "Preface," *The American Credo,* pp. 48–65; "Introduction" in E.W. Howe, *Ventures in Common Sense* (New York: Knopf, 1919), pp. 11–13.

10. *Prejudices: Second Series,* pp. 31–32.

11. "Répétition Générale," *SS,* LX (September 1919), 42–43; Sinclair Lewis to HLM, January 21, [1922], EPL, quoted in Mark Schorer, *Sinclair Lewis: An American Life* (New York: McGraw-Hill, 1961), pp. 290–91.

12. "Nothing Much Is Here, Alas!" *SS,* LVIII (January 1919), 138–39.

13. The interrelationships between the two groups of writers are well illustrated in *Between Friends: Letters of James Branch Cabell and Others,* ed. Padraic Colum and Margaret Freeman Cabell (New York: Harcourt, Brace, 1962).

14. HLM to Fielding H. Garrison, November 17, 1919, *Letters of H.L. Mencken,* p. 162; HLM, *James Branch Cabell* (New York: Robert M. McBride & Co., 1927), pp. 11, 13. "Some Ladies and Jurgen," a short story which foreshadowed the novel, was published in the July 1918 issue of *SS.*

15. *Prejudices: Second Series,* pp. 136–37.

16. Davidson, "The Trend of Literature, a Partisan View" in *Culture in the South,* ed. W.T. Couch (Chapel Hill: University of North Carolina Press, 1935), p. 196. See also George Brown Tindall, *The Emergence of the New South, 1913–1945,* A History of the South, X ([Baton Rouge]: Louisiana State University Press, 1967), pp. 208–11, 285–96, and passim.

17. Quoted in Emily Clark, *Innocence Abroad* (New York: Knopf, 1931), p. 112; *SS,* LXV (August 1921), 138–40, 144; "Morning Song in C Major," *The Reviewer,* II (October 1921), 4.

18. *The New Republic,* XIII (November 24, 1917), 102–3; Pound to HLM, [January 1919], *The Letters of Ezra Pound,* p. 146.

19. "The American Critic," in Rascoe, O'Sullivan, and Henderson [HLM], *H.L. Mencken,* p. 17; Rascoe, "Fanfare," ibid., p. 11; "H.L. Mencken," *The New Republic,* XXVII (June 1, 1921), 10–13; *SS,* LXV (August 1921), 139.

20. *The American Language* (New York: Knopf, 1919), pp. 19, 23.

21. "Preface," ibid., pp. vi-vii.

22. *The American Language,* p. 321.

23. "Baltimore Anti-Christ," *The Bookman,* LIII (March 1921), 81; Boyd, *H.L. Mencken,* pp. 78–80.

24. "Répétition Générale," *SS*, LXIII (October 1920), p. 44; "Thoughts on Being Bibliographed," *Classics and Commercials* (New York: Farrar, Strauss, 1950), pp. 114–15.
25. HLM to Louis Untermeyer, November 25, [1918], PL; "Introduction," *In Defense of Women*, pp. xvi-xvii.
26. "Introduction," in E.W. Howe, *Ventures in Common Sense*, pp. 15–22.
27. Ibid., p. 7; "Répétition Générale," *SS*, LXII (June 1920), 43–44. Amos Pinchot, to whom HLM refers in this quotation, was the leader of the Committee of Forty-Eight, a group of liberals and ex-Bull Moosers. In July 1920 the committee and the recently organized Labor Party merged to form the Farmer-Labor Party.
28. "Introduction," in E.W. Howe, *Ventures in Common Sense*, p. 16; "Preface" [1898], *Selected Plays*, III, ix.

8. CONCLUSION

1. HLM to Dreiser, October 11, [1920], *Letters of H.L. Mencken*, p. 203.
2. HLM to Dreiser, December 11, [1920], PaL.
3. "The Men Who Rule Us," *Baltimore Evening Sun*, October 5, 1931, reprinted in *A Carnival of Buncombe*, ed. Malcolm Moos, pp. 248–49; "Footnote on Criticism," *Prejudices: Third Series*, p. 84.
4. Goldberg, *The Man Mencken*, p. 247; HLM, *Nietzsche*, p. 320; "Preface by the Editor," Johann Burkhard Mencken, *The Charlatanry of the Learned*, p. 44; autobiographical notes sent to Burton Rascoe [Summer 1920?], *Letters of H.L. Mencken*, p. 188.
5. *Minority Report*, p. 292.
6. "The Tune Changes," *Baltimore Evening Sun*, March 27, 1933, reprinted in *A Carnival of Buncombe*, p. 278.
7. HLM to Will Durant, n.d., quoted in Durant, *On the Meaning of Life*, p. 33; "Miscellaneous Notes, continued," XXII, 4, IGP; HLM to Dreiser, February 5, [1926], *Letters of H.L. Mencken*, pp. 288–89; *In Defense of Women*, p. 103.
8. HLM to Ellery Sedgwick, June 7, [1935], *Letters of H.L. Mencken*, p. 392.
   Sara Mayfield, *The Constant Circle: H.L. Mencken and His Friends* (New York: Delacorte Press, 1968), sympathetically portrays Sara Haardt and her relationship with HLM both before and after their marriage.
9. *SS*, LXV (August 1921), 140; *The Reviewer*, II (October 1921), 4.

Index